*Books of Merit*

*What I Meant to Say*

David Macfarlane

Brian D. Johnson

Greg Hollingshead

Ian Brown

Bert Archer

Douglas Bell

J. M. Kearns

Bruce Grierson

Martin Levin

Russell Smith

David Hayes

Ted Bishop

Ian Pearson

Jake MacDonald

David Eddie

Geoff Heinricks

Philip Preville

Max Fawcett

Don Gillmor

Chris Koentges

Ray Robertson

Ron Graham

William Randall

Russell Wangersky

Michael Redhill

Chris Nuttall-Smith

David Hollingshead

Andrew Pyper

# WHAT I

# MEANT TO SAY

## the private lives of men

EDITED BY

**Ian Brown**

Thomas Allen Publishers

Toronto

**Library and Archives Canada Cataloguing in Publication**

What I meant to say : the private lives of men / edited by Ian Brown.

ISBN 0-88762-190-2

1. Men—Psychology. 2. Masculinity. 3. Men—Identity.
I. Brown, Ian, 1954–

HQ1090.W48 2005          155.3'32          C2005-904985-5

Editor: Janice Zawerbny
Jacket and text design: Gordon Robertson
Cover image: Big Shot Media

Published by Thomas Allen Publishers,
a division of Thomas Allen & Son Limited,
145 Front Street East, Suite 209,
Toronto, Ontario M5A 1E3 Canada

www.thomas-allen.com

  **Canada Council
for the Arts**

ONTARIO ARTS COUNCIL
CONSEIL DES ARTS DE L'ONTARIO

The publisher gratefully acknowledges the support of The Ontario
Arts Council for its publishing program.

We acknowledge the support of the Canada Council for the Arts, which last
year invested $21.7 million in writing and publishing throughout Canada.

We acknowledge the Government of Ontario through the Ontario
Media Development Corporation's Ontario Book Initiative.

We acknowledge the financial support of the Government of Canada
through the Book Publishing Industry Development Program (BPIDP)
for our publishing activities.

09 08 07 06 05     2 3 4 5 6

Printed and bound in Canada

. . . if there is a sin against life, it lies perhaps less in despairing of it than in hoping for another life, and evading the implacable grandeur of the one we have. These men have not cheated. They were gods of the summer at twenty in their thirst for life, and they are still gods today stripped of all hope.

— ALBERT CAMUS, *Summer in Algiers*

lovely daughter, Hayley, did what she always does, which is to gently remind me what makes a good story good. My thanks to them all.

But finally, I owe the greatest thanks to my contributors, whom I can only describe as a great bunch of guys. Their enthusiasm for this project (despite the pittance I could pay them), their professionalism, their patience, their graciousness and their talent made editing them that rarest thing—a pleasure of work. I have lived with many of these stories in one form or another for nearly a year, and have read them more times than I can count. But even today, every time I reread one, I get the same thrill—the thrill that comes from reading a story its writer truly cared about. It is for their company on the page these many months that I am most grateful.

# Acknowledgements

This book was a collaboration in every way, and I owe a number of people a debt of thanks for seeing it through. Patrick Crean and Jim Allen, the publisher and president of Thomas Allen Publishers, encouraged this project from the start, and gave me free rein to run it as I wanted. This makes them rare publishers. Senior editor Janice Zawerbny, an organizational genius, is entirely responsible for the fact that you are now actually holding this book in your hands, and possibly for the fact that I am not—at least at writing—in a mental institution. Alyssa Stuart, Thomas Allen's publicity manager, has also been tireless in her efforts to bring the book to a wider audience. I happen to think Gord Robertson did a great job on the cover, as well. And I am grateful to Bruce Westwood for brokering the deal.

I am also indebted to several good friends and colleagues, all of whom helped bring this collection together. My old friend Ian Pearson, the most gifted of editors, turned me on to several brilliant young writers whose essays now grace these pages. Marni Jackson gave me the title. Cathrin Bradbury, my editor at *The Globe and Mail*, offered wise counsel and trained her unerring eye on several essays. Edward Greenspon gave me time away from my job. Bruce Barnes gave me advice. My brother, Tim Brown, gave me a quiet place to work when I most needed it. Meanwhile my wife, Johanna Schneller, provided key editing and another pair of eyes, even as she kept track of thirty pieces of writing. Even my children helped: my dear son, Walker, inspired an essay, and my

# *Contents*

## MIND

## SOUL

*Introduction*

Maybe George Orwell and William Blake were right when they insisted there are no fundamental differences between men and women; that we all, deep down, want the same thing: the lineaments of desire. On the other hand, that didn't explain the look on my friend Janice's face as I explained my thing about female signatures.

"Signatures?" she said.

"You know," I said, "whenever a woman signs a note—say, when a waitress writes "Thanks!" and signs her name on your lunch bill? Say her name's Betty."

"Betty."

"Yeah. And say she makes the B with really round, bulbous loops." I wrote out "Betty" on a napkin the way I remembered seeing it.

*Betty*

"Okay."

"Well," I said, "when I look at that B—and I know I'm not the only guy who does this—I think she's telling me her breasts are available to me." I paused, and polished the signature up a bit. "Right?"

I looked up from my napkin. Janice was staring at me.

"Oh my God," she said.

Apparently women don't think they send secret sexual messages in their signatures.

■

*What I Meant to Say* grew out of a meeting I had in the spring of 2004 with Patrick Crean, the publisher of Thomas Allen Publishers. Patrick asked me if I thought men would read a book like *Dropped Threads*.

Edited by Carol Shields and Marjorie Anderson, *Dropped Threads* was a remarkable anthology of writing by women, about women, for an audience of women readers. I had read *Dropped Threads*; I admired the way it avoided a rigid feminist ideology, and instead let women tell stories about their lives, as they lived through the thirty-year-long earthquake known as late-twentieth-century women's liberation.

On the other hand, I didn't think men would read a book about men, written by men, for men. "In my experience," I told Patrick, "men don't read books like that, if they read much of anything."

"That's what I was afraid of," Patrick said.

"But maybe women would," I said.

"What do you mean?"

"Maybe women would read a book about men, written by men, if it were written with women readers in mind. If it were a group of articulate men trying to explain their privates selves, to women, in the aftermath of the women's movement. That way men might find it interesting too."

This book is the result of that conversation.

■

Certainly there is plenty for men to write about and explain. Over the past thirty years, the institution of manhood—the experience of being a man, largely unchanged since time immemorial—has been ripped apart, burned, repaired, reinvented, rediscovered and remade, almost beyond recognition.

Men are no longer the overwhelming breadwinners in North America, and no longer comprise the majority of the working population. But other changes have occurred as a result of these fundamental demographic tremors. Men no longer commit the vast majority of infidelities in marriage: the more women work outside the home, the more unfaithful they are. Men no longer account for even half the new entrants at many of North America's business, medical and law schools. We certainly no longer dominate the moral, ethical, intellectual, political, financial, athletic and spiritual high ground of North American society; we no longer control the conversation of the culture.

Instead, men are now partners to women—and sometimes to each other, in quasi-legal marriages, with children. Instead, there is now a creature called a metrosexual, who cares as much about his grooming and his hair and his dermabrasion quotient as a woman has been allowed (or forced) to care for hers. Viagra can eliminate any anxiety a man might once have felt about his sexual performance—which in turn has raised the bar of expectation among women to the point where even young men are forced to take Viagra because they're anxious all over again, in a whole new way. Instead of an unwritten and largely unspoken and often unquestioned code of manhood, there are now many codes. The definition of what a man is changes from one *New York Times* Sunday Styles section to the next.

Some of these changes have been a mixed blessing for both men and women. Men have been liberated (sometimes forcibly) from the cast-iron strictures of 1950s lockstep maleness (strong, silent, suicidal), only to be caught up in new strictures and new conventions. Very few truthful men can claim they do fifty percent of the child rearing, even if their wives also work outside the home. But fifty percent of the housework is now a more arguable proposition. And men shoulder more of the work of the home—cooking, cleaning, diapering—in addition to their usual chores (fixing, earning, defending). This is why leisure time surveys repeatedly reveal that married men between the ages of thirty-five and fifty who work outside the home but also have families have less free time than any other comparable demographic group—women included. That's a big change, and it means big changes in the way men live, and how we define our private selves. To cite just one example—and read

Russell Wangersky's excellent essay, "Ways of Seeing," if you don't believe me—we are more involved in our children's lives, as a general rule, than our fathers were in ours; hence we have more at stake in our children's lives, and are even more hostage to that fortune than our fathers were—a development that is as bewildering as it is welcome, as several of the essayists in this book reveal.

At the same time, the age-old challenges of a man's life—the physical dangers; the thankless duties; the trenchant, incommunicable loneliness and guilt; the unspeakable, sometimes unstoppable physicality of male desire; our relations with unreachable fathers and insatiable mothers, or vice versa; our alleged preference for convincing action over persuasive words, to name just a few—all remain as mysterious and under-mapped as ever. This sense of isolation—the inheritance of silence that was bequeathed to our fathers, that our dads in turn bequeathed to us—may only now, with this generation of fathers, be dwindling. But I'll believe that when I see it. In his groundbreaking book *Manhood in the Making*, anthropologist David D. Gilmore surveyed the masculinity rituals of dozens of societies around the globe. In all but two he found the definition of what constitutes a man, and what marks the public onset of masculinity, to be the same: socially acceptable manhood is defined overwhelmingly as sacrifice and service to others. It is a fact most men acknowledge, privately. But it is also a fact about which men have been shamed into silence. That is, until now, when the very definition of what it means to be a man is being directly questioned by more and more male writers.

None of which is to say that any of the men in this book feel entitled to complain, and none of them do (at least not very often). But they do feel a great need to explain—at least if the alacrity with which they responded to my call for submissions is any evidence. With the long-overdue recognition of women as equals, most of the public attention paid to gender relations in the past thirty years has been aimed at women. In the meantime, we boys have been thinking. We thought you might like to know about what.

■

This habit, of men explaining their selves and lives and thoughts in prose to women, has a robust past that runs from ancient Seneca through Shakespeare's sonnets and Montaigne's essays, to the contemporary work of writers such as Phillip Roth and Mordecai Richler and David Foster Wallace and Nicholson Baker, to cite but a handful. The difference between then and now is that in the past, men wrote from a position of privilege in a world where women were second-class citizens, and they wrote for readers who understood that fact. Today North American men write in and to a world where women are at least men's equals as tastemakers and thinkers. That change alone, and the squabbling that comes out of it—it's your turn to look after the kids, why can't you bring home more money, and so on—is worth volumes, as men and women bang out a new set of rules governing our now more or less equal coexistence.

Unfortunately, the male side of the story—men writing about what it's like to be a man—had a bad bump roughly fifteen years ago, with the publication of a book called *Iron John*, by the poet Robert Bly. It was an interesting enough book about the symbolic meaning of masculinity and its many rituals (it called on men to renounce war, among other details, which always struck me as fanciful), but it did some damage by spawning a school of imitators, the so-called "men's movement." These guys liked to dance naked in sweat lodges and write long, theoretical screeds full of complaint about the original wound perpetrated by our fathers and the injustices visited on men in the wake of feminism—writing that was much too on the money, that was more interested in confession and attention than it was in telling a story, and that had no sense of humour whatsoever. And I do mean whatsoever. The men's movement had its strengths, I suppose—divorce laws are arguably a little fairer to men now, thanks to what Bly started—but the writing (and therefore the thinking) it produced was dreck. Bly's acolytes couldn't tell a story to save themselves. They lacked distance and discipline; they mistook confession for candour; they were ideologues, rather than storytellers.

*What I Meant to Say* is not that kind of book. My first criterion for including a piece in the collection was the quality of its writing:

it had to give me pleasure, aesthetic or otherwise, and it had to tell me something fresh about being a man.

My second criterion was that the essays be candid. Candour is not the same as confession, which proceeds from an inference of guilt; candour is more useful, and a little goes a long way. It's also a challenge for a book that wants to be read by women, for one main reason: the truth about the way men think and feel and act may offend some female readers.

So while *What I Meant to Say* is candid, its writers also explain themselves gracefully. This isn't to say they pull their punches, or apologize, or kowtow, or are anything less than provocative. But no matter how many objections a woman may have to passages in this book, I hope she will want to read on, so admiring will she be of the originality of its thinking and the abs and delts of its storytelling. As I explained to every contributor, if it was his lifelong ambition to tell women that he could henceforth happily exist on hot dogs and a lifetime subscription to *Tits 'n' Hitler Magazine* without ever seeing another woman again, I was all for his saying so. But he had to explain himself properly, and give good and honest and convincing reasons, and give them in such a way that a woman would want to keep reading. In other words, this book is not a Rolfing session to vent unfiltered male anger. It's also anything but politically correct. It's not even comprehensive: there are vast swaths of male experience, from money to race, that are not touched on here (though not for lack of trying), that I hope we will get to in a sequel. My ambitions for the book have been more modest, and more serious: that it be nothing more or less than a book of true stories, told well by men, about what it's like to be a man, a male human. I'm not interested in gender ideology. I'm interested in the way a guy tells the truth, especially when he's talking to a girl. Ironically, this approach may have produced a book that is equally appealing to men. Don't ask me why.

■

What have these men written about? Sex, for starters—that can't come as a surprise. What will surprise, I suspect, is the fluidity of the way men think about sex, which goes against the stereotype of men as permanently horny imbeciles. David Macfarlane kicks the book off in this regard with a hilarious (and classy) discussion of erections and why they occur—if they occur for any reason at all, which Macfarlane doubts. This is an idea that has profound consequences: if the man you love has erections for no reason, what does that say about his desire for you?

This isn't to say sex isn't important. J.M. Kearns approaches the subject like a man in "How Men Choose Women," an essay so straight-forward it's almost an instruction manual. Ted Bishop's moving and funny essay, about what a casual passing touch can mean to a man, will surprise women all over again. (If you think my signature reading is absurd, wait till you read Bishop on the subject of receiving change from a cashier in a grocery store.) Bert Archer's "Why Boys are Better Than Girls" is a shocking dispatch from the bedroom of gay maledom. Russell Smith, a novelist and tireless chronicler of male habits, takes several steps sideways in his defence of bondage and his affection for women with flaws. Douglas Bell, a writer and actor, goes a step further still and explains—this has to be a first—not just his bouts of premature ejaculation but the substantial anger and loss he feels as women become more and more demanding about male sexual performance. All these are not new ideas, necessarily, but they feel new next to the traditional silence men once maintained on sexual matters—a silence David Hayes describes in his compelling account of his father's sexual secrets.

This new sexual candour—one reward for making women our equals—has also helped men be less sexually stereotypical. While there is no shortage in this book of men who admit to philandering, it also boasts something rarer: men who try to be faithful, as described by David Eddie in his spirited defence of fidelity, and by Andrew Pyper in his panegyric to his new wife. This new candour has also freed men to talk about physical failure, the terrifying possibility of which occupies a huge space in the mental basement of every man I know. Because of course when our bodies go, so does our sense of certainty as men, as strong and brave and even dangerous beings. Russell Wangersky does a beautiful job exploring this idea and many others as he relates his harrowing adventures as a volunteer fireman; Brian D. Johnson, the well-known film critic and writer, does an equally impressive job, and made me laugh out loud again and again, telling the hilarious story of his hernia. Apparently he was in some pain. But this is the way men are: our bodies know our inner being, our "feelings," far sooner than our minds ever do.

But however physical men are, we sometimes live entirely outside our bodies. When men go mental, they go all the way, as novelist Greg Hollingshead (Governor General's Award for fiction, Giller Prize finalist) reveals in his gorgeous account of how a brainy boy becomes one, despite all the rewards of going in the other, jockish direction. His son, David Hollingshead, is meanwhile caught up in thoughts of his father, and the old man's ever encroaching death. Bruce Grierson, a lovely writer who makes his home out West, may have coined a new phrase—"gratuitous precision"—for the male passion for irrelevant detail; Martin Levin, meanwhile, who in his less secret life is books editor of *The Globe and Mail*, delves into the mind of a confirmed bachelor, a man who loves women but is phobic about commitment—the best explanation of that state I've ever read. Ian Pearson, an editor and record producer, does a brilliantly funny job explaining the psyche of a man with a lifelong Joni Mitchell obsession. Geoff Heinricks, now a vintner (his first barrel of commercially available wine was released this summer, after ten years' trying), spends long parts of his day thinking, and writing, about drinking—a subject that here puts him in the good stylistic company of Kingsley Amis and J. P. Donleavy. Then there's the ineffable Jake MacDonald, the author of *Houseboat Chronicles,* although here he's dreaming about cars and women and ambition, all in the person of the late, great Carol Shields (who was, of course, the inspiration behind *Dropped Threads*). These male obsessions start young, too: Max Fawcett is barely in his twenties, and he's already obsessed with home renovations. Novelist Ray Robertson prefers guns, while I (for a while, anyway) watched strippers. Some modern male obsessions are even more recherché: Chris Nuttall-Smith, for instance, is wrestling with the dilemma of whether his child will take his surname or his wife's. (I predict his essay alone will arouse great arguments among readers.) Philip Preville is trying to learn to shop like a girl, though he writes about it like a man. And all the incomparable Don Gillmor wants is a room—or, make that a house—of his own.

Of course, for all the changes that have occurred in the past thirty years—it's impossible to imagine a man writing what Nuttall-Smith writes, forty years ago—some guy things never do change. It has been said that women's lives are created anew every time they mother a child, whereas men live out their inheritance from the past. Chris Koentges, a young writer just coming onto the Canadian scene, offers a moving diary of a strange trip with his father after the death of his mother, in "Wings of Thatched Moustache"; Ron Graham, the journalist and writer, performs a masterful analysis of his own father's legendary (and ultimately fateful) silence. Meanwhile, William Randall, a young writer and geologist, offers a poetic eulogy to his late grandfather, from whom William inherited his love of books. Mothers get theirs, too, among other places in Michael Redhill's charming "Motherhood: Three *pensées* and an interview with the author's mother."

All of which is to say that, in my opinion, there has never been a better or more receptive time to explore and reveal the old and new terrain of manhood. That is my greatest hope—that for once it may have been possible to write about the sexes in such a way, with sufficient style and verve and nerve, that both men and women will want to read this book. That would be heartening: to explain ourselves candidly—not just to other men but to women, the very people from whom we have allegedly been most alienated since Betty Friedan kicked off the action nearly four decades ago. Strange, how it feels like coming home again.

Ian Brown
Toronto
August 2005

BODY

# David Macfarlane

■

## BONER AND

## NOTHINGNESS

It is a misconception, common to women and men alike, that an erection necessarily has something to do with sex. It is easy to see how such a fallacy takes hold. One need only spend a short time in a barnyard before the connection is made. But I'm not so sure. Frankly, I'm inclined—so to speak—to a more holistic explanation.

My misgivings first arose. . . . (Look. The subject is so rife with cheap double-entendres, I think we should ignore them whenever they pop up, don't you?) As I was saying, my doubts on this matter first arose in math class in Grade Six.

Depending on how a man measures these things (you see what I mean?), you might put the *Sports Illustrated* Swimsuit Issue or the Victoria's Secret catalogue at one end of the sexual excitement graph. And, speaking of graphs, you'd put Miss Peebles's Grade Six math class at the other.

Sex and Miss Peebles seemed worlds apart—even at a time in my life when I knew less about sex than I did about math. There are Zen masters who spend years attempting to find the emptiness that I attained whenever Miss Peebles shut the door behind her and said, "Good morning, class." It's safe to say there was not a thought in my head for the ensuing forty minutes. Certainly, Miss Peebles herself—her hair rolled into what looked like a bullet-proof bun; her eyes, small and piercing and shielded by rimless spectacles—was a source of no fascination. Neither sex nor arithmetic crossed my mind while in her presence. And yet, every math class, there I was: a hypotenuse more than equal to the sum of the other two sides.

Tight white jeans were popular with boys at the time. A mistake for all kinds of reasons—not the least of which was Miss Peebles's insistence that pupils stand beside their desks when answering questions.

Teachers in those days were uniformly ancient. Miss Peebles, for instance, was widely known on the playground to be 107. It must have been some kind of union regulation. And, having passed their formative years under canvas at Mafeking or in the typhoid wards with Florence Nightingale, our teachers had a certain enthusiasm for things military. Standing at attention, for instance.

An unnecessary injunction. The tight white jeans were not much of a disguise. When I was called upon by Miss Peebles to take a wild stab at what x might be, I was often obliged to stand as slowly as possible. Much the same technique was used by dying bad-guys in western movies when they struggled stubbornly to their feet after taking a few rounds in the stomach from the sheriff's Colt .45. Sometimes it took me a good fifteen seconds to unfold. And all the while I was trying to think, as vividly as I could, of the high-waisted, broad-beamed, Band-Aid-coloured bloomers that Miss Hendershot wore in gym.

Miss Hendershot taught the girls gym during those periods when Mr. McCairns taught the boys health. Why someone so unathletic as Miss Hendershot should teach gym and somebody so unhealthy as Mr. McCairns should teach health were among those mysteries that children learn not to question. Even then, a discerning child could see a pattern developing. The drama teacher liked us to spend our time memorizing lines but she hated plays. The civics teacher fondled the girls and kept a strap in his top drawer for delinquent boys. The gym teacher had a rear end like a tractor seat. And the health teacher was an overweight, out-of-breath, red-nosed chain-smoker. A useful life lesson, actually. Forty years later, few of us would be surprised when George Bush became president.

But Mr. McCairns did have one notable characteristic. He was boring. He had a mind that was so unoccupied by imagination he devoted himself with religious-like fervour to one measurement of excellence and one measurement only: how well we underlined the subject headings in our notebooks. In Mr. McCairns's class we rose or fell on the basis of how firmly we could hold a red pencil crayon against the edge of a ruler.

But being boring may have counted as an advantage for teaching health class. For all I know, it may have been a requirement. Health was promising in the abstract: teenage pregnancies and wild-eyed enslavement to dope sounded a good deal more interesting than long division. In reality, though, health was an unending tedium that had largely to do with <u>Dental Hygiene</u>, <u>The Reproductive System</u>, and the dangers of <u>Marijuana</u>. Occasionally, while being paraded— "Straight line, boys. Hands at your sides"—from health class to the darkened room where we watched films (pronounced fil-ums) about cavities, fallopian tubes and drug fiends we caught a glimpse, through the gym doors, of Miss Hendershot. In her bloomers.

An unsettling sight. But a sight that would prove to have its uses. I had not yet discovered sex. But I had, somehow, figured out the opposite of sex.

Calling Miss Hendershot's bloomers to mind worked reasonably well during emergency situations in math class. And, as a matter of fact, I employed the memory at Vespers just the other day when, having daydreamed my way through the *Nunc Dimittis*, I was called upon to stand for the Apostles' Creed.

These things happen. But what is not said as loudly and clearly as it might be is that often they happen for no reason. None what-soever. Erections are frequently caused, in other words, by nothing.

It is women who are largely responsible for the popularly held belief that an erection necessarily has something to do with some-thing. Sex, to be specific. They imagine that we men think about sex at times in our lives when we should be thinking about integers or the mystery of the Holy Trinity. The error is understandable—in part because men have been less than forthcoming on the subject.

"What are you thinking about?" is a question that women often ask by way of breaking the polar ice cap of silence over which men so eternally trudge. And here's how natural selection works. Over the centuries, men—those men whose bloodlines have continued, at any rate—have learned to answer: "You."

To admit to thinking of nothing is not a wise tactic for a man to employ in his relationship with a woman. It's not as bad an answer as "Your sister," but it can still create unnecessary problems. Men understand this—if not much else. To say that you're thinking about nothing conveys an impression of either indolence, vacancy or the ability to think about something that doesn't go to pilates class. None of which will get you laid—unless, of course, you're cute, in which case women drop their rigorously high standards surprisingly quickly. If you're cute you can say or do whatever you want.

However, most of us are not cute. Which leaves lying as pretty much the only thing that works. So men learn to lie—not that it's in our nature to lie. We are honest fellows. It's just that we recognize that it's necessary for the species to survive. Procreation is a social imperative, and we like to do our bit. Because as bad as it is to admit to thinking about nothing when a woman asks you what you're thinking about, admitting to getting an erection while thinking about nothing is much, much worse.

A friend of mine—a solid, down-to-earth fellow who is as heterosexual as the day is long—told me that he was troubled when he realized he was getting an erection during a massage. Hold the presses, I thought. But then, as he provided further details, I could see the reason for his concern.

Carl was the reason for his concern. Carl, the masseur. And yet, as far as my friend knew, he was entertaining no fantasies about the large, hairy male who was giving him his rubdown. It's not as if he found the Brut particularly fetching. It's not as if he was irresistibly drawn to the nose hairs or to the little thatch under Carl's chin that his razor had missed. My friend didn't think that he'd given Carl much thought after things got underway. In fact, he didn't think he'd been thinking about anything. "What could this mean?" he asked me.

I used to wonder the same thing about the Aberdeen bus. In my youth, I often took the bus. Perhaps you remember buses. They were a bit like SUVs, only they had no cup-holders, sat a little lower to the ground, used less gasoline and carried more people.

I took the bus downtown. There were always two or three other passengers—all elderly women—sitting primly near the front.

Frequently when I climbed on board the Aberdeen bus—on my way to the "Y" or to what, in those innocent days before multiplexes and fourteen-dollar movies, we called "the show"—I got the impression that I was interrupting a meeting of the Women's Christian Temperance Union.

I suppose my average ride would have been about fifteen minutes' duration. And I was never entirely sure about what happened during those fifteen minutes. Nothing, so far as I could ever recall. I sat. I peered from the window at a streetscape of humdrum, grey houses as the bus groaned and bounced and shuddered toward my destination. I don't think my brain ever shifted from neutral. But however blank my travels, the result of the trip was always disturbingly similar. I rang the bell. I stood. And I always left the bus a few stalwart inches ahead of my feet.

Now, of course, I realize that my condition was caused by haphazard road maintenance and poor suspension. But I was not so wise then. For years I worried that, hideous as the notion was, I was attracted to fox-wrapped old ladies who kept their senior citizen bus tokens in clasped change purses, who smelled faintly of lavender and who were constantly on their way home from downtown after purchasing a few new doilies and antimacassars and another packet of After Eights.

No doubt you noticed the space between this paragraph and its predecessor. Well, that's what I'm talking about. That's exactly the kind of thing that so often gets me into trouble. Nothing, I mean.

Miss Hendershot also wore a kind of deodorant that left faint splotches of green on the underarms of her gym tunic.

There. That's better. Now, where was I? Ah, yes. What I was about to say, apropos of nothing, is this: the truth is, men are drawn to nothingness. Sports radio. Neo-conservatism. Celebrity poker. It's in our nature.

We have passed an infinity prior to our births thinking about nothing much. We are destined to spend an equal amount of time thinking about the same thing after our deaths. Thus it is that men—freed as we are from the rigours of making sure there's enough toilet paper and remembering everybody's birthdays—are predisposed to admitting a little of the truth of the universe into our lives. Thinking about nothing is what men do best. Apparently, there are times when it gets quite exciting.

The proof of this is that men often wake with erections. God knows why. It's quarter to eight in the morning. You forgot to set the alarm. The kids are going to be late for school, the garbage isn't out, the dog hasn't been walked, the carpet cleaners are arriving in fifteen minutes and camels could take shelter under the top sheet should the dust storms get bad.

Women have no parallel to this in their lives. They have no idea about the moral complexities that frequently greet a man before he is even out of bed. The equivalent, perhaps, would be for a woman to wake with a martini in one hand and a lit joint in the other. For no apparent reason. What to do?

Take baseball bats. They have many uses. Laying down a bunt. Fouling off enough full-count fastballs to draw a walk. Defending 7-Elevens. As well, a Louisville Slugger is a nice thing to look at. It need have no purpose other than inspiring contemplation. I find it quite pleasant to have a long, firm, wooden rod of ash around for no particular reason. You never know when a batting cage and a hanging slider will present themselves. If, however, the makers of baseball bats were to insist that the only purpose of their product was a ninth-inning, bases-loaded, come-from-behind home-run with the crowd cheering and the fireworks bursting over the stadium, you can imagine how diminished the sales of baseball bats would be. My guess is that they would fall until they equalled the precise number of Corvette Sting Rays on the road.

This is not to say that erections do not have a role to play. For one thing, their presence, much like the presence of a scented candle, may signal that the act of love is imminent. Or, if not imminent, at least a possible alternative to television. With an erection, it's possible to run desire up the flagpole, so to speak, and see who salutes.

But are erections central to lovemaking? Or entirely peripheral? That can be a bewildering question. For a man. In these confusing times. Let me explain.

In part, the confusion arises because it often seems that the only times that erections are absolutely obligatory are those rare (or so one hopes, for all the good hoping will do) occasions when you don't have one. If, on the other hand, some serendipitous combination of raw oysters, ginseng tea, prescription drugs, rare steak, ground rhinoceros horn and not-having-had-sex-for-three-weeks means that your bowsprit is proudly leading you home to port, you will be informed, coolly, that there's a good deal more to sex than your penis. She will ask: Can't you be a little more considerate? A little more generous? A little more loving? A little less self-obsessed?

We can, of course. Anything's possible. We could get out the Scrabble board if anyone thought it would help. But unfortunately, at such a juncture, an erection is difficult to ignore—both emotionally and geometrically. And when you get down to it—and you might as well; there will be hell to pay if you don't every now and then—there's not a lot for an erection to do during foreplay. During foreplay, an erection sits on the bench, its throwing arm throbbing in the keen anticipation of a ninety-yard Hail Mary. It watches from the sidelines as the second-string quarterback calls draw play after draw play through the middle. This is excitement? the erection asks. Sheesh. How long, it wonders, can a human jaw hold out?

Another common misconception is the widely held belief that having an erection and having a social conscience are mutually exclusive activities. Far from it. As the baby-boom generation slouches toward the nothingness from whence it came I'm beginning to think that they might be the same thing.

Consider the eerie parallels:

Erections are most readily and abundantly available to those who can't use them for very much. There are times when I lie abed and ruefully consider the untapped hydraulics that went to waste in Miss Peebles's math class.

And precisely the same is true of social consciences. Intent on social justice, environmental responsibility, and Third World debt relief, an idealistic youth might as well have a hard-on in a sleeping bag at summer camp for all the good his passion will do him. But the great irony—the tragedy, in fact—is that by the time that idealistic youth, along with the better part of the enormous bulge of his generation, becomes established enough, and influential enough, and affluent enough to effect meaningful social change, he isn't much interested in meaningful social change anymore.

What can be said of something that sprang so frequently into action when action was not a possibility, and now retreats so unceremoniously when it is? Not much, I daresay. Perhaps it wasn't called the Woodstock Generation for nothing. Once firm in his conviction that he would change the world, the aging male baby boomer now thinks that the ten minutes he spends once a week walking a blue box to the curb is a rock-solid act of social responsibility.

How the mighty have fallen.

# Russell Wangersky

■

## HEROES

Her hair was piled like white candy floss, as soft as feathers. I knew how soft it would feel, just by the way the individual hairs shivered in the breeze. Hard to escape from that, holding a fire hose just three or four feet from her face.

Running up to the car, still thinking there was something that could be done, carrying the trauma kit and already going through the sequence of things to do. Another K-car in a crash, another victim. Thank God her eyes were closed.

And it was summer, and the cows were out in the fields, huge and wandering, udders distended. The window on her side was down, and I was reaching in to see if there was a pulse in her neck, carotid artery, the easy one, just like we were taught.

And Al MacDonald, Big Al, grabbed my arm before I touched her, grabbed my arm and looking at me as if I were stupid.

"There's an engine block in her lap," he said, incredulous that I hadn't noticed something so obvious.

And there was. Torn from its engine mounts, pushed in through the firewall, tucked between her forced knees as neatly as a lover. And I wonder how I hadn't noticed something as simple as that, when I could notice so much else: the smell of fuel oil and summer grass, the first because the car had sheered off the filler cap to the oil tank in the basement of the house she had hit, the second because it was high summer, and the hay mowers had been out, turning the grass and clover in long, tumbled green lines, ready for the baler.

When I could notice how hard the car had hit the chimney, and that bricks were scattered loose across the hood, but I didn't notice that she was crushed beyond any hope.

And they had me stand there with the hose until the medical examiner came to confirm what we already knew, that she was dead, dead enough for everyone else to walk away and pack up the gear, and the milkweed pods were breaking apart, the lightest of air currents catching the thin, almost crystalline tufts of seeds and carrying them up, up so that the sunlight caught them glinting, always rising. High summer in Nova Scotia's Annapolis Valley, the grass on the shoulder of the road already past green to yellow-brown, the air holding steady like a breath drawn all the way in and waiting.

The lady with the candy-floss hair was the first person I had ever seen dead: no family members, waxy and hands folded across their stomachs in their coffins, not even a closed-casket, distant dead cousin found gripping the stock of a shotgun.

It's hard to imagine how I got there—and at the same time it isn't. Boys and heroes—I suppose that's the beginning. A boy's belief that you just might be Superman, that you might be a firefighter or a policeman, that sometime, for some moment, your talents might be called upon to do something great. Not something complicated— something great, something that involves nothing more than your muscles working in the calm, straightforward, ordered way that muscles are supposed to work. The way they work for someone else, the way they work for someone in a comic book, or for the square-jawed guy who can stretch his body out horizontal to the ground and, diving, always catch the crucial long fly ball.

You don't think about being a university professor or a newspaper editor. Not ever. (My father was the first, and I am the second.) But I was a volunteer firefighter before almost everything else, trained at eighteen to do CPR and to stop arterial bleeding, to use the heavy tools to cut people out of cars smashed up in highway accidents. The Jaws of Life, the air chisels, the Vetter bags—big, reinforced rubber bags that can lift whole vehicles with air pressure—I was trained for all of it. I was even trained for things I'd never want to see: what to do about "flail chest," when all the ribs are broken on one side and can't help the lungs inflate. For choking, for full-thickness burns, for the shock of accidental amputation.

I jumped at the chance while I was still in university, eager to do something that had been denied me because of my poor eyesight. Paid, full-time firefighters are a particular type—big enough and strong enough, and always with 20/20 vision.

When you've been ruled out for something, and then you get the chance for it anyway, the chance to do the training and wear the gear, wide red suspenders and all, well, you jump at it.

And after a while, you realize it's crystallized into something more: if you're really unlucky, you realize you've always hoped—and now, I realize, almost planned, and eventually virtually expected—to one day do something heroic. You look around at the other firefighters, and imagine that it's something they're thinking, too. But it's not something you're likely to talk about. Talk in the fire hall skids along the surface: there are rules—say too much, and you get the sideways look.

Perhaps, however unlikely, my belief was that maybe I'd help someone, and they would just sit up, brush themselves off, and say "thanks." And the crowd that invariably gathers in any public place where someone has collapsed would spontaneously burst into applause. People I didn't know would pound congratulations on my back. You see men who can do that: mostly on television, occasionally in person, the kind who takes charge and does things right.

But it's not that simple. I can remember every single person I've ever done CPR on, can remember the feel of their skin, the stubble of their whiskers, the sounds and smells that come from them, the invaded privacy of their living rooms or bedrooms or front halls.

You end up in a relationship you can't shake, with a person you don't even know.

I was in the fire department for a few months before the night with the drunk-tank man, just long enough to have gone to the riveting excitement of a van fire where a burning right-side tire exploded, dropping frightened firefighters to the pavement. Long enough to go to a car accident where a single car had jumped a guardrail into the Gaspereau River, where I was assigned to sit and talk to the panicked driver, both of us in the rescue truck, while more experienced firefighters were cutting her injured passenger out of the wreck.

I had the basics by then, the emergency first aid, the CPR, the nuts and bolts of the breathing gear, and what to do if the air suddenly cuts out, sticking the mask tight to your face. And I had crawled around the firehouse in the pitch black, a garbage bag tied over my breathing gear so that I couldn't see, imagining I was heading up the stairs to rescue frightened children from smoky closets. But the skills hadn't become habit yet.

The lockup was next door to the fire station, so it wasn't hard to get there. There, where a drunk threw up into another firefighter's mouth during artificial respiration. Threw up, even though he was already dead. Back then, before HIV and AIDS, when you did artificial respiration without a mask between you and the victim. When the training films used to say, "Pinch their nose, tilt their head back, and make a seal on their mouth with your lips." Obscenely, graphically close, a horrible pantomime of a kiss.

It makes me think that's why people want firefighters to stay just professional enough, just distant enough that they could cut away your shirt, put their hands on your warm, naked skin, and walk away afterwards without thinking about it, without ever thinking about you again. Walk away without ever giving away how much they now know about you. That you have a mole that your lover might touch with a fingertip, just there. That, if you die, your mouth will hang open, and I might wonder how it is that you ended up with so many fillings.

In the back of the fire hall, then, the other firefighter was rinsing his mouth with distilled water from the back of the rescue truck, saying wryly, "Now, *he* was dead drunk." Then he threw up himself, threw up into the long drain grate that the slush melted into when we backed in after driving the big trucks in snow.

The trainers might have had the decency to have taught me the averages. They might have taught me up front, as I understand they do now, that only one out of every ten people you treat with CPR will actually survive—and by survive, I just mean they will make it to the hospital with something close to a beating heart and a working brain.

Years later, on the night of the March social for a volunteer fire department in the small Newfoundland town of St. Philip's—working at a new newspaper, volunteering with a new fire department— I remember that I was sound asleep when the pager went off, and the paramedics needed help on Bradbury's Road. That's all the dispatcher said.

Waking from a sound sleep, there's always that immediate dislocation, that inability, for an instant, to figure out where you are or what you are doing, until the pieces fall together and you fall into the place: the light from the hall, the hulk of the dresser against the wall, the curtains, wavering where they should be in the half-light. No wonder I always leave my clothes laid out in the same order, socks on top, then pants. Your stomach is already half in your mouth from the shock of being woken so suddenly, of being dragged upright and trying to catch everything that's being said on the pager.

That night, it was icy roads, and no one on the radio. No sign that anyone else was responding, no trucks keying up their microphones to say that anyone else had even left the station. The swing of the back end of my pickup through the slush and snowdrifts, so that I was always fighting against the rear wheels, cutting the front wheels too far over and trying to stay out of the ditch. The night both empty and lonely, snow drifting across the road in the way that suggested no one had been there in hours, the long, gilled, breathing snowdrifts, cut in the rearview mirror only by my own wheel marks. Turning into the driveway, seeing the rescue truck abandoned, its lights spinning, its doors yawning open, in the driveway with no one in sight.

And everyone was there in the living room—husband, wife, the two firefighters. The house would go on the market a couple of weeks later, a blue and white sign swinging in the wind in the front yard.

The husband was on the floor in the living room, and immediacy makes things simple; the room was muddy, everything the same set of earth colours. The husband, flat on his back near the stairs, the couch pushed back out of the way. The brightest light on in the kitchen, casting a long yellow triangle across the carpet. The staircase behind, angled up.

An airway down his throat, obscene, so that his mouth was a small and unyielding white plastic "O," and the two firefighters were alone there from the rescue truck, no one to drive, no one else to help, and what kind of trust is that: they were out beyond the reach of the radios, both working, both trusting that someone else would eventually show up. You don't know how physical it is unless you've done it; they were working him, sweating already. His skin was too, too white, and it was shivering away from their hands in ripples—they pushed, and his stomach shimmied reflexively away in fleshy little waves. They wanted the backboard, and the gurney. They wanted someone to help them lift him onto the board, and no one in the world would ever want to be in that room. They needed help, in the kind of place anyone would just want to walk away from.

And when the big pumper came, it drove spinning right across the lawn, the big truck sliding sideways away across the grass, tearing up great trenches down through the snow to the soil.

And I wound up driving the man's wife into the city: you're supposed to be able to do something, to fold people into your big, strong arms, to make things right through sheer strength. But you can't—you simply can't do it, and that's crushing, too. She sat beside me in the front seat while the red light spun on its almost noiseless axis just inside the windshield.

Asking that Faustian question: Do you want me to put the siren on?

Of course you do. If you could press a button and make the truck sprout wings to get there even faster, you would. But no one will ever say "Yes." No one ever really wants the siren. Embarrassed that its wail might be unnecessary, embarrassed because of the attention it will inevitably draw. Embarrassed, because someone has sadistically put that choice into your hands.

Coming into the emergency room with her—a woman who sat next to me in my truck, so close that I could hear her stifled sobs, but whose name I never knew—I watched the emergency room nurse spot me in my firefighting gear, put the pieces together and give her head that final, warning half-shake. The shake that means, don't tell her yet, but he's dead.

Don't make promises; don't even begin to suggest that things might be all right. Wash your hands of her in the waiting room cleanly and walk away, as clean as you can, as clean as you can be when you're lying by not telling what is obviously now the truth. That's what the look is supposed to do; it's supposed to give you the clue to disengage, to get away while you can. It's a throwaway, a kindness, a warning, and your heart falls.

But someone still has to wait to pick up the backboard, someone still has to wash it off and collect the loose tangle of black nylon strapping that holds the patient on the board, someone still has to slide it back into the empty, cooling rescue truck and imagine that there's nothing important about it, that it doesn't ride always with its own ghosts.

No one ever tells you what it will do to you—sure, they tell you that you can't help but be affected by what you will see, how it may come at you strangely, in your dreams, or even in the daylight, triggered by something as simple as driving by a particular house again. But they don't tell you how it will pick you up by the neck and shake you silly, how it will blast your nights with doubt and leave you cringing. I picture myself in my head fighting fires in all my bunker gear: the image isn't of me, naked except for my boxer shorts, sitting in the moonlit midnight emptiness of my living room, tears streaming uncontrollably down my face. But the man on the scene gets both.

And they don't tell you about the sex. They really should tell you about the sex, at least so it doesn't smack into you unexpectedly. They should have told me that I would come home with the death-smell still in my nose, with the powder from the gloves still on my hands, with it all still clinging, impermeable, to my clothes. That I would think I should be monastic, that I should be saintly and thoughtful and religious in what everyone considers a solemn moment. They should tell you that in reality all you will want to do is to rip the clothes off someone you love. That you want to roll wild, that you want to boil, that you want your flesh to shiver, that you want to tremble and fall.

That you want to howl at the night that they're dead, they're dead—but I'm still alive. Damn you all, I'm still alive.

And since they don't tell you, afterwards you can look forward to spending the rest of the night ashamed for just that, listening to the even breathing of someone sleeping next to you, sleeping with their damned clear conscience. And it will happen again, and again, and again.

I can count them off, as familiar as my own fingertips. I can see them, and I know each one.

Rita.

Wilkin's dad.

The snowplow driver.

But perhaps you need more than that.

A woman, Rita, somewhere over seventy years old, and then a man, Wilkin's dad, in the same age range, both dead less than a month apart on the same floor of the same Royal Canadian Legion Hall. She, spread like an unlikely lime-green starfish on the wooden parquet floor, he in grey flannel pants, suspenders, and a shirt that stayed pressed at the collar even when he didn't. She, toppling over at a seniors' dance, and he, at a wedding reception. Looking at Rita, I remember thinking, "The odds are against this." It's mostly men in cardiac arrest, and even though she was clearly over seventy, the books say she was more likely to be toppled by stroke or by congestive heart failure, a heart muscle in there somewhere fluttering like a desperate little bird. Looking at Wilkin's dad, his mouth gaping in that slack-ligament way, I was only able to conjure up one thought: "Here we go again."

And we did go there, again. Breathing for them when they didn't breathe, leaning into their chests to make the oxygenated blood circulate. Breaking ribs. Cracking, snapping ribs, but never slowing the pace, never deviating from the pattern. Checking for a pulse, checking for breathing, then starting it all again by rote when they didn't breathe, and the ambulance didn't come. They tell you when you should start; they've left out the opportunity to ever, ever, stop.

Doctors decide when people are dead. Emergency workers just keep going. Volunteer firefighters are right down there at the bottom of the ladder, doing basic lifesaving and waiting—always waiting—for help to arrive.

They were classic coronaries, both. The snowplow driver, too, and he wasn't that far away, plowing the Legion lot. The plow blade of his truck ended up against the corner of the building, wheels still turning, tires smoking and squealing, because his foot didn't leave the gas pedal. And he was like waxwork coming out of the cab of the truck, as if he would never unbend from the curled position into which he had bent himself around the unyielding curve of the steering wheel. Reach in to turn off the ignition, and know that the last fingers to touch that key had no idea, no idea whatsoever, that anything was wrong, that anything was going to happen.

Then it was a small, delicate woman who died in front of a television, bleeding silently from dental surgery while she slept. Bleeding into her belly. Once we started working on her, it got messy fast.

I picked things up in instants then. She was as white as clean bond paper. Even her lips were washed out and pale. Her skin under my hands felt empty, drained, as if there was nothing left inside her—or maybe I just imagined that afterwards. One thing I didn't imagine is that she didn't really have anything close to a chance, that every chance had bled away, moment by moment. We were the denouement to a story that had played out everything except the last word of its ending.

The Red Cross once had a slogan, a slogan that sold CPR as a way of becoming a hero—they used those exact words. Learn first aid and be a hero. You don't know how seductive an offer that is, to the right man, to the skinny boy who watched the fire trucks stop, red lights flashing, and the big men piling off the truck. And maybe the Red Cross learned somewhere along the way that there is nothing as shattered as a fallen hero, that instead of losing one person, sometimes you might well wind up losing two. Maybe, in the great scheme of having someone step forward, take control of the scene and act—perhaps saving a life—maybe in that, the chances of losing two people really didn't matter.

People do learn, sometimes, because they did stop calling artificial respiration "the kiss of life."

They would have stopped that anyway, if they'd met the cold man.

Not much more I need to say than that. It should have been enough, all by itself. Twenty-three years old, in the dark back bedroom of a white bungalow—a one-storey, with green shingles and the street number big and black next to the front door. An easy address to find, not like some. He had the blankets up to his chin, and he was cold to the touch, and stiff. He had a heart defect, it turned out. A clock that just stopped, a spring that wound down.

But that didn't keep anyone from working on him just the same.

"Stop, boys. Just stop."

The fire captain actually had to grab one of the firefighters by the wrists. You follow the routine, just the way you're trained to—you get past the horrible by focusing on the mechanical.

And sometimes I would sit and wonder why I did it at all, the feeling rushing up over me and clenching at my chest so tightly I could barely even breathe. It pulls back like a wave, and you feel yourself twisting and rolling, caught in underneath and unable to surface.

For a while, as an officer, it was part of my job to look for the firefighters who might need help, talking to them back at the station and watching for the ones who squirm and won't hold your eyes. The younger firefighters who one day just stop talking. Two new firefighters find a suicide in the water supply; an experienced guy, a captain, decides to treat a bad facial cut at a wild accident scene and misses the teenager with the skull fracture, and suddenly can't make decisions anymore. Cut the quiet ones out from the herd, get them aside on their own, quietly hand them the counsellor's number. I never, ever thought to call that number myself.

Because there's a secret to it, a secret to the whole business. A secret I'd lose if there was ever any reason for them to decide to take me off the job.

When you leave an accident scene in the middle of the night, around three o'clock, when you've rolled up all the hose and swept the broken glass off the pavement and watched the ambulance roll away, then everything is in sharper focus. Robins sing liquid in the first light, and there's the sharp smell of wet pavement, and truly, your vision is sharper, and the things you hear are clearer, more distinct, more beautiful. Maybe it's adrenalin, maybe it's the strange security of having dodged someone else's fate. But the scales fall away from the night, and the sky is never more blue.

Then Craig's dad. The last. Two, three years ago—I don't remember. But every time I shave, I can draw a diagram of his living room in the mist on the mirror.

Craig, a reporter at my newspaper, suddenly jumping up at the office, dropping the phone on his desk. Yelling "Call 911 to my house! My dad's down on the floor!" And me, running after him, thinking at the time that he shouldn't drive: nothing more than that, just that he shouldn't drive. Not even on call as a firefighter then, just a co-worker. And the road was wet, greasy wet, glassy wet, and I put the light on the dashboard, white and red, white and red, spinning, and the toggle switch for the siren was right there by my left knee— I can feel it now, know the angle my arm needs to take to touch it. I've turned it on in the pitch black on the first try—up for yelp, down for wail. It is silver, and the end of the switch is a smooth teardrop shape. I can feel it, feel it between my fingers—and if I look down, I know exactly how far apart the index finger and thumb on my left hand will be from one another.

I ran three sets of lights—Canada Drive, Blackmarsh Road and Mundy Pond Road—and I can remember slowing for each one, looking for traffic. I can remember seeing the faces of startled drivers at each one, and that the road was as shiny and black as licorice. I also remember that I didn't ever touch the siren. I parked on the wrong side of the road, driver's side wheels thumped up over the curb on the sidewalk, and we ran in through the shining rain. And the truck was silent.

Just inside the door, and he was lying there. Craig had to step over him to get to his mother, in the kitchen. And I remember thinking, coming through that door, that this time I had really fenced myself in, that, just by being there, there was nothing I could do except help; I had absolutely no choice but to do something.

And with it, a feeling you get sometimes when you're the first one on a scene, even when you have had every single scrap of training, a feeling somewhere between indecision and a crisis of confidence, even when you've done it all before: "It's too bad, guys. It's too bad you got the fake firefighter."

Then I was alone in the front hall with him, an overweight man stretched out like an unlikely door mat right there, his small dog wheeling and barking.

Lying in a place where I knew he would always be remembered by his family, every time they came in that door, as indelibly as if his outline were painted right there on the floor forever. Harder still because his parents lived with Craig in the same small house.

I remember thinking, if anyone, let me save this one. They'll never get over this, not in this house, not in this home. So let me save just this one. Just one. And I remember his purple mouth, the rasping last two breaths that shook the great curve of his stomach. Stomach breaths, reflex breaths, those great shudders that you dread seeing, the ones they sometimes call a death rattle. And the skin on his chest was impossibly soft, like the underside of your arm, there almost to your armpit.

His lips were darkening to blue, his face devolving through red to purple, and the ambulance still hadn't come. And Craig was yelling into the phone for the paramedics—"Just get here, just get here fast" and his mother was still sitting in a chair in the kitchen, resigned, her back to us, and the dog was circling the living room, barking, sometimes biting my pant leg.

Shouting to Craig between breaths, telling him to tell the 911 operator it was a Code-4 medical, which is emergency room shorthand for moments—mere instants—from death, and I hoped he hadn't ever heard enough to understand what I meant. My own little head-shake, and I didn't know if anyone would even see it.

One, two, three, four, five. It's easy, you think in a detached way, to understand why CPR is taught the way it is, like a mnemonic, but in numbers. So you won't forget. So your hands take over, and your mind checks out. Or tries to. Tries desperately to check out, to get away from all the information it's collecting to let spill out later in your dreams. One, two, three, four, five. One, two, three, four, five. Tilt the head back. Breathe, breathe. One, two, three, four, five.

Then help came through the door all at once, scattering equipment and medical packaging. Trauma kit and heart-start monitor, the blue nylon bag that always holds the suction kit; things bang and crash on the hardwood floor, and the noise is angular and sharp, far from the rolling wail of grief. The paramedic had gloves on already, her hair tied back, and I remember that she was attractive—and I don't like to think why that still bothers me. With one pass of the round-nosed scissors, she had the rest of his shirt off, from bottom to top, so that he was lying on the floor naked from the waist up.

"He's packed solid," she said, taking the suction kit and clearing vomit from his throat. I knew all about that already, I just couldn't do anything about it. She peeled the covers from the monitor pads, stuck them onto his chest.

Twice, the heart monitor said his heart was beating again, and she said, "He's back," and you wonder, like you always do, who's going to be back, what kind of person will be there, and if they will be anything like the person their family used to know. Because it's always hard to get enough air through. Harder still when the airway is blocked, harder still when it's taken you so long to get there. So are you saving someone, or just finding someone new, someone quite different? And then, twice, his heart stopped again, and the monitor croaked its mechanical message, "Start compressions, start compressions."

Her partner fighting with the gurney, trying to get the wheeled stretcher in through the crowded front hall. People still coming in, and the last man through the door swept everything up in his arms. Craig's dad's heart was beating at that point, and I was kneeling, sweating, my hands flat on my knees. The last man through the door kicked the screen door open again, and with a heave, all the hockey sticks, the coats, the coat rack, everything that was wrapped up in his arms was thrown out into the melting snow. As simple and thoughtless as a shrug, because it had to be done. It was like a switch thrown in my head—don't think, just do.

Too late, though. Too, too much thinking already.

I remember going in the ambulance, Craig's father's chest hooked up to the heart monitor, and the paramedic was telling me that I was doing fine, that the chest compressions were clear and sharp and strong on the monitor. And that's the first time I'd ever known that. About an inch and a half to two inches, they tell you for some compressions, but everyone is different; maybe they have a big barrel chest, maybe they're fat. With an infant, you use two fingers, and you only press down about half an inch to an inch, your fingers at the centre of the chest, just half an inch below the nipples. Everything so neat, so fine, so perfect, so small, that you feel like you are imagining it all. But believe me, you don't ever want to have to think about that. Not ever. Even when you're practising on the training doll, it just comes home too quickly, goes stomping right up the stairs and looks into the crib at your own kid.

There's a chrome bar that runs along the ceiling, and everything in the narrow, cramped space of the back of an ambulance is planned. Spread your legs, hold onto the bar, and you're at exactly the right height to keep doing CPR with one hand, while the ambulance throws itself around corners and you keep your balance, holding onto the ceiling bar. And the ambulance tries to throw you again and again, and it can't.

Eventually, when the sweat is pouring down into your eyes, when every single thing has already happened, you're at the hospital, and it all ends. And everything you're doing is taken away from you. Not passed off, not picked up by someone else, but somehow, taken away.

Watching the doctors wheel Craig's father away from the ambulance entrance, still pressing on his chest, watching the doors swing closed behind the gurney, and knowing then, even without the shake of a head. Knowing that I'd actually done it all right, and he'd died anyway. I knew from their stride, I knew the difference in their movements between trying and really trying. I knew when the minister came out and grabbed Craig by the elbow. And I knew Craig didn't know, so I went out and got in a cab.

Disengage.

I went back to Craig's house to get my jacket, and my truck was still on the curb, and the red and white light was still circling blindly on the dashboard. I remember Craig's wife and his mother still in the living room, my coat lying on the floor where I had thrown it, and I can still feel the heat of the emergency light, hot on the heel of my right hand when I took it off the dash and pulled its plug out of the cigarette lighter.

The next morning, his obituary was in the paper, and I found out his name was Frederick. At the bottom, "a very special thank you to," and then my name. I have that obituary somewhere, folded in my wallet, I think, the newsprint soft and ragged at the edges, starting to yellow, the ink smudging from body heat.

Special thanks.

Special thanks for nothing.

And there aren't heroes, anymore than there are lottery winners who know anything else but luck. Here's the hard statistic; even if you're there in less than four minutes, something like 93 percent of people who get CPR will die.

There's the funny thing about kids and the men they become—and the heroes they both want to become. Funny how deeply you can be betrayed by reaching for something, failing in the attempt, and still find yourself waiting eagerly at the edge of the curb.

I remember every person I've ever done CPR on. And I remember, too, that not one of nine survived. But I know where to put my hands. I will always know where to start—three fingers above the bottom of the rib cage, one hand folded over the other.

*Brian D. Johnson*

■

# ROCK 'N' ROLL

## HERNIA

Men prefer not to over-think the pelvis. Generally speaking, our attitude is: let that whole mysterious region enjoy its sovereignty, like a small but spirited principality that defies understanding. We see "down there" as kindergarten geometry, a holy trinity of one cock and two balls, all of which move of their own accord. Spare us the details.

Women, from what I can gather, are more savvy about things pelvic. Pelvic histories, pelvic futures, pelvic scars, pelvic memoirs—there's a constant awareness, and discussion, of how this baroque cartography of reproductive channels, chambers, valves and (above all) the womb is knowable. Mix in feminism, and the notion of "our bodies, ourselves," and it becomes clear that women have a vital controlling interest in their sexual *terroir*. And because the female anatomy has been the testing ground of the sexual revolution—doped by The Pill, invaded by IUDs and STDs, scarred by abortion, colonized via in vitro, automated by Caesarean, mothballed by hysterectomy, women have learned to pay attention to what's going on inside their bodies, and to compare notes.

Guys, on the other hand, like to be a bit thick about how it all works. We don't have to go looking for our genitals. They're on the outside, overt. We deal with impediments as they arise (or not). The holy trinity is expected to be self-governing, and when there are issues they tend to be mechanical, like a bicycle catching a tack in the back tire. Nothing as exotic, or Cronenbergian, as endometriosis.

(Scary: uterine tissue that grows wild outside the womb.) Elephantiasis of the genitals is always a slim possibility, but for the most part men deal with sexually transmitted diseases, erectile dysfunction, enlarged prostates and—that most mundane of manly afflictions—hernias.

Usually we're taking about an *inguinal* hernia. It's not a direct assault on the trinity as such, but it's perilously close—a breaching of the abdominal wall just above the groin. And when most men discover they have a hernia, the usual course of action is to pretend that it's not there, like the San Andreas Fault, and to ignore it for as long as humanly possible. Sure, you might get a bit of intestine that starts bulging through, like ripe Camembert. But you just poke it back in. And that actually works for a while. If we could fix a hernia with duct tape, we would.

Finally I went to my doctor.

When he diagnosed me, he seemed almost pleased. "Yep, you've a got a little hernia there," he said, with the satisfaction of someone putting his finger on something tangible and familiar, a cute little ailment that's not life-threatening. He seemed almost pleased. It must be pretty boring having guys cough day in day out while you hold their groin and don't find anything. The doctor said there was nothing to worry about, but eventually I would have to "take care of it," as they say on *The Sopranos*.

So Little Hernia became my abdominal Chia Pet, growing by increments over the years. It wasn't much, but it was mine. And if it weren't for rock 'n' roll, maybe I'd still have it. But I happen to be one of those fifty-five-year-old men who still find it necessary to be in a band. I play congas, a set of three heavy oak drums hand-carved out of staves from Jamaican rum barrels. Lugging these things in and out of the trunk of the car was bad enough. But when I played, seated with a drum between my legs, Little Hernia would start to scream. It seemed especially responsive to the kinds of stimulants that nourish the rock 'n' roll lifestyle. One night, as I was playing a gig, the pain became excruciating, but I couldn't exactly leave in mid-performance, and the agony got worse as the night wore on. Somewhere between *My Generation* and *Gimme Shelter*,

I discreetly slipped a finger under my waistband and tried to pop the hernia back in, but to no avail. I had a "wide on" that just wouldn't go away. So I went back to the doctor, who offered a cheerful warning about the danger of dying from a strangulated intestine. It was time to put Little Hernia out of its misery.

■

It's hard to get much sympathy for a hernia operation. This is the most minor, lowest-risk surgery you could possibly imagine. Not only that, but if you live in Ontario, you will probably end up at the luxurious Shouldice Hospital, a country club clinic in a former mansion on twenty acres of rolling grounds north of Toronto. The place was founded by Dr. Edward Earle Shouldice, an army major during the First World War. He developed his own technique for repairing hernias and getting men back on their feet in record time—so that they could enlist. What kind of man would let a hernia stop him from dying for Queen and country? Shouldice's technique was so effective, civilians began to line-up for it.

The Shouldice now draws patients from all over the world. It does nothing but hernias, a dozen a day. It's a private hospital, but Ontario residents get reimbursed by medicare, except for the semi-private room charge, which is covered by most corporate health plans. The Shouldice likes to keep its patients sequestered for three to four nights. They say it helps them recover more smoothly. No kidding. When I told this to a former emergency room doctor in Quebec, he practically fell over laughing. "That's a total milk job," he said, "a four-day milk job. In Montreal a hernia is day surgery."

And of course he's right. While women are being whisked through hospitals, having breasts and uteruses and babies removed with barely a sleepover, I would spend three nights enjoying one of the most benign surgical experiences on earth. Apparently I had stumbled upon one of the few remaining niches of male privilege; Little Hernia would be served like a princeling while newborn babes are sent home in a cab.

Still, I worried. I didn't want to lose my surgical virginity just yet. I'd never been cut. Well, at least not through the outer perimeter of the flesh. A few years earlier I had what was euphemistically called a "procedure" in the same pelvic triangle—a trans-urethral section. For some reason, there was scar tissue blocking the neck of my bladder, which caused the walls to pouch into rococo little sub-bladders called diverticula. Under general anesthetic, I had a doctor insert a small power tool up my penis to cut away the blockage. I got a good look at the implement. It was the Swiss Army Knife of surgical gear—a combination scalpel and periscope. Afterwards, I spent several days convalescing in the hospital, tethered to a catheter.

What? No, no, really, I'm fine, thanks. The only reason I bring this up is to make a point about the overwhelming stupidity of the penis, which often doesn't know what's good for it. While catheterized and asleep, I'd be woken up by the searing pain of an unwelcome erection. The idiot penis, interpreting the pain as another indiscriminate sensation, would just get stubbornly harder. More evidence that the cock has a mind of its own—one that understands only "on" and "off," like Robin Williams with a microphone. But that experience taught me something I'll never forget: it's always better to have your penis inside something—anything really—than it is to have something inside your penis.

In other words, I'd had some rather perverse dentistry done on my pelvis, a little root canal. But I'd never been cut open. So as the date for my first "real" operation approached, I felt pretty jittery. My wife dismissed my fears out of hand, said there was nothing to worry about. She thought I was fetishizing my beloved skin, as if this were just more Peter Pan behaviour—grow up, her attitude seemed to say, get surgery. But I felt there was more to it, that my fear had something to do with just where the surgery would take place, this delta of male vulnerability. And although I hadn't become overly attached to my hernia, I confessed to my wife that, as a pelvic opening, it was like a mini-vagina. That produced howls of laughter. At least she didn't say, "Go fuck yourself."

A few days later, however, I consulted an anatomy book and looked up inguinal hernia. Vindication! This common ailment, as it turns out, is located in a spooky little site called "the inguinal triangle." And it's defined as the protrusion of an organ, usually the intestine, through an invagination in the abdominal wall, caused by the *processus vaginalis*.

Allow me to quote from a racy little volume titled *Clinically Oriented Anatomy*: "Normally, most of the processus vaginalis disappears before birth . . . if the entire stalk of the processus vaginalis persists, the hernia extends into the scrotum superior to the testis, forming a complete indirect inguinal hernia." So there you have it, the entire stalk of some vaginal procession was causing a dent in my abdomen. If you could stick your baby finger through this dent, you'd spear something called the superficial inguinal ring, which lies at the headwaters of the inguinal canal. In the male, this originated as the birth canal for the testicles—a chute through which they drop to the scrotum when the fetus is about eight months old. The canal also encases the spermatic cord and the infamous cremaster muscle—the weirdly involuntary hoist that raises and lowers the testicles. This bit of yoyo engineering inspired avant-garde impresario Matthew Barney to make *The Cremaster Cycle*, a wildly ambitious suite of five feature films that examine the groined fork of sexual differentiation through performance art, Vaseline sculpture, geometric arcana and surreal pageantry.

The cremaster: now we were getting somewhere. A manly name evoking in equal parts "master," "masturbate" and the exquisite *crema* of an Italian espresso. It also conjures an image of a high-end food processor with Porsche-like styling.

But I digress. Here's the thing. By coincidence, I went directly from booking my operation at Shouldice's downtown clinic to a screening of Matthew Barney's *Cremaster 3*—a three-hour Wagnerian opus in which the director magnifies his anatomical metaphor into a blockbuster film, a high-brow answer to a Jerry Bruckheimer action flick. Serial killer Gary Gilmore's body, as a woman, is interred in one of five vintage Chrysler Imperials, which converge in a pentagram of automotive menace in the lobby of the Chrysler Building. Slowly, they begin a demolition derby that continues until the floor is a blackened action painting of debris and grime, and all that's left of Gilmore's Imperial hearse is a compressed cube of steel. Barney himself, resembling Indiana Jones, plays a mountaineer who scales the elevator cables of the Chrysler Building, a leather tool belt of jade obelisks hanging off his waist. Those cables, that shaft . . . it's all *beyond* phallic. Here's an exceptionally well-endowed artist (he has a serious budget) taking male sexual mythology upriver, right up the inguinal canal, to create some mad Masonic Stonehenge. The film feels more erected than directed.

And there, on the top floor of the Chrysler Building, I caught a glimpse of my hernia! Like a vision of the Virgin Mary on a piece of toast. I saw it in the bulging slit between a pair of elevator doors that would not quite close, as a bagpipe drone sifted through the crack, modulating the sound of wind bellowing up the shaft.

So . . . primed by this hyperbolic prologue, I felt I wasn't just going to have an operation. I was going to have a medical-mystical experience. Must prepare. As my surgery grew near, I went from being nervous about this procedure to treating it as a kind of ritual circumcision. On the night before the operation, I found myself writing questionable poetry.

> *waiting for the incision*
> *an early morning skate*
> *down the inguinal canal*
> *begat in the prenatal night*
> *as a fetal flume ride for the descending grape*
> *which now rappels up and down the sex cliffs*
> *of the cremaster muscle*
> *on braided winds*
> *of temperature*
> *and desire*

The Shouldice, like a package-holiday resort, works on a double-occupancy basis. The rooms look like they belong in a hotel, not a hospital. I was billeted with Tim, a corporate accountant who was roughly my age. A decent guy. He seemed utterly normal, even though he was a member of the Anglican Church and played the bagpipes. Tim was the kind of guy you wouldn't mind getting stuck beside on a long flight. He kept to his side of the room and was affable company, but he'd let you read in silence. We usually went down to the dining room for meals together. The food was better than hospital food had any right to be. It was actually very good. And the surroundings were pleasant. We'd sit around a table, half a dozen patients who were at various stages of the assembly line, from pre-op to post-op to healing-up-very-nicely, thank you. It was reassuring to hear people who had been through it talk about how it was no big deal. (Although I did end up playing a distressing game of pool with a post-op Hassidic Jew who said he was in considerable pain, I dismissed him as a malcontent.) I was turned off initially by the cult-like notion of patient solidarity that the Shouldice promotes (they even have patient reunions), but when you're about to go under the knife, you're happy to get with the program. It made me wonder why all operations weren't organized like this, like club activities.

All but two of the four dozen patients were male. Hernia is twenty times more common in men than in women. When a woman gets one, according to my anatomy text, it forms an abdominal pouch called the canal of Nuck (*sic*), which can produce a bulge in the labia. Wild. The two women at the Shouldice were both young athletes, one a volleyball player. The men seemed to take great interest in them.

I had a briefing session with my surgeon, a middle-aged Asian man who answered my journalistic interrogation with offhand quips ("I haven't lost anyone yet"), then apologized, explaining that doing the same thing over and over is so boring you've got to find a way of staying interested. He explained the operation, which involved cutting through the abdominal wall and interleafing layers of muscle to make an unbreakable seam. He told me I would be sedated and frozen with a local anesthetic but awake during the operation. I could bring my own music for the CD player, but no earphones. That bothered me. I was hoping it would be like dentistry. Ever since I started using nitrous oxide and listening to the Rolling Stones on earphones, I'd come to enjoy dental work. The drill became just another electric guitar, and what better accompaniment for oral surgery than the band that trademarked the tongue?

However, I'd never deejayed a hernia operation. This presented quite a challenge. I'd brought a CD wallet with me, and spent hours on the eve of the Cut trying to decide what music would work for both calming a drugged-out patient and keeping a potentially bored surgeon on his toes. In the end, I opted for *Talking Timbuktu*, Ry Cooder's collaboration with African musician Ali Farke Toure. Upbeat but not jagged, it has long sinuous guitar lines (like confident sutures, I thought) and lyrics that lofted on thermal rhythms in a safe haze of foreign language.

Operation Day. They wake you up early. You shower, change into a skimpy gown, swallow a whack of valium and wait. Then they take you to a dimly lit ward lined with cots and ask you to lie down and relax. It looks like a military field hospital, and the low lighting even gives it a period feel. People snoring. I lie down and do not sleep. I feel like the only kid awake in the dorm. I remember the time I was found sleepwalking in the infirmary at Camp Min-e-o-wee. A nurse comes by to see if I'm dopey enough. I feel totally alert, more alert than usual (I tend to treat all drugs, even downers, as stimulating invitations to altered consciousness).

In the operating theatre, they seem concerned that I'm talking too much and cracking lame jokes. They decide I need a little something extra, and hook me up to a morphine drip. I remember feeling very happy, awake but floating free from the force of emotional gravity, unable to imagine any pain. I continue to talk. I'm exceptionally funny, and surprised that those focusing on the operation aren't paying more attention.

When it's over I go back to the room and lie around in a stupor. They want you walking within four hours, to stretch the scar tissue. I make it to the end of the corridor after two hours. In midafternoon Tim and I, still slightly stoned, walk about a mile through the grounds. We walk in slow motion, like monks patrolling a large monastery. Later, at magic hour, I smoke a joint and take photographs of the Shouldice putting green, which has been fenced off by a pentagram of yellow police tape. It seems to have huge significance. I feel a bit like Matthew Barney.

That night they offer me a choice of painkillers. Extra-strength Advil, Tylenol or Demerol. No contest. I choose a shot of Demerol, and they spike it with Gravol to cut the nausea. I can't tell them I won't be feeling any nausea because I just smoked some dope.

All the drugs are synergizing nicely. I have an iBook full of tunes set up beside my bed with headphones. Fire up Leonard Cohen's *Ten New Songs*. The barbiturate slows my brain to a velvet crawl, and Leonard takes me down, "a thousand kisses deep," like an ancient mariner of the heart, a narcotic Nemo. You haven't heard Leonard Cohen until you've heard him on Demerol.

The next day I look at the incision as they take out the staples, which are clamped along a bruised ridge of yellow flesh, like a Cerlox binding. Later that day my roommate was sitting on his bed, examining himself.

"Hey, have you checked out your balls?" he said.

"No."

"Well, take a look at them."

I did as instructed and saw that my scrotum and most of my penis was the colour of a ripe plum, literally black and blue. In what I now assume was the apotheosis of the hernia bonding experience at Shouldice, we made a comparison, and decided that mine was darker.

The next day was spent reading and walking, much walking. At bedtime I reported to the nurses' station as instructed for my meds. I was offered a choice of Tylenol or Advil.

"Can I have what I had last night?" I asked weakly.

"What did you have last night?"

"Demerol."

The nurse scowled. "I can give it to you by mouth, but I'm not giving you another shot."

Sure. Whatever. Like most things, it wasn't as good the second time.

I went home the next day, although the Shouldice would have been happy to keep me for yet another night. I went right back to work, and discovered that, while I had no problem walking for several hours, sitting wasn't comfortable, because it bent the incision. And while writing is not, strictly speaking, physical work, it does generate a lot of tension, which triggers pain.

Now, a year later, I still get the odd twinge, a faint reminder that something down there once got rearranged with a knife.

The scar, by the way, is impressive: a five-inch diagonal slash that runs from just below the waist to my genitals. My wife said it looked "rakish." After nine months it's still red, with a hard narrow ridge of scar tissue, which I'm told is normal. For no good reason, I'd come to regard hernia as an injury from the sex wars, as if I'd used my pelvis the wrong way, or too often, and worn it out. It felt like a mid-life fault line, a moral rift. Now that I've been shored up, and there's no longer a danger of my organs escaping through a slit in my groin, I feel I'm one step closer to that elusive mirage called manhood.

# Greg Hollingshead

■

## ON KNOWING

## EVERYTHING

### Brain

I can still remember the moment it came to me that I was *this close* to knowing everything. Nothing happened. It just came to me. This was on a hot weekday afternoon the August after Grade Eight. I was twelve, sitting in the maple tree in the middle of the driveway we shared with the Ancasters. My valedictory address that June had been the work of an iconoclast: "This is not the end but the beginning!" For myself, the beginning of clearing up a few details. What I knew so far was as solid and familiar to me as the hot, bright neighbourhood down there through the leaves. If only I could count on my body and other people the way I could count on the contents of my mind. But could I? At graduation, Audrey Ancaster—between whose legs my eyes, nose and mouth had spent the best hours of my life so far—exclaimed to my mother, "I always knew Greggie was a Brain!" Audrey had a good backhand when it came to candour. How many different ways can one cry of praise throw years of physical intimacy into doubt? A Brain knows and a Brain remembers, but what does it mean, *Greggie*, if for one like you that's all there is and ever will be? What do all your knowledge and precious memories amount to then?

## *Embarrassment*

I needed to know everything because I wasn't comfortable in the world. I liked my body fine. Stretched out in the tub, it was slender and fair as a girl's. But with a ball or a puck coming at it, it became a problem. I didn't avoid sports, I wanted to play. Take wrestling with Baird Buntz, from two doors down: Baird pinned me every time—crushing my biceps with his knees, threatening to drool on my face, the whole production—but next morning I was at Baird's door, ready to wrestle again. Softball, touch football, ice and road hockey, by season. It was what we did. Ping-pong and badminton, later soccer, volleyball, tennis. I could do everything except move with grace and not choke at crucial moments, my brain in a stammer of confusion, my visual field gone jerky like the world through the lens of a camera held by a man stumbling backward as the ball swells. The only school team I made was soccer, but they wouldn't let me off the bench. In house basketball I once had a breakaway that was less astonishing after I scored on our own basket. "Let's get this one back for the team," Lawrence Frapp said grimly, with a team captain's it-could-happen-to-anybody-but-it-better-not-happen-again glance at me.

*Shame* is from a root meaning to cover yourself, as in Genesis or the dream of finding yourself naked in public. *Embarrassment* originates in the experience of being hampered, obstructed, barred, like an animal in a cage, like a mind in a body. The mind needs to give over and let the body handle it, but when it doesn't know how it makes stabs at this and that. The result is harsh, robotic, like being slammed around behind the wheel of a vehicle you have no feel for. You jolt to a stop, and the embarrassment is everywhere, in the silence of the air. Yet nobody ever said anything. If they did, it wasn't to me. A boo or a jeer would have been pretty bad, probably more than I could handle without tears, but a boo or a jeer would at least have let me know my performance was *conceivable*.

To compensate for this predilection for screwing up, I fell a lot, elaborately and dramatically. I made a show of trying so hard that I had no choice but to go flying. When you can't relax into the move, just relax. It was an obvious ploy. If there were no comments about the clumsiness, there were about the falling, which disgusted people. Falling dramatically is not what sports are about. Sports are about winning. Falling is about the faller. I grew so attached to falling dramatically that when we played guns I'd make sure I got shot in the best locations for falls: out of trees, over cliffs. I learned how to give myself over to Gravity as to the arms of God. As a kid I always wanted to be a stuntman. I couldn't imagine a more satisfying life.

One of the things a Brain knows is that the true possession of the world resides with the coordinated, who, like the animals, are unequipped to appreciate what they have. By Grade Seven, even the smart girls were showing an unwholesome interest in the jocks. What were they thinking? Did this special connection I felt to their sympathetic intelligences and their fantastically aromatic and not-so-coordinated bodies mean nothing at all? Had Audrey put her finger on the truth? How incredibly unworthily they'd slip away, like camp followers, checking their hemlines, dumbing themselves down as they went. Watching the couples pass in the hallway, girls I loved clinging like kewpies to grace and muscle, I would think, *Forgive them, for they know not what they do.* I would think, *My God, the waste.* Later, walking home alone, weeping, I would softly sing to them as they made fools of themselves watching ball practice on the other side of the playing field. *You always hurt the one you love.*

## The Fear

The worst thing about believing you can know everything is the fear that comes of the deeper knowledge that this belief is insane. By Grade Eight, my desktop was ground zero for such knowledge and such fear, particularly the pattern of the grain in the wood and the fifty years of initials, ruts, scratches, nicks, gouges, burns, cracks and ink stains. I'd been hoping a two-week module after Christmas on trees, logging, photosynthesis, growth rings and so on would help me to understand why the pattern of the grain in this particular piece of wood was as it was *and not some other way.* But the module came and went, the information sketchy. How could a surface so familiar to me be so mysterious? Who was this "B.T."? And what was this two-inch runnel along here about? How long did that take, and what did he use? If I couldn't know these things, what could I know? If these were mysteries, the whole world was a Sea of Unknowing.

When my father said that the problem with old things was they were dirty and the problem with nature was it was dangerous, I knew exactly what he meant. As town councillor, he voted consistently for demolition, development and asphalt. As a child, I aspired to know everything. That there was something psychologically ill-advised about this was suggested by the way the familiarity of things would detach and lift off without warning, like a decal in hot water. This revealed them in their true aspect, seething with annoyance that I'd presume to draw comfort from a crackpot illusion of familiarity with them. Where did I get off? You have an accident, all pretense of grace in the world falls away, and its malice is right in your face. You reach bare-handed for a plate in the oven—*Ouch! Smash!*—and that's when you hear it: the chorus, from every utensil, every dish, every chair and cupboard in the kitchen: *Ha! ha! ha!*

That moment in the maple tree must have come toward the end of my dream of knowing everything. By winter, the choice was clear: either commit to me—this fearful little guy clinging to these pathetic hopes, fears, memories, ideas, ambitions, to this whole interior rigmarole—or commit to the world, which was more complicated, more mysterious, more likely to be right and more merciless than I could ever anticipate. The world didn't care whether I lived or died, except—as I knew from a thousand fumbled catches, bad throws, bad kicks, and glimpses into the abyss of unknowing and the fundamental hostility in things—when there was no doubt whatsoever it preferred the latter.

What kind of a choice was this?

## The Glove

One day as I was playing catch with Harry Hawkhurst on Church Street, our big old Buick Luxus cruised past. I concentrated on making my next throw as little like a girl's as I could. A few minutes later the Luxus cruised back. Stopped. The driver's window came down. My father leaned across and told me to get in. I thought he'd been drinking. I thought he was going to tell me how to throw a ball. Instead he said, "It's time you had a proper glove." I was astonished. One, father was an athlete: lacrosse and hockey (Junior B). "When I was young," he once told me, "all I cared about was being strong." Two, he'd never said or done anything to make me feel bad about my lousy coordination. Three, he didn't do things like pick me up from playing with a friend to drive me to the store to buy me something I hadn't dared even to wish for. His behaviour was all the more astonishing because the reason he was driving around in the afternoon was that he was unemployed and broke.

He bought me a new fielder's glove, a good one. Light brown in colour, properly padded. A beautiful glove, with that high, thin smell of cured leather cutting through a bigger, muskier aroma. My face in that glove was like being back between Audrey's legs.

Here's what happened to it. When it was too dark out to see to catch a ball, I'd come into the house and toss the glove onto the little table in the front hall. On the table were a few other things: the phone, a notepad, a comb, my mother's aerosol hairspray. She used to fix her hair in the mirror above the table before she left the house. One day she left the cap off the hairspray. Maybe the phone rang, making her late, causing her to rush, and she forgot to put the cap back on. That evening my glove landed on the nozzle, and the can of hairspray slowly and quietly emptied into the leather.

The next day I couldn't believe it. I hadn't had the glove a month. On the padded area opposite the thumb was a large dark stain resembling an ice burn, with a dark core like an inverted nipple where the nozzle had impressed itself. Like a weird scar, the burn wasn't so bad. But now when I played baseball or catch, in place of the beautiful wild aroma of the glove was the scent of cheap perfume. There was something appropriate about this, I knew, but also something too cruel, too perverse, too much in the nature of things for this not to be the world letting me know that, whatever my father might pretend, my performance had always been, and would remain, unworthy of such a glove.

## My Leg

When I was eight, my right knee had started to hurt. When I complained, my parents told me it was growing pains. Everything was growing pains. I also had headaches. "Kids don't have headaches," my father would say, shaking his head. Eventually he took me to see Dr. McDuff, who thought I must have twisted my knee from wrestling so much with Baird Buntz, so he bound it. When that didn't work, he bound it again. When nothing changed, he let the grass-stained bandages fall into the wastebasket with a little smile. In those days I was an elocutionist. My mother used to do the books at the hardware store, and she and Laetitia Whelpdale, who owned the store, attended the York Music Festival in 1956 to hear me recite "The House with Nobody in It."

"Why's he limping?" Laetitia asked my mother as I crossed the stage.

My mother said my knee hurt.

"It's more than that, darling."

When Laetitia got home she called her orthopedic surgeon in the city, who called us in for an examination, during which he diagnosed Perthes. Caucasian boys between the ages of two and ten whose parents smoke in the home are susceptible to Perthes. It's a bone disease caused by insufficient oxygen reaching, in my case, the spongy bone toward the head of my right femur, which was withering and twisting and no longer moving properly in the socket. This, for some reason, was causing pain in the knee. Now they operate immediately. In 1956, treatment was six weeks in traction to pull the ball out of the socket, followed by two years in a brace, a steel and leather contraption that kept your leg straight and locked into the specially built heel of your shoe, so you bore your weight in your crotch, in the space between the top of your leg and your testicle.

Perthes was a godsend. The brace absolved me of responsibility for my lousy coordination at the same time as it conferred the conceivability I'd been missing. I was now obviously a cripple—a fact the most casual observer could see at a glance. The pity that came my way was overt and out of all proportion to my suffering. In hospital, the nurses kept the toenails on my traction leg painted red, and that set the tone for my brace years. Every day was Christmas, and I was Tiny Tim. Everybody loves the little guy. Pities him, yes, but *he* knows the pity's misplaced. Also, any physical achievement at all is now met with wonder and approval. My mother still talks about me riding my bike in my brace, kicking the pedal around with my good foot. And the brace added a touch of surreal pathos to my falls off cliffs. I could really whip that thing around.

When the brace came off, the leg, not having been walked on for a couple of years, was blanched and wasted, like something that had been left under the dock. I walked again but still with a limp, partly because the leg often hurt—though no longer at the knee—and partly because it was nearly half an inch shorter. The limp was worse when it hurt, but also when I was tired, felt sorry for myself or wanted attention. You put a brace on a limb, or it stops working properly, and it becomes a suburb of the Self. Such a private, complex little world of pain, solicitude and specialness lit up when I said the words *my leg*.

## Spaz

In September, I started Grade Nine at a day school for boys, in the city, a school for Brains. My parents' friends and the teachers at my grade school were embarrassed for my mother when she signed me up to write the entrance exams, but after an interview with the headmaster—during which my father tried to sell him a car—I was in. The most important thing a Brain learns at a school for Brains is that he's actually not all that smart. Not here. Here he's a slow learner and something of an ignoramus. Less fortunately, at a school for Brains, a Brain learns that what counts most at such a school is sports, because physical skill and strength is what every Brain—who isn't dumb—wishes he had. Even here, jocks ruled. But at least smart jocks, who didn't have heartbreaking girls hanging off them.

By this time, with the brace gone, the old coordination problem was back. The limp came and went, and many people took years to notice it. "What happened to your leg?" they'd suddenly ask, thinking I'd done something to it on the weekend. Then one day in gym class as I was bouncing wildly on the trampoline, Mr. Spiggot, the phys-ed master, shouted, "Come on, Hollingshead, you spaz!" This was said in a tone of cheerful contempt, and when I looked at him, he was already turning away. *Spaz.* What a strange and unexpected assault, revelation and gift, all in one casual piece of abuse. I know this sounds like my father telling me that a teacher who threw a blackboard eraser at him and, when my father ducked, threw him down a flight of stairs, was the best teacher he ever had, but the thing is, Mr. Spiggot was the first adult who ever acknowledged my problem, the only one who had the . . . what? . . . hostility? insensitivity? confidence? honesty? to place it in the realm of the conceivable. A few years later, when I was nineteen or twenty, I was trying to back my father's old Chev Impala out of our driveway. My father was standing with Baird Buntz, watching me. When I nearly hit the old maple, I looked around and saw my father make a comment to Baird. Afterwards I asked Baird what my father had said.

"'He can't drive,'" Baird replied.

## Later

As the girls turned into women, the smart ones returned to their senses. I still hadn't been to mine. According to the Oxford English Dictionary, in females adolescence extends from ages twelve to twenty-one, in males fourteen to twenty-five. A four-year lag sounds right to me. Not that before age twenty-six I didn't find in the arms of some of the finest post-adolescent females on earth the physical happiness the world had consistently refused me. Upon meeting a woman I liked, if I didn't lightly touch her upper arm or shoulder with the tips of the fingers of my right hand as we talked, I'd lift off and spin away. I needed grounding. Of course, this was the '60s. But I did always feel that women and I had a lot in common.

Then again, I had a long way to go. In his twenties, a man forgoes the playing fields of his youth for the company of women, who have much to teach him. As when he's confiding to a woman that sometimes he feels so close to people it's like they're his own ideas, and the look on her face is alarm. Or when he's demonstrating to a woman as they undress for bed how he can make his erection go up and down with his mind, and she bursts into tears. Or when a woman says to him, "You think you know everything, don't you?"

To which he replies, "Not anymore. Now I don't think I know anything at all."

To which she replies, "Same problem, right?"

*Right.*

Like kinder, gentler Audrey Ancasters, women continue his education, delivering him into the world, if they can.

# Ian Brown

■

## LOOK AND SEE

There have been three stretches in my life when I wanted to watch live naked women more or less incessantly. I don't mean to say there have been other stretches when I haven't. But in those three phases the desire mounted to a compulsion.

I was a new young man, the first time, with a job for the first time, and hence for the first time enough money to get into a strip club. Phase one lasted six months. I had a girlfriend, but she came with strict conditions, whereas naked strippers did not. What made me suddenly want to run, not walk, to the peeler bar when the need unexpectedly overcame me was the simple opportunity—the chance to see what I had never been able to see enough of (naked female bodies) and to be, for however short a time, what I was, without apology—a young man interested in being near naked women.

Not touching. Near was enough.

The place was on the verge of downtown Toronto, which meant I could slip over from work, at lunch. The girls danced in a minia-ture boxing ring, ten feet square. If you sat next to the rope you could tuck a few dollars into a garter or a bra, which in turn might win you a more private glimpse from the dancer. I had no spare dollars and was too shy to do anything that venturesome, so I sat halfway back and watched. It was a jaunty, good-natured place— not at all like the darkened cattle yards out in the suburbs, where mobsters lived, or the soulless holes on the so-called airport strip, where everyone seemed to be doing his and her best not to feel any-thing—more like a well-intentioned community centre for young men, a place we could work off our primitive tendencies without threatening society at large. There was no such thing as MTV then, where female nakedness was just a channel away, and there was certainly no such thing as lap dancing—girls weren't even allowed to take off their panties at that point in the history of the degradation of women.

The waitresses were the only competition for our attention, which may be why I remember the dancers smiling a lot. I especially remember one girl—Suzie? Deeana? Some bright, extroverted gleam of a name, anyway—a natural blond with a ponytail, an open smile and a short, athletic body, who wore white cutoff jeans (cut off all the way to Norway) and white disco boots. For a couple of weeks she seemed like the sexiest person in the world to me.

Most of the other men wore ties and suits. They were traders and brokers from the financial district who were always there when I arrived and still there when I left. I could watch five dancers, and then I had to exit the premises—whether because it was too arousing, or too frustrating, or too embarrassing, I am still not sure (and it could easily have been all three). But for an hour I was excited and felt daring and happy. I often ordered lunch—the burger was excellent—and sometimes I read the newspaper. I just wanted to be near some nakedness. I was a free man: I could experience lust, and admit to it, on my lunch hour. ("To be surrounded by beautiful, curious, breathing, laughing flesh is enough . . ." Walt Whitman wrote in *I Sing The Body Electric*: "I do not ask anymore delight—I swim in it as in a sea.") At work there were rules, hierarchies, exclusions, secrets. The strip club was more democratic: its pornography "transgressed" the differences between the genders, as feminists were prone to say, albeit not about strip clubs. If the business of girls taking their clothes off for men was invented to democratize human impulses—and that was what I believed—then shame was invented to regulate that levelling. I wanted to be an enemy of shame.

Then one day there was an accident at the bar. An older man who liked to sit by the corner of the dancing ring and look up into the girls' darknesses was in his regular spot when a dancer took pity on him. As I heard the story, she squatted down in his corner with her back to him, and pushed her buttocks through the ropes at his face. The experience was apparently too much: overcome with desire, he thrust his entire face into the crack of her ass, much to her surprise and very much against the rules of the club, which forbade all touching. The bouncers—two big square guys shaped like fridges—threw the old guy out the door, but alas with such force that they killed him.

I seem to recall it made the papers. I stopped going after that, and shortly thereafter the club closed. It's a café now, the kind that sells large muffins and a healthy lifestyle. That was the first time I realized that my simple desire to see a girl take off her clothes was not as simple as I wanted it to be. Looking is complicated.

■

"Tell me honestly," my wife says, standing in front of the bathroom mirror. "Am I too fat to wear this?"

She's looking at her reflection. I'm looking at her, looking at her own reflection. Her eyes are hard, appraising. She could be buying a second-hand car.

"Am I? Why won't you answer me?"

Do you know this nightmare? It's a nightmare for a man because *there's no entirely acceptable answer*. It doesn't matter that she's a well-dressed woman, my wife—slim, fashionable, a clever shopper. (Loehmann's, mostly.) She wants me to tell her she looks great—

"You look great, honey."

—but she wants to feel that my answer is believable—

"Don't just say it because I want you to say it!"

—so it has to be discerning as well:

"I'm not. Turn around? Right around. Are you going to wear those shoes?"

"Do you like these others better?" Whatever I say, the problem has to be fixable.

"Yeah, the second ones."

She's pleased now. She has an answer, she believes I have been straight and truthful. One more reassurance, and she will be done.

"You didn't used to think I was too fat."

"I don't think you're fat."

"But everybody else does?"

"That's not what I said!"

"Is there a reason why you're speaking to me in that tone of voice?"

Etc.

This is another reason I went to strip clubs from time to time: because no one ever says, "Do I look fat in this?"—even if they do. Because at a strip club it is very hard for a man to come up with the wrong answer.

∎

The second phase of my addiction began after we moved to Los Angeles. My wife was in the movie business, and had a demanding job that left me even more on my own than I was already.

The Star Strip wasn't far from our apartment—a heavy door up the street from Frederick's of Hollywood, the lingerie store, in an otherwise residential neighbourhood. The girls were astonishing, Hollywood pretty: I remember a slim brunette with a face so beautiful she made the breath rush out of my chest whenever she walked through the club. I went perhaps once a month, mostly between October and February when it rained, mostly when my wife was away, in that first lonely year in that huge circuit board of a city; every time I did I hoped to see that girl there. I wasn't in love with her.* I just liked her face, and the gentle, unforced way her body seemed to follow her mind around the room. (As opposed to another kind of woman whose mind follows her body, equally charming.) I had the impression, looking at her, that she would not defeat me sexually, and that I would not defeat her.

---

* There's an extensive body of writing by strippers and "sex industry workers," as they like to call themselves, and their advice to male sex work clients is always the same. 1. Bathe. 2. Be direct, and tip generously. 3. Don't fall in love.

I didn't keep my visits a secret from my wife: I was writing a book about men I had known, and she knew going to a strip club was a reliable way for me to see men at their most unfiltered. In a strip bar you can see what attracts you and what doesn't; I find I need to be reminded occasionally. Men are often strangers to themselves, in my experience, but in a strip club, in a room full of naked girls, a man can see who he is and isn't, because men often define themselves by who and what we want. Sometimes after I'd spent an evening happily watching TV with my wife, after I'd been sufficiently domestic, the urge to see a naked female stranger was like a small sharp hunger in my stomach. I didn't need much more than a snack: there was no cover charge at the Star Strip, and you could pop in and out as you would at Starbucks for a creamy *latte*. Some nights all I did was watch busloads of Japanese tourists pour in. Japanese guys smoked Marlborough Reds and went berserk for the same kind of girl: the blonder, the bigger her breasts, the better. But I preferred them to some of the other mutants who showed up. They were the guys who never looked anywhere but at the prize, men who spent hundreds of dollars to have a girl stick her ass in their faces for an hour at a time—and not just buttocks, but specifically anuses, "monocles tiny as dimes," as John Updike once described them. Nights like that, the Star Strip was exactly the kind of place you found in Updike's Rabbit Angstrom novels, full of guys who wanted to be, not think, guys who wanted to believe that life was better, truer somehow, when it just happened. The place seemed more old-fashioned on nights like that.

In any event the club was no threat to my marriage. I loved my wife endlessly in those days, and she loved me, especially in that strange and remarkable city, where we were on our own and everything was new and hilarious to us, where there were celebrities buying tofu in the supermarkets and riots and earthquakes—details we would later remember as undeniable evidence that we had lived, been here, seen this, had known the world in a way no one else could because we were there in each other's company. I never had and still haven't loved anyone quite as properly as I did my wife in that lucky stretch of years away— and yet none of that was changed by my slipouts to the peeler bar, where I just needed to take the burr off the edge of physical longing that rasps a man, to see what I was missing and remind myself why I didn't mind missing it; to feel the headlong lurch of the need for friction, and see the scrap pile where that ride always ends. Going to a strip club was like enrolling in a night school sociology course: Alternative Ways of Male Being. It was as much adventure as I could handle, as much temptation as I could turn down. Surely it is not so much of a sin for a man to remind himself, in the end, how lucky he is. Anyway, I came home calmer.

■

A few years later we had a baby, a little girl, and I stopped feeling the need to see naked women for a while. A few years after that we had another child, a boy. He surprised us: he was born with an impossibly rare syndrome, something almost no one had heard of. He can't speak, or reason, or walk too well, or protect himself, or eat without a tube in his belly. At nine, he has the body of a four-year-old and the mind of an infant. He has no eyebrows, or eyelashes; what he does have is patulous lips and thin but wildly curly hair, and low ears the way developmentally retarded people often do. He is what doctors call an FLK, "a funny-looking kid," but that is putting it medically. He hits his head with his fists, often brutally, and is often in pain; but sometimes he has enormous bursts of happiness, great gusts of glee that are capable of charming anyone.

So he too is something to look at, though I have never been ashamed of him. To calm him down I take him out for marathon rides in his stroller, sometimes for hours at a time. I like to talk to him as I walk, though I'm not sure he understands any of it. People look at us, often can't help themselves. Some people peek and glance away; others make an effort to meet my eye and smile, to convince me they accept us both. Others are too shocked to do anything but goggle. Children stare blatantly, and some parents don't even tell them not to.

Sometimes pregnant women, or youngish women who have begun to experience the lust to have a child of their own, come upon my boy and me clattering down the street, and a look of alarm passes over their faces: what if they have such a child? It's a reasonable enough fear. Then they seek my face out, to see what I look like, to see if there is some hint in me that I could be the father of such a being—because if there is something to spot in me, I can see them clearly thinking, they will be able to spot it in their own men, and thus avoid the terror of a deviant baby. But I am quite normal looking—even fairly robust, genetically speaking—and so the look of fear on their young smooth faces often turns to terror. Then they look away.

The worst offenders are thirteen-year-old girls, to whom appearance is so paramount, who cannot stop wishing or fearing that the entire world is gazing upon them in rapture. (In some ways they are the exact opposite of strippers, who never assume anyone is interested until money changes hands.) A few springs ago, at the opening of the baseball season, I took my son—his name is Walker (ironically enough, given that he barely is one)—to see a Toronto Blue Jays game. His entire school, populated exclusively by disabled children, went along: thirty bent and broken bodies, beeping and whooping and squawking in wheelchairs and carts, travelling in single file along the sidewalk for twenty blocks through the centre of the city: now, *that* people watched. But we broke up when we arrived at the stadium, and I walked my Walkie through the crowd.

It was School Day, or Bat Day, or some unthinkable combination of the two at the stadium, and the place was overrun with raucous teenagers. Again and again the same thing happened: some tall, good-looking fourteen-year-old girl, in a pink or blue pop top and a white miniskirt and flip-flops, the leader of a tiny gang of three shorter girls dressed exactly the same way, would spot Walker and me coming at them, Quasimodo and his handler.

Then, when she thought I was not looking, she would lean over and whisper to her idiot cronies.

Then they would all look, and put their hands over their mouths.

Then they would pretend to hide what they were doing.

So while I may be a man who goes to strip clubs and objectifies women who are willing to take their clothes off, I too know what it is like to be an object, of fear and pity and even scorn. And I guarantee this: unless you are up there on the stage, or pushing that carriage, being looked at, naked—and Walker and I are psychologically bared and even stripped when we walk down the street—it probably doesn't feel like you think it does.

It's not depressing, for starters. Sometimes it's the opposite: stark, but clear, and clean, even slightly belligerent. I never feel a need to apologize. (That's a rare feeling for a man these days.) I don't even mind the looks, most of the time: I figure you need to see us, the way a stripper figures a man needs to see her. At least when you are looking at me with Walker, or I am looking at a naked woman, at least by the act of *looking* we each declare our desire to see something true. I want to see her, unadorned. And I know you want to look at him, at my boy; you want to know what his darkness is, and why the light comes off him too. I am no different.

Then one day two years ago a woman from the government called: after seven years of worry and despair and sleeplessness, after seven years of counting the unspeakable cost of one broken child's life on those around him, an agency found a home for my son. Suddenly, after nearly a decade, Walker had another place to live, a place where children like him live together, a place he could go home to and come home from. My broken boy was going away. I didn't know which was worse: the fact that I had to give him up, or that part of me wanted to.

■

It took a long time to work out the details, and it was in that grey time, after we knew Walker would be leaving but before he actually left, that I began to visit strippers again. This time the urges were sharper, more impatient, but also shorter lasting, and less satisfying when indulged. At least it wasn't Internet porn, that sterile repetitive motion machine. At least these women were living flesh and real.

This time the club was ten minutes from my home by car, on the way home from our nanny's apartment. It was a rambling three-storey place, always busy. Downstairs was cheaper, more crowded, younger guys; upstairs, where I went, had pretensions to sophistication: upstairs you sometimes saw businessmen banging away on their BlackBerrys. The music was uniformly terrible, disco shit and bad rap, pretend instincts and fake chants, nothing more. For a nominal fee (the price of a drink) you could watch the "featured dancer" take her clothes off on stage. For a less nominal sum (twenty dollars a dance, which made ten minutes with a girl more expensive than a night of cocaine) it was possible to have a girl take her clothes off and writhe naked on your lap and in your arms in the cushioned booths that lined the perimeter of the room.

Each booth had a crimson velvet curtain, but you couldn't draw it—presumably a regulation. You sat with your back to the wall, looking into the club: the girl faced you, or faced in too. Most of the girls would let you touch their skin, their hips, their breasts, their bums. This arrangement made it possible to sit in the audience watching the featured dancer while all around you in open booths naked women were being felt up by male hands and arms: it was surrealistic, sometimes even sexy. Some guys had enough money for two girls at once. The stage was red, the carpet was red, the ceiling was black. The backdrop on the stage was a series of vaguely cornucopic, concentrically receding red velvet-covered foam circles, as if the stage were a giant red velvet sphincter, or (on good nights) a womb. But the action was definitely in the booths.

I never wanted the girls to writhe on me, and mostly asked them not to, nervous though I was that they would be offended. I very seldom even touched them. They were interesting women just to talk to: realistic, often articulate, financially acute—I was never charged for fewer dances than I watched—and sometimes hilariously manipulative, as when they walked up and sat down, in their peignoirs and bikinis, on your lap, and asked why you were still alone, and pouted when you said you preferred it that way, and wanted to be left alone. Most of the time I would say I had just arrived, and wanted to relax, which especially pissed the South Americans off. "I dint e'en ask you anything," they'd huff, "but I could tell you was cheap anyway." None of them asked if she was too fat or too thin: they appreciated honesty if it saved them time they could more profitably spend on other clients. Still: it was nice to chat with a naked pretty girl. The last thing it felt was middle class and ordinary.

In the hole in my head and my heart where my boy had lived, where my duty had done its bit, other longings now began to appear, and they were not always simple. There was a dancer named Cheryl, for instance, whose hips called to me from across the room—there's no other way I can put it. This, as I say, is the existential mystery of the strip club, the best of the few good reasons for going: to find out what will catch your eye, or hold your glimmer of interest, or turn you off and away, whether there are still some undiscovered corners in you. There seldom are, but it is a question we boys like to ask again and again, in the hope the answer has changed.

Most of the time, I didn't feel a connection. I realize I'm talking about a financial transaction. I have no illusions that the come-ons of a lap dancers are genuine. I'm talking about what I felt, about the presence or absence of the vibe men feel in the company of a woman they connect to, for whatever obscure reasons. It's the same democratic longing, the search for an unpredictable adventure, that makes a man walk down the street and privately scrutinize every woman he passes, no matter how young or old or big or small she is, and silently ask himself the famous private male question: *would I sleep with her?* Not *could* I, or *should* I, or *do I want to* (often especially not *do I want to*): just *would I? And if I would, what does that make me? What would happen to us? Where would that adventure lead? To a kitchen filled with children and bread? Or just to bed, and then nowhere?*

For instance: there was a thoroughly gorgeous Chinese-Thai girl at the club, Pin Li, whose skin was the colour of sand. She was polite, even fawning, articulate and well informed (she liked to talk about Communist China), and she declared herself willing to do anything I might want. By that definition, then, she had everything a man might want: the face, the body, the mind, the willingness to serve. But for reasons I can't fathom I never felt any real physical passion for her. I admired her, respected her, even thought I ought to be getting off on her. But beyond that it was flat, and I found her attempts at intimacy glaringly false. There was a luscious girl named

Natasha who called herself Stephanie and drank a lot, and talked a blue mile; there was a sexy Jewish girl, a mother of two, curvy and always friendly. I loved to look at them both. But I never felt their draw, though I looked again and again. Then someone comes along and you feel it.

I found Cheryl more intriguing—thin, and tall, but by her own admission bisexual. (She wanted me to bring my wife. I said I thought that was unlikely.) Her breasts had been surgically augmented, and up close were almost absurdly out of proportion to her slim body; but they looked bombshell from ten feet away, the distance at which she made most of her money. The first time I met her, she tried to sit down on my lap, but I told her it was too much, and after that we started to talk. She said she rarely got turned on by the men she danced for—maybe once every couple of years—and she said the majority of the men she danced for never climaxed. She didn't appear to be enslaved to a pimp or addicted to coke. Instead, she was working on her master's degree.

One evening as Cheryl was sitting semi-clothed on a chair next to me, drinking Perrier, I tried to explain why it was that only certain dancers appealed to me—how some women made me think they would crush me, sexually, while others didn't. Cheryl didn't, for instance.

"Sure," she said. "Men have control issues."

"What do you mean?"

"It makes sense. A man's never sure a woman's baby is his. Whereas the woman knows it's hers, no matter who the father is." She was twenty-six-years-old. Two days later in *The New York Times*, I read the same theory, espoused by an internationally acclaimed anthropologist. I felt like I'd had the winner of the Nobel prize for physics sitting next to me with her top off.

Every month or so, sometimes more, generally on a Tuesday night, as my week at work geared up, I felt the urge to slip by the club. I didn't always go, and I didn't always stay; I just wanted to see some flesh, to calm the lurching in my head. It was like taking an aspirin. I would walk into the club and dozens of semi-naked women would waft by in a wake of perfume, and sometimes even that was too intimate, enough to make me leave, and therefore instructive: the lesson was *slow down*. I was always wrestling with myself in that place. Often I was no sooner inside when I began picking and choosing in my mind, deciding who appealed to me and who didn't, based on the slightest and vaguest of twinges I nevertheless thought I could sense in my chest: yes to the Jamaican girl in the red bikini, no to the parabolic blond, maybe to the Romanian, the older one with the hips—or perhaps that immensely tall Nordic bombshell, yes, she would be different, she might provide me with some new definition of myself, some new outline that might disappoint me less than the one I had. (She didn't, in fact. That lesson was *the twinge can lie*.)

Some nights, slow nights—I always went on slow nights, early in the week, it was less intimidating—girls would say, "Hi, baby" or "You gonna take that overcoat off?" before I was even in the door. It didn't matter that I knew this was a come-on to make money, a way to get at me fast, before my doubts set in: I still managed to feel flattered. Flattery from a woman is such a rare thing in most men's lives—there's always something we tend to do wrong—that we'll take even the blatantly insincere variety.

Mostly I liked watching it all. I liked to see the way the girls dressed, to see what they had discovered was sexy to men: it was remarkably uniform, geared to a guy's instinct, not to the eye of women. There was a blond, for instance, who wore a red baby doll camisole and a red thong that cut across the middle of her ass with two red satin strings. I thought it looked stupid and infantile, but she got a lot of attention. There were a lot of peroxide blondes with huge breasts packed into fluorescent yellow and pink bikinis; there were even girls who seemed comfortable in unconventional bodies, heavy in places you wouldn't expect it, and that seemed to work for them too, though less reliably. Some traded on youth, some on tits, some on their eyes. Sometimes I felt sorry for the girls who couldn't find a customer. I most liked the girls who didn't put on airs, who had some enthusiasm for whatever bodies they had, who weren't embarrassed but who didn't have to be hard or tough about not being embarrassed, either. The waitresses alone got me going—sexy *and* hard-working, beautiful *and* practical. Sex and life, hand in hand! Real life, and real desire! This was the dream of a lot of men I knew, myself included, but it sometimes seemed like an impossible combination to hope for, at least outside of a strip club. And whatever else it was—calculated, transactional, efficient—I knew the strip club was a fantasy too. It was the fantasy that sexual desire could be simple: that one of these women might incite a desire that would simply overcome me, that I would never have to work at, that would be taken out of my hands, a desire that I could simply not avoid, the way desire operated in Flaubert's novels, for instance. A woman who would make my flickering, wandering, inconstant male desire finally blameless, unashamed, unavoidable—something that simply washed up like the sea.

Less romantically, I went to the club to bring lust into a more honourable place in my life, to normalize desire, to make it less of a big deal. And not just my sexual desire, but (by inference) all my desires—to be a man, but to be human; to be a good father, but to be a man; to be a husband, but not the sole foundation of a woman's existence. To be all I could be, and nothing that I could not. Maybe that was why I found Cheryl sexy—not just because she was, but because she was realistic. I never went home longing for her; she was a stripper, after all. Instead, back in bed at home, I dreamed I could fly. Being superficial at night made me more serious by day: it was during this stretch of looking that I took up gardening; that I took up painting again; that I began to try to find a straighter road to satisfaction, one that didn't lead through a strip club.

For a man, looking is part of his education. It's one way he learns the difference between what he wants, and what he can have; or between what he thinks he wants, is supposed to want, and what he actually needs. My boy taught me that. And so did the strippers, albeit from the opposite direction.

Look, one night, a girl came up to me while I was still in my big grey overcoat, and the first thing she said was "I'm a little bit horny." She was a gorgeous Czech girl, a natural blond in an all-natural body and a red sequined gown. Her accent made her sound faintly ridiculous, as if she was acting in a TV sketch about desirous foreigners. But her long curves could have incited coronary thrombosis in a plank of wood. In any event, I laughed. This was the wrong thing to do.

"What?" she said. "I am."

"That's not what most dancers say. They say they never get turned on, they just say it for the customers."

"Not me! I am, every night!"

"I believe you."

"I am going to think of you at home tonight," she said then, and stood up. I cannot say I believed her. Her glittery eyes were already dancing about for a more pliable conquest. I did admire her directness. She was on her way across the room when suddenly she reached back, took my pen out of my shirt pocket, unscrewed the cap, saw it was a fountain pen, screwed it back on, put it back. "Nice," she said. I'd filled it earlier in the evening. "See you sometime, maybe," she said. Then she left. And I was free: free of her, free of my desire. A strange place to come to that conclusion.

That was the last evening I spent in a strip bar. Of course, I'm not saying it won't happen again.

The next morning my boy visited his new home for the first time. Afterwards, I rode to work on my bicycle and burst into tears: it took me by surprise. I'd sob for a couple of blocks, trying to hide my face from passersby; but before long I was back to normal, trying not to stare at the girls on the sidewalk, feeling the morning sun on my arms, trying to work up a less tumultuous feeling than grief. I even thought about Cheryl. I'd run into her the night before, on my way out of the cave of nudes.

"Fancy seeing you here," she said, with a big smile, and that great way she had of standing with her body to the fore, as if her hips were asking a question.

"Yes," I said, "fancy that. But I'm just on my way."

In the end, I used her. She helped me back to a place in myself. True, I paid her. But she showed me money isn't everything, and neither is love.

*Bert Archer*

∎

# WHY BOYS
# ARE BETTER
# THAN GIRLS

To answer your first question: No, I have never felt that any aspect of my masculinity has been blunted for having sex with men. Quite the opposite. I don't understand why it is that the men who regularly make the sorts of compromises men must in order to have sex with women are mostly considered more manly. When men have sex with women, they are politicians, possibly inept ones, not understanding this or that element of rhetoric or compromise, but dealmakers nonetheless. When a man has sex with a man, he is a purist, an activist, a sexual idealist. It is a stereotype, but also true, that a man can suggest sex with another man without an opening line, and without any thought that the disengagement after it's over will be anymore complicated than wiping off. There could also be a round of quick negotiation: fuck, suck, top, bottom, safe, bareback, fist, piss, facial, no scat, keep your socks on (only if they're tube), call me Chet, the amyl's on the table, bite my nipple, twist my balls, hard. If you're online, or in a bathhouse, or on the street, it really is mostly as simple as that.

Which is not to say that there's never any conversation or embraces; it's just that any mixed signals that might come up tend to be fairly basic ones ("I said no kissing"; "That was a nibble!"; "That was a kiss and you know it"), but rarely, in these contexts, are they the complex, "What, you're leaving, just like that?" variety.

Oh, now, I know, that's an awful stereotype, too, and there are plenty of women who just want a good, uncomplicated fuck. But they're not the norm, just as men who will turn down string-free sex aren't the norm. Most of us are still out there playing the averages, running into those norms far more often than we run into those delightful, surprising exceptions, and that's one of the reasons I've chosen guys.

Which may go some way toward answering your second question. It was, indeed, just like all those awful men and women in the States have been trying to convince everyone, a choice, one I was led to through the usual astronomically complex series of pointers and suasions, incidents and accidents, hints and allegations. I wasn't born this or any other sexual way, as far as I've been able to tell. My very first, prepubescent attractions were almost exclusively to girls, as makes sense when your father, mother, aunt, uncle, brother and sister asks you if you made any girlfriends your first day of kindergarten. Think it's natural? What would your impression be if I came over to your house and asked your five-year-old son if he's got a boyfriend yet? You'd think I was trying to plant ideas in his head. You'd be right, and that's just what those aunts and uncles are doing, too.

True, I did think my little sister's best friend was cute when I was ten and he was eight, but my first, full-fledged, complete-with-pubic-hair-and-penetration fantasy was about Sabrina in Grade Six, my second involved twins named Richard and Christian that same year, my third serious set revolved around Jennifer in Grade Seven, and they came pretty fast and furious after that.

My choice had something to do with how Christopher Atkins in *The Blue Lagoon* could be both sexy and aggressive, able to just go with his hard-on when he got one, where Brooke Shields was unsure, confused, turned her shoulder away and was upset by the onset of sex rather than immediately invigorated by it. It had something to do with the fact that Barbara, my first straight-ahead postpubescent girlfriend, seemed similarly nonplussed and had a tendency, in order to keep sex at bay, of using it as a tool, a game or a prize rather than simply as a fuck. There's a discussion to be had about the sorts of forces that led Randal Kleiser to have his actors act the way they did in *The Blue Lagoon* which, if we were to focus on those forces, would almost certainly turn out to be much the same ones that led Barbara to act the way she did.

But that's women's studies. And we're engaged in some men's studies here. So let's just say that no matter what the causes behind Brooke's and Barbara's attitudes, the effects on me were primarily confusion and frustration in the face of alien behaviour. After a while, after the front seat of the car was too awkward, the couch was too public and the waterbed too wavy, I just stopped trying with Barbara. Maybe if I'd been born a few decades earlier and about a thousand kilometres to the south, my dad would have hired me a prostitute when I turned fourteen, exposing me early on to the sort of female sexuality that's tailor-made for men, rather than the sort that more regularly crops up, and I would have locked my sights on getting more of that, of convincing women to want to cater to me the way the hooker had. Or maybe if I'd grown up in San Francisco or Toronto or Ottawa down the street from stores like Good Vibrations or Come As You Are or Venus Envy, I might have met women doing some mother-and-daughter dildo shopping, getting in touch with their G spots and learning to ejaculate, who could have jumped me and shown me what sex was like with a woman who liked it for what it was, seeing it as neither a joke nor a sacrament.

But Vancouver in the '80s was not that kind of place, at least not for my family, and so I was left with the usual conversations about sex with boys and various attempts at sex with girls. As my sexuality was developing—by which I mean my general approach to the subject rather than my specific tastes and preferred practices—I got the distinct sense that boys understood me, that I understood boys. On the other hand, what I, and all the guys I talked to about it, understood about girls convinced us that communicating with them about love and sex was like learning another dialect, possibly even another language.

I still remember the conversations with my friend Justin. He was big, a rugby player, but also kind of sweet and a little pretty and therefore among the first of any of us to have a real girlfriend. By the time I was sixteen and figuring out the first stages of dating and sexual negotiations, he'd already been with Diane for ages. But he was still having problems. It hurt. He was too big, she told him. They'd been going out for more than a year and still no fucking. He was genuinely distraught. Worse, there were all these emotional misunderstandings and miscommunications. In the words of the father of all teenage boys who are trying and failing to live as if the world could accommodate teenage boys, they were tearing him apart. Meanwhile, having dated Barbara for only a few months by the time Justin and I started having these 2 a.m. discussions (we'd both just got our licences and our first cars), I was not so much torn apart as frustrated. He didn't want to hurt her, didn't want to disrespect her; he loved her. But still. Why can't she just open her goddamned legs and let me fuck her? Yeah, really. "Hand jobs are gross," she says. Yeah, and like, "Blow jobs taste yucky." I know what you mean. Fucking chicks. Like their business isn't all slimy and stinky too. But it's good, right? Fuckin' A.

Most of us decide, like immigrants, to learn to speak the way we must, the way everyone around us is urging us to. Why I ended up choosing to spend most of my time in this little expat community called gay, while Justin went on to become fluent in girl, is the crux of the thing that has most people convinced that there must be something innate, something genetic, something preordained about how we spend our sexual and romantic lives. If I were less presumptuous, I would say that I can only speak for myself, but in matters of sexuality, as in many and possibly most things, I think you can, if you're responsible about it, generalize outward from personal experience. (If I'm wrong, then novels, and most art forms, are pointless entertainments.) My personal experience, as I've said, was that my prepubescence was, if anything, girl oriented, and that when puberty hit, I was focused on sex, not on girls or boys—I distinctly remember having sexual fantasies, waking and sleeping, about having sex with furniture, trees, horses, maybe a cow, definitely a Volkswagen Beetle—and that in those crucial years between twelve and about seventeen, I was schooled. Status came into it, of course: having a hot girlfriend was a definite social booster. So did peer pressure, the media, and so on. All influences, but not deciding factors. I certainly thought some boys were sexy, and when I fanta-sized about them, I didn't stop myself for fear I was a fag; even then, I didn't see the connection.

But the same went for girls. And there were a lot more attractive girls in my high school than there were boys. The fact that I ended up fucking and falling in love with mostly boys while some of my friends ended up fucking and falling in love with mostly girls has, I'm convinced (though they for the most part do not agree), no more profound implications than when a group of friends in high school, all taking the same courses, get more or less out of one class or another and go off in their separate professional ways. I'm sure that in the final analysis, it's all explicable, having to do with trian-gulations and quadrangulations of various genes for risk-taking and chocolate-loving and whatnot. But since there is no final analysis, it doesn't matter much.

But that's all history, and history is not destiny. There's some-thing that keeps it going for me, something beyond habit and con-ditioning (though it'd be silly to underestimate the importance of those: the longer I'm with the guy that I'm with, the less likely it becomes that I'm going to have another relationship with a woman) that overcomes the enormous and—despite *Ellen* and *Will & Grace* and Elton John and the collected works of Joel Schumacher—still overwhelming and mostly quite active social pressure pushing us all toward our opposites. And that is the really interesting part. One of the primary things that makes sex interesting, to men and women, is transgression. For women, as a sex-columnist friend of mine has suggested to me, it most often takes the form of an imposition of commitment and marriage on men when it is so obviously contrary to a their nature; as she said, "Forcing someone to do your bidding is pretty intoxicating." Which makes bonds of matrimony seem an awful lot closer to bonds of leather than one usually assumes them to be, but it makes sense. The triumph of one will over another is not only at the root of war, business and bondage, but one of the chief satisfactions of child-rearing and pet ownership, as well. It's basic, it's fundamental and it's not gender-specific, merely gender-spun.

The kind of transgression men find sexy is considerably less nuanced. For the vast majority of men (and I'd say I've had sex with a good cross-section of the ones living in this part of the world), sex is distinct from love, intimacy, cuddling and spiritual exchange, no matter what outliers like Sting and Woody Harrelson say. Check out your local porn shop. Notice the section specializing in facials (you know what facials are, yes? It involves semen on the face; in these films, impossibly great torrents of it) and blow jobs and barely legals and twins (twins tend to be sisters, and, in porn, tend to spend a fair bit of time on each other, which makes for yummy incest) and "lesbians" and anal sex. And that's all before you get to the fetish sections. Breaking the rules, even being disgusting, is men's mainstream. Recognizing this provides a key to understanding all sorts of things about men and their love and sex lives: why they so love having sex with people other than their primary partners, for instance, and why Gérard Depardieu cheats on Josiane Balasko (total babe) with Carole Bouquet (pretty much Ethel Mertz) in *Trop Belle Pour Toi*. It is a guy, I can assure you, who first called sex "doing the nasty."

This rule-flouting may come from our distant history, in which all sex was, as it still is in the animal kingdom, ad hoc, foreplayless and dangerous (very difficult to defend yourself against attackers while you're copulating—I imagine there were quite a few *grands morts* following hard on the *petit* ones among our Cro-Magnon and Neanderthal forebears). I've no idea why it is, but it most certainly is. It's also—though most men would balk at actual incest, and the more judicious or timid possibly even step back from a genuinely barely legal girl—why so many men are appalled and enthralled by the idea of fucking their wives/girlfriends/sex workers in the ass. It's nasty. It's degrading, mostly to the women; it's gotta be. It reveals their dirty, poopy shame, the kind of physicality they try to distance themselves from—for our benefit, for their benefit—with makeup and diets and hairdos. In fact, anal sex is at its most exquisite when the woman's otherwise pristine; it heightens the defilement factor. And they can't really like it—there's no clitoris there, right? There's not even a prostate—so it's all for you, like a blow job, only with maybe just a little bit of pain. She's sacrificing for you. In other words, it's way cool.

And guess what it is that guys tend to do when they have sex with each other? It's a kiss on the cheek, a twist of the nipple and right up the butt. We can do it missionary style when we're feeling kissy, a reminder, if one is ever needed, that this kind of sex is every bit as natural, every bit as much a part of the anatomical design as what some are convinced is the way God intended. Then there's the porn version of missionary, the one people who've never done it but who've seen people do it on screen think of as gay-missionary, the heels-under-head position, a kind of *bouleversement* of standard man-on-man missionary with good sight lines that dirties it up a little, making everything a little more explicit, giving both guys more visual and tactile cues that they're butthole-surfing the border between making love and fucking. Then, of course, there's doggy style, for the man who wants to pretend he's a wolf, or Ron Perlman in *Quest for Fire*. Visual stimuli are important, as are mental ones, and the immediate meaning behind having sex with someone this way is that you've overtaken them, that you're in the middle of over-taking them, dominating them, without all the leather and rope stuff (though, you know, some of my best friends . . .); you're out for yourself, your own pleasure, which you're grabbing from the other guy, your hands clasping his hips, pulling him onto you, whether he likes it or not. And when you're doing it with a guy, the pleasure is only increased by the fact that what you're overcoming is not the thing that every guy is expected to overcome (that is, a chick), but another guy, someone who could maybe beat you up, someone who moves through the world—and will move through the world as soon as you're done with him—with the presumptive power of his gender.

But he does like it, and so do you, which is another thing that keeps me in this particular game. (In addition to the fact that, as I've come to notice over the years, guys can be really hot and, as you may have heard, rather better natural blow job artists than the aver-age non-professional woman, who seems to see the penis, at least initially, as a rather large clitoris to be treated very, very gently— have you never seen us jerk off?) And that means you can switch it up at the drop of a condom. Tits are nice, hips are great, the placement of the pussy is a marvel of versatility, and supple, soft, mostly hairless skin is wonderful to plunge into. John Mayer's right, women's bodies are wonderlands. But men's are paintball ranges, they're wrestling matches, amusement parks where there are no lines and the rides are free. And the reason is that top is bottom and bottom top and that, my friends, is all we know and all we really need to know about one of the very specific pleasures and fundamental equities of hot man-on-man love. When a woman gets on top of a man, it's a nice variation on a theme. But between men, unless one of you has got a hang-up about a domineering mother or absent father and thinks that only girly men take it up the ass (or if you're anal retentive enough to think it's gross, or girly enough to think it'll hurt), who's in and who's into are as up in the air as your legs, and not only are the sensations and orgasms different, the whole experience changes. For all the disturbingly equalizing talk about the empowerment of the pussy and bottoms, there is something viscerally different about penetrating and being penetrated, and it's not something that can be reproduced by all the silicon and latex technology Come As You Are and Good Vibrations can stick up us. Those experiences are not necessarily inferior, but they are different. Having flesh in your flesh gives you—gives me, anyway—a feeling of voraciousness, that you could go on forever, take all comers; you want it deeper, faster, harder, grasping, always on the verge of fulfillment, never getting enough, and there's a unique pleasure in having someone come in you that even dildoes that squirt whipped cream can't duplicate; in other words, an entirely different experience than the penetrative or typical male masturbatory orgasm, which always has an assured and singular end in sight and can often be had, if required or simply selfish, in under a minute— and which is, I should add, always awesome. The penetrated experience is more extensive than intensive, though the more typical male orgasm is also a part of it (he jerks you off while he's fucking you, you do it yourself), giving the experience a Teiresian quality, a both/and rather than an either/or.

There are many, many other positions in which to boink, as a quick look through Edmund White's or Felice Picano's *The Joy of*

*Gay Sex* will affirm. The porn industry has also been quite generous in its suggestions, letting generations of boys in on the secret that tabletops can be the perfect height for a smooth, satisfying fuck. But look, if you can find it, at that first Edmund White edition of *Gay Sex* and you'll see a brief discussion of rape that, though extreme almost to the point of Juvenalian satire, illustrates another reason I choose guys. White and his co-author, Charles Silverstein, suggest in this '70s breakthrough book that if you find yourself being raped, the best thing to do is lie back and enjoy it. Though police have been known to give similar suggestions (without the enjoyment part) as a technique to avoid any further violence (a suggestion, I should add, that most everyone else utterly repudiates), this piece of advice came from a different place. The notion was that sex was sex and sex was good, or at least not bad. It was the result of decades, centuries, of men being told that sex with each other was disordered, evil. So guys got a little reactionary at the dawn of gay lib and added righteous stridency to their usual sense of entitlement in the sexual realm and were, for a decade or more till they started dying off in rather large numbers, quite unbearable.

I don't suspect that anyone believes that stuff about rape anymore or even that anyone, including White and Silverstein, ever really did. But the underlying principle, that sex is fine and not cause to get overwrought, remains current among men who've discovered they like having sex with each other. It's a result, to a great extent, of that equity I mentioned earlier. Between two men, there is no natural oppressor. Or more properly, no natural victim. Though partner and spousal abuse is not unheard of in same-sex relationships, this basic gender equality changes the social dynamic as much as it changes the sexual one. At least until recently—when this whole same-sex marriage struggle started convincing guys that they were just like het couples, only with extra penises—things like leering, uninvited sexual touching, even what in other contexts would be considered full-fledged molestation have not been the issues they have been, in various ways, between men and women. It's the same reason there are same-sex bathhouses and no sustainable public mixed ones. None of the guys at Steamworks is worried about being assaulted. Though bathhouses have gotten quite public-minded since AIDS happened, after two decades of management thinking about things other than how to get the stains off the walls—there are posters around reminding guys to wear condoms, that there's this or that outbreak of syphilis or herpes to worry about, that those really hot young guys who are inexplicably coming on to you are actually hookers—still there has been, to my knowledge, not a single flyer concerning sexual assault. It doesn't mean it doesn't ever happen, but it does mean that we're not worried about it, and it's that worry, however justified, that prevents women from being a part of the great sexual freedom men are now enjoying with each other.

You might think things are changing, what with gender equity maturing, if not yet actually a fact, and with the general sexual candour in North America and Western Europe leading to ever more empowered women and actualized men. And I'm sure things are. Though I've got to wonder to what extent, or in what way. I was talking to a het friend of mine a while ago, when we were both using online and phone sex services quite a lot, ordering in or getting take-out. We were both thrilled with the whole thing, obviously. He told me about how he had hooked up with a woman and went over to her place. When he got there, she was waiting for him at the front door, and they dropped to the floor right there in the front hall and fucked in a very neat, efficient fashion and, as soon as they'd finished, they got up and she saw him to the door. It was great, he said. It was also, for him, a singular experience, one worthy of comment, even though he'd hooked up with women what I gathered was dozens of times. I smiled and congratulated him and resisted mentioning that out of the thirty or forty times (maybe fifty, but not sixty, I'm pretty sure of that) I'd hooked up with guys using the same methods, there was only one instance in which we did not have sex, and only a few in which that sex had not occurred in the first three minutes after one of us showed up at the other's door (or his car or, once, his roof). In the course of telling me about his success, my friend explained how any number of his dates ended up just wanting to talk, or not being that into him, or who sounded like nice big sluts on the phone or instant messaging but ended up really looking for a boyfriend. Now, I have no doubt that any number of guys I had sex with were looking for boyfriends. I was. And if we happened to find one in the course of our fuckings, we'd have been pleased (as I was when I did). But one thing did not get in the way of the other, as it seemed to at an alarming rate for my poor buddy. And if I ever thought the guy was unpleasant, or not as pretty or as young or as svelte as he'd implied, as I often did— well, fat ugly old jerks can be fucked, too; and the approach seemed to be mutual.

I had another friend once, a guy who mostly had sex with guys, who told me that, after giving the matter a lot of thought, he figured that the biggest thing he was attracted to in anyone was their attitude toward sex, and that if he ever ran into a woman who was as into threesomes, getting fucked against the back of a building, fucking him, fisting him, and maybe renting themselves out as a pair from time to time (he was young and hot and why not?), that he'd be as into her as he was the sexually adventurous guys he liked. He found a couple (one was, I believe, a she-male), and it turned out he was right. I hadn't thought about it in quite this way before, but I immediately agreed with him. The cocks are nice, as are the roughly equivalent levels of physical strength that, among other things, allow you to absolve yourself of the worry that you're ever bodily forcing someone to do anything they'd rather not. But a huge part of it is the feeling you get that you're both playing the same game by the same rules. There's a great comfort in that, one that fosters a truly fine ease of mind. It's not like there are no women who are overtly sexual along these lines, they're just difficult to find. And despite whatever cultural forces there are still militating against it, in many important respects, having a sexual and romantic relationship with a guy is just easier.

So maybe that's it. Maybe I'm lazy.

# Douglas Bell

∎

## FIRST AND FOREMOST

In my experience men rarely trade in the specific qualities of their sex life. Among my gender it's little more than a conversation starter, a foot in the door, a way station to the real conversations: how much money one makes, what kind of car one drives, and one's views as to which Red Sox or Blue Jay outfielder moves best to his left on a line drive hit over his right shoulder.

The seemingly infinite interest that women take in the details of how and under what circumstance other women make love is the antipode of the male sensibility. That the other bloke has sex is all one needs to know; how he has sex is way, way, way too much information. It's just a bad idea for men to talk to each other about this stuff.

So it is with considerable trepidation that I embark upon this subject. What I know is this: from the first stirrings of puberty, until the last grey days of dimming potency, *do not under any circumstance come first.*

There. I've said it. I believe it. I stand by it. I don't care if you're having it off in the john at a Wendy's beside the highway or serving yourself up in the hereafter as a man sandwich to a gaggle of virgins: *do not jump the queue.*

If my say-so isn't sufficient for you, there's plenty of hard-won scientific evidence to suggest that this is a good idea. But let's start with me.

My first girlfriend was a chesty redhead for whom I would happily have bounced a striped rubber ball on the point of my nose and swallowed raw herring as my reward. Among the first things she told me about herself was that her previous boyfriend, a hockey star at the university we were attending (with whom she had last "made love" only a few weeks before we met and many, many months after they had "broken up"), had made her come by just kissing her. (I prefer the word *come* to *climax* due to its unisex connotation. Whereas *climax* suggests a George Lucas production, in which the empire of femdom overcomes the brutality of the mute and evil penis, *come* at least holds out the possibility of equivalent status between consenting adults.) She furthermore shared with me their "record" for lovemaking in one evening, a figure so intimidating it made me queasy.

■

The first time we fucked—well, first let me say that as a rule I prefer the word *fuck* to all other expressions for the physical act of love. And while I might occasionally give in to a synonym for the sake of style, I favour a crisp one-word verb—shtup, shag, rail, etc. And I solemnly swear to never, ever use the phrase "make love"—because like the phrase "military intelligence," it's a priggish oxymoron, or ought to be. In any event, that first time, and seconds after I came and began to wilt in grateful ecstasy, she took my tool in hand and made it clear that there was a good deal more work to be done. Now, luckily, on this occasion, the fresh and tender consolations of the act were such that my response was prompt and enthusiastic. Still, it's safe to say that on the whole my understanding of lovemaking tactics and strategies was, at this stage, primitive. Using the ascent of man as a rough analogy, fire and the wheel were a couple of valleys over. Put more baldly, I couldn't take a hint. As time went on, the consequences of my ignorance snowballed.

Whereas our inclination to spontaneous sex born of necessity and passion seemed entirely satisfying and prolific, the more planned the lead-up to, and consummation of, the act, the less competent I appeared. Whenever we weren't rutting in a public park, the choreographed lovemaking of *l'amour propre* (note to reviewers: this is a play on words. I know what it actually means and I don't particularly care if you do or not)—dinner, a movie, several glasses of wine and then to bed—was invariably a tragedy. By tragedy I mean in the sense that when someone else slips and falls on a banana peel it's comedy, but when I slip on a banana peel it's tragedy. What I particularly remember about these sessions was that in the afterglow of what I found to be a perfectly satisfying experience, I would begin to drift into a gauzy slumber, only to be disturbed by a handshaking to my shoulder or, worse, a knee to my groin.

"Asleep?"

Now, there are any number of suitable answers to this question. The best of these of course is to say nothing, present arms and commence firing. I, on the other hand, would emit a bearish grumble and bury my head under the pillows. This was a mistake. Or not so much a mistake, really, as an indicator that she should dump me as soon as possible in favour of someone closer to her genetic/evolutionary station. Which she did. But only after hanging on for a couple of years or so hoping, I suppose, that my number-one deficiency, my inability to control my ejaculations, would pass; that somehow I would grow out of it. To me, at the time, this didn't seem like a deal-breaker. After all, from my point of view the sex was pretty good. I mean, I was getting off and she wasn't complaining that much or at least wasn't at the time. I mean, she might well have been storing up certain resentments. (Which of course is exactly what she was doing.) Still, when she suggested we might want to take a break, I didn't see what was coming—or not, so to speak. Six weeks later she was engaged to marry a tall, muscular, Finnish accountant. This turn of fortune rather put me off sex. I decided that since lovemaking and love were too closely associated in my mind—and to no good effect— I needed to decouple sex from affection.

In any event, time passed. I studied the sexual act like a monk in a cell, at least when I got out of the cell. I learned to control myself and my eructations. I'm not saying I developed the disciplined sustain of a porn star, but I got the basics down well enough. I played good college intramural ball, sex-wise. Whereupon I proceeded to marry a kind, decent, generous and honourable woman whose life I made miserable for nearly twenty years while I came to the realization that no matter how painful sexual relations could be, they are as nothing compared to going without.

I'm sure you have theories about this. Perhaps you think it's telling that a man who had a problem with sexual incontinence would marry a woman who didn't much like having sex. Maybe you think A caused B. But you would be wrong. Before we had children, we had a sex life. After my children were born, we did not. This was not my fault.

I'm not talking about once a month here. And I'm not talking about once a year. I'm talking about losing track altogether. I'm talking about replacing even the abstract distant flickering memory of sex with some phony consolation prize: our marriage is more about the children or companionship or some other conforming nostrum—even, this is what I owe her gender in payment for the crimes of my gender. I even thought it was my idea.

In any event, when this low-watt light bulb turned on, I got, as they say, "bizzy." I did what any married dolt in my position would do: I had extra-marital affairs. So many, that a chum suggested this particular volume chronicling my life's progress ought to have been titled (after a recurring feature in *Playboy*) "The Girls of Doug Bell." It was true. I spent my time staring soulfully into the eyes of as many women as I could get to sit still. If I got them to lie down, even better. If I fell "in love," and I did—with all of them—or they with me (and that sometimes happened), so much the better; it helped ease my guilt. Sex was shameful, but love sublime—or some such other rationale. As appalling as all this unfaithful stepping out might sound to non-combatants and my wife's friends, in retro-spect I can't imagine I was alone or even in a distinct minority.

Let me make myself clear: I had sex three times in six years. Santa Claus slid down our chimney three times more.

In his book on the pro golf tour, *The Bogey Man*, George Plimpton described the motion of his golf swing as though his mechanics were controlled by a phalanx of excitable and inconstant Japanese naval officers. I had a similar sensation when it came to my amorous doings during this period. Only in my case the mechanics were con-trolled by an alternately surly or saccharine group of drunken Albertan machine operators on a CP rail gang. I realize this is an obscure reference, so let me elaborate. (Having spent a summer working on one of these gangs I know whereof I speak.) Drunk most of the time and consigned to working and living on a steel track, Albertan railway workers are either incredibly angry or incredibly sentimental. Their capacity for feeling the one is dependent on their capacity for feeling the other. Unearned self-righteous raging at the fates leads to guilt. This, in turn, leads to the desire to be forgiven which, when unremarked, leads back to anger. And so it was with me.

As a result I was particularly attractive to a genus of the feminine I'll call the Florence Nightingale; that is, the kind of woman who seeks to save her man from himself—willing and happy to bathe with him in this swirling love soup of anger, sadness, self-pity and all-round self-righteous *amore*. A number of optimal conditions are required for the Florence Nightingale to feel fulfilled on the way to her destiny. It is important that you, the recipient of her ministrations, be unhappily married. It is important that you suffer from some sort of sexual dysfunction, real or imagined. In my case and in my mind, the problem was that I couldn't make love to my wife enough, or well enough. (She doesn't want to have sex, so of course there must be something wrong with me.) It is also important that you be the protagonist in a vast melodramatic movie titled, oddly enough, *The Florence Nightingale Story*, starring Florence, written and directed by Florence and, not surprisingly, produced by Florence.

In it you play the part of a guy either marching down the road to an epiphanic insight, and Florence holds the key to a better future; or careening down that same road toward a monstrous act of self-destruction which, while temporarily breaking the heart of our heroine (and making her stronger and more resolute in her search for true love), leads to the ultimate and conclusive repudiation of all that you might hope and dream. Strange how something conceived in such misplaced idealism can end up making both of you feel like Dresden—after the fire.

As for sex with the Florence Nightingale—well, it's a very big deal. Not necessarily for you; not even for her, really, at least as sex. Sex is merely a symbol, a crude and barely necessary expression of the much greater and vaster and more eloquent *feeling* between you. The two of you are tapping into a holy communion of sincerity, integrity, social justice—love and sex (which for those of you scoring at home is really only love!) as the grand analogy and as the Second Coming, and as the renewal of the entire world, at the very least.

Now, you'd think that in these sacramental circumstances, where love is all and sex is merely its by-product, that who gets off when (and especially first) would be kind of irrelevant—or at least not the primary issue. Yes, women's right to sexual satisfaction is equal to men's. But women are the ones who convinced me that love was more important than sex in the first place. Now they say it's not? Perhaps you can begin to understand my confusion.

■

Among the legion examples that come to mind when I think of how to illustrate the sacred importance of order and precedence in the great chain of orgasm, two stand out for me.

The first features a woman of unparalleled status and breeding in Montreal with whom I slept for six consecutive nights at her house in Westmount. This was shortly before she made my life a living hell for six consecutive months. (Okay, sorry. Must control irrational rage. I made my life a living hell. She just happened to be around at the time.) This is what happened: in the midst of applying her oral technique to my fundament the woman in question (let's call her Taffy, since after all that is her name) succeeded in eliciting the desired effect. But at the exact, crucial moment of ultimate tenderness, Taffy snapped at me. In a tone suggestive of an irate desk clerk calling at 12:30 p.m. to remind me that check-out was at noon, she said: "We don't swallow."

At a bare minimum, I wondered who the hell "we" were. It was only later that I realized Taffy resented my presumptuous desire to fulfill my evolutionary destiny—my getting off before she'd climaxed—before she'd had a chance to get hers first. She was pissed because I hadn't demonstrated sufficient gratitude for her having given up her entitled spot in the orgasmic line-up. But—that having been said—why on earth would she blow me before she got off, and then resent me for it? I suppose one answer is that it was all a sort of Indonesian shadow play, that I was meant to understand that she was to come first, or at least that I was not to come until modern protocol had been observed. She is the modern woman, after all, the oppressed gender, now self-reliant and self-financing. And yes, we're all pigs nosing about the orgasmic trough; we'll all say or do just about anything to get some. Both sexes will dress up this desire in whatever manner suits their interests in the moment. Recently *The New York Times* reported that medical researchers have isolated the part of the brain—the caudate nucleus—that demonstrates heightened activity among men and women reporting themselves to be smitten with another. "It all happens," said the chief researcher, "in an area of the mammalian brain that takes care of most basic functions." Duh. We're all slaves to our primitive biology, and the more we reconcile ourselves to our common fate, irrespective of gender, the better off we'll be. Fine. But I wish the rainbow of emotions available to men and women in bed under this grand new shining convenant included gratitude and generosity. I appreciate the sex; I want you to get off too. But does it have to be an exercise in higher actuarial accounting?

The other occasion on which I was forced to learn the hard lesson of orgasmic precedence also involves Taffy and the last time we had sex. By that time I had figured out that the only way to protect myself in our particular brand of blood sport was to ensure that somehow I organize a brain-crushing orgasm for her before even thinking about taking the stops off my various inhibitions. This I did, and if I do say so myself, with more than a little flourish. And then following on in the natural order, it was my turn to fire the old retro rockets.

But by then, time and again, as I called my internal capcom countdown, I felt my engines shutting down. What was it? Too much self-abuse? Or was it a subconscious revolt against her endless positing of romantic and sexual formulae that made me feel as if I were stuck in a first-year political theory course long after the drop date? Yes, women have a right to their own orgasm. But must it come at the expense of extemporaneous and inarticulate passion? Does a woman's politics, and her right to her orgasm, immunize her from having to feel compassion or empathy toward me? Does her status as a modern, sexually emancipated woman mean that I have no right to any insecurities or—heaven forfend!—neuroses? So she's equal: unfortunately, that seems to mean I no longer have a chance to be loved as I am.

You can say this is my problem. But it's your problem too. I mean, is it remotely possible that sex is . . . *not that important*? Or at least that it's secondary to the shared experience of the total self, in all of its imperfect complexity? It certainly should have been for Taffy and me; we might still be together. Instead, we had these modern conversational transactions, after she came, of course:

Her: "Why didn't you come?"

Me: "Well, I was enjoying it and I just didn't feel like I had to."

Her: "Didn't feel like it, or didn't want to?"

This last query was delivered with a certain, how to say, edge. And had I had the courage of future conviction I might have told her that the best idea would have been for her to have fucked *herself*: that I'd performed my human duties and she could have been grateful at least for the chance to be gracious and human; that what I didn't say (out of fear, not compassion) was *that she didn't always turn me on*, especially when she behaved in bed the way Ivan Boesky behaved in the middle of a corporate takeover: as if she owned every part of me. In the event, I fell rather short of this noble ambition. I mumbled something like an apology, seeking to assuage her wrath by suggesting that it wasn't her; that my not coming was in fact not a sort of slandering of the genius of her technique; that—well, it wouldn't happen again.

That much, at least, turned out to be true.

Still, for all the competitiveness that marked our sexual congress, I suppose that my efforts at formalizing and rationalizing my experience in retrospect are nothing compared to the simple desire we both evinced for sex, which worked to make our time together mutually consoling for as long as it lasted. I suppose if there was a difference between us, it was that I had little or nothing in mind as to what would count as good sex or a fulfilling relationship: I was simply a man, and therefore a naïf, compared to a modern woman replete with a sophisticated agenda as to what constitutes love. You see, in the end, no matter who's supposed to come first or how often or how well, *I wanted to be with someone who would help me forget that there ever were rules.* And now that I've found her—a younger woman, as it turns out, less burdened by the struggle to balance the scales—I'm going to stop writing about this, because no matter how much the chatterers would have us believe otherwise, love is ineffable and beyond the reach of mere formulation.

# *J. M. Kearns*

∎

## HOW MEN

## CHOOSE WOMEN

Let me say at the start, I don't mean to imply that men get to do the choosing. It isn't like a vegetable stand, where a man can say, "I'll take this onion here, not these others," and the onion has nothing to say about it. What we're talking about is, how do men pick out which women they are going to *try* for. Nor am I condoning, excusing or endorsing men's methods. Interesting essays could be written on how men *should* choose women, or how men *wish* they chose women. But we will focus on a topic of more practical interest: in the real world, how do men actually choose women? We will take a clear-eyed look at that question, and maybe we will find that the truth has some redeeming qualities.

The first thing we need to face about men is this: they are animals. More accurately, they are loons. They have their own ways of doing things. They don't proceed in a politically correct, enlightened way to select a woman. They may end up valuing her for the "right" things, the things she wants to be valued for. But that is not how they start.

Men are hard-wired to look for certain features. Evolution wants the mating process to succeed, and so it makes sure that men home in on that which will be conducive to success, regardless of how unrefined this strategy may be.

But no matter how strange men are, if you're a woman who wants to meet the right man, you have to clue in to how men think. (Okay, "think" is a bit of a stretch.) If you try to change men or just don't get them, you'll be stymied—but if you accept how they are and forgive them and work with them, you will have enormous power and effectiveness.

Men want to look. First, foremost and always, men are visual. Men's eyes are always wandering, seeking out that which they could and would impregnate. Why is this so, Mr. Darwin? "Well, it's because the genes that triggered that kind of behaviour had the best chance of survival down through the ages, until all the men who were left had those genes." In other words, an obsession with reproduction leads to a better reproductive score . . . or something—let's not get too technical. The fact is men can't help looking, even happily married men, even codgers who think Viagra is better than money.

So the first rule is, *let men see you*. This may seem too obvious to even mention, but in fact it is the key to the whole thing. If you make it difficult to be seen—for instance, if you sit in the back booth with shades on—you stop Step One from happening. So none of the other steps can happen. (Note that being seen is particularly crucial—and achievable—if you are trying to meet Mr. Right online.)

Now let us ask, what are men looking *for*? What are they hoping to see? If you're feeling cynical, your answer may be, "Cameron Diaz." Or if you happen to look like Cameron Diaz, your equally discouraged answer may be "Kiera Knightly." But this is so wrong it is laughable.

Men are, in the first place, looking for "attractive." Now what on earth does that mean? Well, the good news is, it means completely different things to different men—but it almost always involves a combination of face, and body shape and size.

Different men like completely different bodies. Many men in our culture like slender, athletic female figures—some men really do, and some *say they do*, because they are ashamed of admitting anything else to their male peer group. Some men want the rail-thin model type. But many men in our culture do not want a slender woman: they want someone with riper curves, someone who is larger, more "Rubenesque." Some men like pear-shaped women;

some men like inverted pears. Some men want very large women. And some men don't really care that much about body size or shape.

Then we have faces. Here there is even less consensus. No one agrees on faces. A face that strikes one man as masculine may seem feminine to another. A face that strikes Tom as sexy may look shallow to Harry. Ralph may hate a lot of makeup on a woman, while Shawn considers it a turn-on. There are no objective standards concerning faces. Even in the realm of extremely good-looking celebrities, you will find a whole gamut of opinions. I know men who think Britney Spears is homely. I know men who think Pamela Anderson is grotesque.

I know men who hate all blondes. Men who hate brunettes. Men who appreciate a good tan. Men who adore very pale skin. Boob men. Leg men. I knew a guy who got very turned on by a woman's handshake, if it was "as strong as a man's." His friends told him he was in the closet, but he stuck to his guns.

All this may strike the sensitive, intelligent woman as superficial, even offensive. "How shallow can guys get?" you may ask. Surely the cultured, educated, spiritual (yet masculine) man of *your* dreams doesn't look only at the outside of a woman. "*True beauty is on the inside,*" women cry out from the salons of the world. "Besides," I hear them say, "we women are forgiving of men's looks—why can't men return the favour?"

Scientists say men and women are both designed to be ruthlessly pragmatic in their criteria for a mate. Women are programmed by evolution to choose men based on their father potential, which is closely associated with status in the group—what we now call money and power. Men—regardless of their conscious attitude to having kids—are designed to look for good reproducers; a low waist-to-hip ratio of around .70 signifies "likely to be a success at bearing children." (Larger waists relative to the hips have been linked to lower estrogen levels, less body fat available to sustain pregnancy and lower fertility.) And in both sexes, facial beauty is associated with grace, intelligence, popularity and, in general, fitness for survival.

So forget about how superficial men may be and realize that they, like you, are hard-wired in mysterious ways, which may or may not be as shallow as you think. (Fortunately, many of them don't toe the evolutionary line anyway—apparently their wiring has come loose.)

Take faces, for example. It's clear that we read far more in a face than looks. We think we are reading souls. We look into the eyes of the person we are talking to, and we feel as if we can tell who they are, deep down—what they value, what they love. With certain people, something about the face feels familiar, even familial. Many people strike us as somehow alien; but some faces arouse in us a strange empathy from the first time we set eyes on them.

What is a man doing when he looks you over? On some level, quite possibly unconscious, he (or his genes) are trying to decide, could this person be a lover or is she just a potential friend? If the answer comes up "lover," his charm will probably kick in, and there will be a lot of twinkling eyes and banter and smiling (read: spreading of plumage) that might not take place if his circuits decided on "friend." And how is the decision made? Let's assume he finds you to be above some basic threshold of attractiveness—what other factors come into play?

Well, as odd as it may sound, you are being checked out in a number of ways to determine whether you are *too intimidating*. You are being studied to see whether you are likely to defeat him as a lover. I mean this in the most literal way: he wants to know whether in your presence he might be *unable to perform*.

The average male who is old enough and mature enough to want to marry has realized that sex is not always a triumph. I'm not saying he is sexually insecure: indeed, with the right woman he may be easygoing, studly and confident. But therein lies the rub: how does he know which women are "right"?

Our evolving male has tried, with those few cells in his brain devoted to self-knowledge, to wrestle with this question. This has made him attentive to factors that influence his chemistry with women. Many of these factors are hard to pin down: who knows what creates that magical heat for some couples? And how many men have bravely catalogued the qualities of particular women that threaten their ego, and thereby their arousal? But one area, at least, seems to be a no-brainer: a man's own physical likes and dislikes. So he tries to screen out anything that might lessen his prowess if a woman invites him to perform.

This isn't all selfish. When a man spies a woman who is really "his type"—whatever this may be—he thinks he has found someone whose sexual needs he could enthusiastically fulfill. Shall we blame him for thinking this is good news for her too?

## Intimidation and Attraction: A Short Vignette

It's lunch time. Randy and Tom find themselves sitting next to a rather elegant woman in a yuppie bar in the business district. They strike up a conversation with her while they wait for their respective tables. The woman, Rachel, is friendly, glad to have someone to talk to while she waits for a friend to show up. The men are responding in kind, but meanwhile they are both, as discreetly as they can, checking Rachel out.

Now it happens that Rachel, though strikingly attractive, has a slightly hawk-like cast to her features, a slight fierceness built into her face, that reads to Randy as intimidating and as slightly masculine. He senses in her an unswerving confidence in herself and in the cosmos, and a capacity for aggression, that make him feel he may be out of his league. So Randy is leaning toward a no on the "lover" issue, except for one thing: he has noticed that Rachel (who is wearing an attractive taupe business suit) has long, very good legs, and Randy is a confirmed leg man. (He is having trouble getting good views of her legs, because he is right next to her, and has to lean back and tilt his head to inspect them.) To make matters worse, Rachel has said she is a criminal lawyer. Randy is a tax lawyer, and they are bantering about the legal scene. But he opted out of court work because it was too scary, and he is very conscious of a threat to his ego in this woman. Those legs make him wish that she didn't intimidate him, but he can't fight the verdict of his genes.

Meanwhile Tom, who is one barstool over, is caught in a different struggle. Tom does not perceive Rachel as hawk-like or aggressive; he came from a family of women who had features somewhat like Rachel's, and to him her face represents not only beauty, but comfort, femininity and warmth. Tom is half in love already. He is not a lawyer and is not directly threatened by any status Rachel may have in that area. Tom's problem is that he can't seem to get into the conversation (because Randy is the one sitting next to Rachel and they're talking shop), and is therefore unable to tell how he and Rachel might get along, or even how she might react to him. Tom is divorced, has been lonely and horny for ages, and he has checked Rachel's hand and found no ring.

Tom has one other problem. Don't laugh at him, girls, or think he's a lout: he didn't choose this problem. Tom is a breast man. This does not mean that Tom thinks he deserves more goodies than the next guy—that he wants a luxury that he could do without. Rather, Tom's problem is that his sexual confidence is tied to the large female bosom: he becomes just a little insecure without it because a large bust is the catalyst that sparks his sexual chemistry.

I said he didn't choose to be this way. Tom didn't sit down with a notepad at age thirteen and write, "I now decide that I will find the following features of the female anatomy unbearably exciting." He just discovered what moved him. Like a man who hears western swing music for the first time and knows he has found his Holy Grail. So what *did* determine the matter? It could be cultural: the TV did it to him, men's magazines did it. The problem with that theory is we have too many different men liking too many different body types: they seem to extract different images from the media. It could be genetic: his grandfather liked the same type. Or perhaps it was early childhood experience, or lack thereof. Maybe he imprinted on the first woman he fell in love with—and maybe that was his art teacher in Grade Four.

At any rate, ever since he noticed how lovely Rachel is, Tom has been trying to lean around his stocky friend Randy and get a gander at Rachel's chest. But Randy is always in the way, and unfortunately Rachel is wearing a business suit and the jacket pretty much hides her shape.

Just as the men's table is announced, two things happen. Rachel says to Randy, "The only place that really matters to me is our family cottage on the lake," and Rachel twists toward them on her stool, her jacket falls open, and Tom has his first unobstructed view of the generous curve of her chest in a cream blouse. Tom is now completely smitten, because his own sacred place happens to be a cottage on a lake, and he is absolutely clear that Rachel, as a physical specimen, is his wet dream.

Tom now has achieved what we will call a "sighting." Tom is beside himself, if you must know the truth. He knows right now, with the same certainty that he knows his own address, that he could be happy with this woman. Behind his exterior calm he is hyperventilating, because *this never happens.* He sees women whom he finds attractive, sometimes, but they are not alone. And they are usually married. Mostly he sees them across a room or across the street. And he never gets to hear them talk about their lives, never gets even a hint as to whether he might be compatible with them in a personal sense. On this occasion in the restaurant, all these sad rules have found an exception.

This woman is classy, she is smart and she cares about lakes. And in Tom's eyes, she is a goddess.

Randy gets up to go to their table. He says goodbye to Rachel, who gives him a warm smile. Tom suspects that Rachel is attracted to Randy. Tom has no sense at all of Rachel even noticing him. He smiles at her but his smile comes out anxious and stiff, because for him there is too much at stake and he has no cards to play. Randy says, "Let's go, bud," a little sarcastically—and Tom realizes he is just standing there in a haze, gazing at Rachel. Randy tugs him away and says to Rachel, "This guy needs to eat."

Tom flushes and follows Randy into the restaurant area, and they order. Randy says dismissively, "She was nice, but kind of butch-looking. A little hefty, too." Tom, who knows his own taste for fuller-figured women is atypical of his male peer group, keeps quiet, doesn't mention that he just lost the love of his life. A few minutes later, they see Rachel sit down in a nearby booth with a very good-looking, well-dressed man, who seems to be locked in constant hilarity with her. Tom abandons a half-formed plan of somehow talking to her before heading back to work.

This is how it happens to us men.

A typical session in the endless male search: what can we learn from it? Let's inventory a few useful points:

1. Facial looks are totally subjective: the same woman can look feminine and pretty to one man and just the opposite to another. Same for body shapes and sizes.

2. Total accidents of seating and attitude can stop major connections from being made.

3. Men very rarely have positive "sightings," and usually are not in a position to act even on those.

4. Men's relentless scrutiny of women, the thing that drives feminists crazy, is just as much *a screening out of that which is intimidating* as it is a judging of whether someone is up to par. If truth be known, Randy's dismissal of Rachel had little to do with her being not pretty or too heavy. These were excuses. The truth was, he found her intimidating as a lawyer and as a woman.

5. The most confident, forward man in the group is not always the most interested one. He may be confident because he isn't interested, and therefore has nothing to lose. The one who can't get a word out may be the one who is stricken with attraction. *Above all, remember this.*

6. Qualities of character are often in play from the beginning. Men may seem to be judging solely on appearance—but in fact *they see in appearance many other levels of humanity.* In Rachel's face, Tom saw warmth, familial comfort, kindness, intelligence. In her words he heard a love for a type of sacred place that he too values. Even her body's sexual appeal to him holds other levels of connection—in her full figure he sees a reassuring quality, and a sensual opulence, that speaks to his emotional needs. (Randy saw qualities of mind that scared him off.) Both men were reacting to a whole person, through her appearance.

And what did Rachel think?

Here we encounter an amazing disparity—a gap like the Grand Canyon. Her experience was so unlike that of the men as to seem like a cruel cosmic joke. Rachel did not have "finding a man" on her agenda. She wanted to meet her friend Pete and have lunch, and she was preoccupied with a trial she is in the middle of. Pete works at the same firm she does, and they hang out together a lot, but there is no chemistry between them and that is why they have the relaxed, hilarious rapport that Tom noticed later.

Rachel broke up with a long-term lover six months ago when she discovered he was cheating on her. Although she is lonely and occasionally makes a slight effort to meet new people, she is skeptical of all men. And anyway, *she does not think of a bar as a place where she could ever meet a man.* She was perfectly happy to talk to Randy, but did not even ask herself whether he was relationship material—he was just a fellow lawyer. Tom she hardly noticed. She did observe that he had a nice face, but it never occurred to her for a moment that he was interested in her, and he seemed sort of uptight and sad compared to his friend.

Rachel's attitude to her body is even more tragically counterproductive. Rachel has regretted since about age sixteen that she is not skinnier. She thinks of herself as full-figured, because although she has a model's legs, she has rounded hips and a full bosom. Actually, she thinks she's fat. If she could only lose thirty pounds, she might be acceptable in her own eyes. She has an older sister who still weighs 115 pounds and this torments her daily. Somewhere inside her, a voice still says, "You're beautiful," but lately she has trouble hearing it.

Oh Rachel! The truth is, you have a classic hourglass figure, and plenty of men would find you almost overwhelmingly sexy if you would let them—and if they could escape the caustic stereotypes of their peer group. So Rachel wears her business jackets in such a way as to conceal her generous chest—she is ambivalent at best about it. It certainly never occurred to her that Tom is a man who absolutely cherishes the very body type that she represents, at the weight where she is. Or that her jacket was preventing such an admirer from even verifying that she is what he admires!

Tom, a man who is normally cheerful and entertaining, managed only to seem a bit sad to her. And if he seemed sad, maybe he had a right to be. Because something sad did just happen. Rachel just walked away from Mr. Right. Tom was it.

Don't get me wrong here: I am not saying that Rachel did anything wrong, though she could be accused of being somewhat unaware.

What I *am* saying is that near-misses like this happen all the time. People who would be perfect together pass like the proverbial ships in the night. Then they trudge on down life's path, forever lonely. Women cruise through situations, blissfully unaware of the life-and-death struggle going on in the man who is right next to them.

For it *is* a life-and-death struggle. Biologically, nothing is more important than successful mating. And for an average male who is old enough and mature enough to want to marry, that challenge is an awesome test, a labour of Hercules, fraught with perils and obstacles. The main peril is rejection (intensified by the competition of other males, many of whom have him beaten in one way or another— looks, money, physique, smarts, style, confidence . . .*). The main obstacle is rarity: too seldom does our eligible male encounter an unattached and approachable female whom he senses could really be the one.

No wonder a man goes a little crazy when a true sighting happens—success and happiness and an end to loneliness are beckoning to him, if he can only make the right moves. In our example, Tom froze up completely, even managed to make himself less attractive! Became stiff and sad-looking, tongue-tied.

---

* Or if he is the rare bird with looks, money, physique, smarts, style and confidence, then he meets some woman who wants him to be more sensitive, more creative, more humble.

In recent years the "Am I as good-looking as the other guys?" issue has intensified, as the media have done to men what they always did to women: assaulted them with a barrage of images of "perfect" male specimens with perfect faces, hair, clothing, pecs and abs, as they conspire to sell exercise machines, diets, erectile dysfunction pills and plastic surgery to men.

Must we leave our little story of the yuppie lovers with a bad ending? Could Rachel have done anything to change the outcome?

Well, suppose we replay the scene with just a few tiny changes. This time, Rachel keeps in mind that any place is a good place to meet Mr. Right.

Let's say that again. *Any place is a good place to meet Mr. Right.*

So she has her antennae switched on. Then she may well notice that lawyer Randy is not really interested in her. And that he is a bit of a bore—too needy in the ego department. And she may well pick up on the fact that Tom is eyeing her in an almost stressed way. Why is he doing that? Maybe he fancies her. Maybe she should make a point to speak to him, instead of letting this insecure tax lawyer hog all her time. Tom does have a very nice face, after all. So she leans across Randy, smiles at Tom, realizes that her jacket has fallen open, which is fine, and says to Tom, "Why do you hang out with this lawyer boy, anyway? Can't you do any better?"

Tom lights up at this suggestion that she has noticed him, at her sense of humour, and at the curves that he has just detected. Tom starts to talk to her; Randy decides to go to the rest room; Tom cannot resist moving over next to her. They discover their mutual love of lakes and cottages. He asks her if she is meeting someone for lunch. She says yes, but he's just a friend. Finally Tom cannot restrain himself. He asks for her card. She gives it to him. They smile at each other. Love is born.

(Somewhere, Cupid frowns: because two people who will be *happy together* have found each other.)

MIND

# *Bruce Grierson*

■

## GRATUITOUS

## PRECISION

A guy was sitting at the kitchen table with the newspaper open. He'd been parked there for fifteen, twenty minutes now, without turning the page. Had he fallen asleep? No. Was he deeply under the spell of some muse: hatching a plan, composing a poem, negotiating a second chance with his god? No. He was as still as a flame in a cup. He was reading the stats page.

"What can possibly occupy you for that long?" this man's wife wanted to know. What are you looking for?"

Not just the scores, obviously. Patterns. Changes in the rankings among teams, changes in point production within teams. Streaks, broken streaks. That all-important stat, "Last 10." Who's got momentum and who's in the breakdown lane. He wanted to see how these trivial things were trending right now, as if such knowledge might give him clues about the larger, less quantifiable world.

Guys can be alarmingly loosey-goosey about things that many women would deem fairly important to get right: whether we locked the front door, whether there's enough money in the joint account to cover the rent cheque, whether the travel medical coverage expires the day we return home or—oops—the day before. What's the procedure in an earthquake? Who knows?

But ask us—come on, ask us—which is the more reliable, Moore's Law of computing power or the Pareto Principle of customer loyalty, and we can give you an explanation that would move a jury. Who performed our wedding ceremony? Her name is . . . gone. But we can tell you the name of the world's fattest man, who was buried in a piano case.

What has happened here is that the culture of precision born with the Scientific Revolution has fallen into the hands, 450 years down the line, of guys with no actual expertise in anything, but with high-speed Internet hookups. And so we immerse ourselves in the minutiae of the few subjects we know a little about and feel comfortable discussing. (Generally these are the same subjects we were interested in, and felt comfortable discussing, when we were nine.) There's a psychological payoff in being able to claim *a mastery of something*; and since it long ago became obvious that we haven't the will or patience to acquire the skills that were once, and may still be, the *sine qua non* of being a man—things like celestial navigation and boatbuilding and animal husbandry—we settle for a comprehensive knowledge of *The Simpsons*.

(A word has emerged in the last decade to describe this phenomenon of micro-overeducation: "wonk." Its origins are murky, but one theory is that it's simply "know" spelled backwards. Which, intriguingly, implies that to be ridiculously informed about something is in some ways the opposite of really knowing it.)

You might think of gratuitous precision as, for modern man, the third behavioural wave. First came postwar, can-do earnestness. Then came chill-out, give-a-crap-about-nothing cool. The third wave is the synthesis. It says, I *am* capable, and I *do* care—but only about things I choose to care about (rather than what they want me to care about). Juvenile? Of course. But that's kind of the point. Such a strategy worked for us once—and we are inclined to stick with a winning game.

In high school, mostly to keep our minds off the dates we weren't getting, I had a contest with my pal John Wetherill to memorize pi as far as we could. I memorized it to forty places. (The trick was to break it into five-digit chunks.) John got fifty. I went home and pushed it to sixty. The next day John had a hundred. I suggested a new game: compiling a list of hair bands of the '70s. The novelist Ron Carlson admits to once, as an elementary school student, writing the numbers from 1 to 120,000 in order in a notebook—which "made me feel pretty much that the sky was the limit in terms of what the future held."

Gratuitous precision involves the art (and of course it's only "art" to the degree that the "sandwich artist" who builds your meatball foot-long at Subway can lay claim to the term) of applying academic rigour to small topics—like, say, the history of the smiley-face button or the bolo tie. The approach leaves no stone unturned, no cavil unanticipated, and when you're done you realize you have sunk an enormous amount of time into the enterprise without regard to whether the subject really warranted it. It's like a whole generation of cancer specialists working round the clock on a cure for baldness.

Not long ago I overheard a guy at the bus stop say to his buddy, "There's between an 85 and 90 percent chance that Larry won't show up at all." Now how'd he arrive at that? The other guy betrayed no hint of skepticism. It was as if it were the most natural thing in the world to at least try to estimate the inestimable—no different from a poet trying to find the exact correlative, in the dawn light or the movement of a locomotive wheel, of an emotion. They were noble archers shooting arrows in the dark, these bus-stop guys, sublime and ridiculous both.

■

I spent months recently researching a series of articles on space exploration. It's a quickly evolving field, and so I didn't so much read books as rummage among the newsgroups and follow the discussion threads there. Largely, it was guys trying to win status points by catching other guys in minor inaccuracies. There was an intensely competitive air to these exchanges. Sci-fi geeks, I thought, dismissively—at first. In time I came to realize that these contests were pretty much the same as those you find in any Internet domain dominated by men; there's some random juking and jiving by a dozen or so entrants, and then a couple of leaders emerge, guys awesomely, masturbatorily dedicated to precision. The topic is almost immaterial: typefaces, baseball closers, the relative merits of antimatter propulsion versus solar sails for interstellar travel. Who committed the most boneheaded miscue: Merkle or Buckner or Corrigan? Where did Barney Rubble work? Is a cheque signed on underpants legal tender? Could you make decent artisanal cheese out of human breast milk? What happened to Howard Hughes's will? A great intellectual levelling is at play: all issues are treated with equal reverence. (That's the fun of it, of course. Except when it isn't.)

What you notice about a lot of the most fiercely argued points is that there is no right answer. What was the best drum solo ever? Was Eliot Smith actually murdered? It's all about how you make your case. (For example, "Ginger Baker's solo in the original version of 'Toad' was great, though the live version verges on self-parody." And so on.) But just because there's no right doesn't mean there is no wrong. The hapless record-shopper who incurred the wrath of the Jack Black character, Barry, in *High Fidelity* learned that it is simply wrong—was wrong then, is wrong now—to like anything by Depeche Mode. The wrongs, in these matters, though, are not wrong in a way that will stick to you and tarnish your name. Long-term public ridicule is unlikely. That's why it's fairly safe to wade in, expounding willy-nilly.

The "what" of gratuitous precision is a lot easier to explain than the "why." I suspect many women who have observed this personality trait in their men, and been driven around the twist with frustration, would argue that it comes from insecurity. More specifically, it comes from men's awareness of their emotional illiteracy. A guy experiences what ought to be an emotional moment—but the emotion doesn't register. So the guy, unable to feel, grasps for something to do in the breach. He describes the moment, makes lists, assigns labels. We name what we can't get close to; what we can really feel we have no need to name.

It's not a bad theory. But it is, I think, incomplete at best.

Anyone who has watched little boys and little girls playing knows there are big gender differences, apparently innate. One of the biggest is precision. Precise is almost definitely what little boys are not. Clay-footed imprecision doesn't temper a little boy's enthusiasm, but it routinely sabotages the results—especially compared to the fine work the girls are doing. So we men, I think, spend the rest of our lives trying to make up for the frustration and inefficiency that so set us back. Once our fine motor skills come in and we learn to keep our butt in a chair, we over-err on the side of precision. Lots of high-end stereo manufacturers make speakers with supertweeters sensitive to sound thousands of kilohertz higher than the human ear can hear. These units are very popular among audiophiles, almost all of them men. I once paid more for a car stereo than the car it went in. Shortly after, somebody in the back seat put their foot through a woofer.

Margaret Atwood has a line that I think is relevant here: "The difference between men and women [I'm paraphrasing] is that men are afraid of being made fun of, while women are afraid of being killed." That seems right. Freed from worry for our physical safety, we promote to the top of the pyramid of concerns those lesser, social fears. (It's no accident that stand-up comics, a largely male lot, call bombing embarrassingly on stage, "dying.") A great unspoken fear for guys is that we will be caught in a "streeter"—a roaming TV crew looking for a common-man perspective—on some subject we haven't really been keeping up on. The lights, the lens: real-time humiliation.

One way to avoid being publicly humiliated, of course, is to be prepared. Notice it was only guys who memorized the Trivial Pursuit cards. It's mostly guys who write out vocabulary with correct pronunciations so we won't be caught saying "yar-moolk." It's guys who find reading a book review a sensible alternative to reading the book itself—which is a little like jogging through the Louvre. Somehow we got confused about the concept of being "cultured." We thought it was the same as being "informed."

It's not really a movement, but gratuitous precision does have its resident gods. Its poet laureate is Nicholson Baker, master of the micro-observation, a man, in poet Ken Babstock's phrase, almost autisticly precise on subjects such as the use of pencils and ice-cube trays. Its *auteur* is Stanley Kubrick, so gratuitiously exacting about details only he would notice that he took decades to finish his films—if they ever got finished at all. Its jock-intellectual is the sabermetrician Bill James, who changed the way owners—and to an extent, fans—think about professional baseball. The success of James's approach to the game supports the argument that the things that are presumed to matter most (batting average, home runs, strikeouts) actually matter less than the things everyone overlooks (swing/miss percentage, run/support ratio). And the It Boy, you could say, of gratuitous precision is the *Jeopardy* whiz Ken Jennings, who threatened us all with his command of information. Except that Jennings seemed to know everything about everything— including things that are not gratuitous at all.

What's the difference between gratuitous and non-gratuitous? Ah, that's the question.

Many guys will try to tell you that even the most trivial-seeming details aren't, because you never know when they will pay out. For instance, if you know the jersey numbers of the '70s Eskimos, '80s Oilers and '90s Bulls, plus the home address of every sitcom character from Lucy to Archie, then you have a vast cache of mnemonic devices in reserve, and you will never forget a phone number or a locker combination as long as you live. McGyver proved the practical value of long-dormant chemistry-class knowledge every time he made a bomb from weed killer, or stopped an acid leak with a chocolate bar. Is it gratuitous to know words you'll never use, the capitals of countries you'll never visit, the names of flowers you'll never encounter? You could argue that information is neither gratuitous nor important; it's value-neutral; it just is. Only when we shoulder it out into the world does it prove useful or not in any given context. It's not really gratuitous to know facts. Stockpiling facts in some area builds a body of knowledge, and that's just being a connoisseur, right?

Well, maybe. A good way to tell if what we're doing is true connoisseurship or mere affectation is to ask the question (or better yet, get us to ask it of ourselves): if there were no one else around, would you still do it? Drink great Scotch instead of merely good Scotch? Listen to vinyl albums instead of CDs? Keep Anne Carson instead of Anne Tyler in the bathroom? The answer could very well be yes. But that may be more out of habit. The real question is, if there were no one else around, would you have developed the habit in the first place? If you were left alone on your trial-and-error fumblings, to sift through the subtle aesthetic distinctions and arrive at perfection on your own terms, would you go to all the trouble?

Not long ago a couple of salvage divers found a sunken German U-boat off the coast of New Jersey, after having spent many years and many perilous dives looking—and their story has been turned into a book. Reviewing it, the writer Mark Bowden, himself no stranger to dangerous undertakings, refused to shower the divers with praise. He didn't doubt that they were brave, he just questioned their motivation. This submarine was a footnote in the war. Why all that risk and effort for a fairly trivial prize? Such intense effort, Bowden suggested, ought to be reserved for "questions that alter our understanding in a significant way." "An extreme concern with relatively minor details," he wrote, "more or less defines hobbyism."

So there it is. We are, we guys, most of us, hobbyists. That may seem strange to say when actual hobbies—have you noticed this?—seem to have vanished. Once hobbies were so essential to our identities that we put them on our resumes. Now that no one has the time, or the will, for discrete hobbies, we have integrated the spirit of hobbyism—that focused reverie, that dreamy Zen-like picking of nits—into our daily routines. In the old days hobby time had a beginning and an end—perhaps after the dinner dishes were done and before *Masterpiece Theatre* began. But when you are a lifestyle hobbyist, life itself becomes your hobby.

One of the more curious gadgets to come out of California recently is a watch that runs on Mars time—that is, it loses thirty-nine minutes a day. It was designed by a Bay Area jeweller, because some scientists from the nearby Jet Propulsion Lab in Berkeley were working on one of the Mars landers, and it was a pain to have to keep converting Earth time to Mars time. They heard that a local watchmaker was a Swiss-trained master, and they handed the problem to him. It turned out to be a bear. I saw a documentary TV show on this fellow. There he was, with gears and springs and lead weights of varying sizes spread out on the table. It took him months and months of tinkering. He looked happy as a clam, utterly absorbed, working right at that coveted attention level of just-manageable difficulty. He was serving the call of his country as it explored the High Frontier. But really, he was just fooling around. There was and is no pressing need for this watch, but there he was shaving down the margin of inaccuracy, grinding ever closer toward the gold standard of an atomic clock. It was just a cool thing to do. And because others said it couldn't be done, it became a contest. Now that the only people who can conceivably make any practical use out of the watch—a hundred or so space scientists at JPL—own one, the watchmaker has begun selling them to the public. And people are snapping them up. Because, hey, these are watches that run on Mars time. (And as one space enthusiast put it, he figured this way he could sleep in an extra thirty-nine minutes.) This is as serviceable a metaphor as you're going to find for the modern guy. The cooler among us are building a Mars watch. The rest of us are wearing one.

# Martin Levin

∎

## CONFESSIONS OF A
## COMMITMENTPHOBE

D. and I see one another only occasionally. When we do, there is essentially but one topic—women: women and their beauty; women and their elegance; women and their charming oddness, veering occasionally into madness; their scent (natural and aided); that hair; those eyes; those lips. I have similar conversations with most of my men friends: books, baseball, blues, beer and B-movies intrude, as a way of keeping us from self-combusting with generalized desire. We discuss the curve of an arm, the lilt of a leg, the reasons why we brainy types find a certain trashy look so appealing—lank straight hair, cheap summer dresses, an artfully misplaced little tattoo do it for me. We talk about why another look just won't do: for me, it's jeans and high heels. Or we talk about how women's alien perception of the workings of the universe is either crazy or, just possibly, salvific. (Of course men are crazy too, only in a more familiar way. I, for instance, would love to sleep with Ann Coulter, not because she's an attractive blond, but because she's an attractive right-wing loony blond.)

The pleasure in such conversation is at least as much aesthetic as it is erotic. For instance, how common it is—I learn at long last, opening up in middle age to other men after decades of the most transparently Freudian clenching of the emotional sphincter—that in the throes of emerging passion/lust/love, we may fail to attend even remotely to the actual woman seated across the table/sofa/car seat from us, not because we're imagining detailing our new Jaguar, or we're wondering which wide receiver to take first in our fantasy football draft, or we're contemplating levelling a Remington .303 (I looked it up) at the heart of a moose, or, furthest thing from our minds, we're thinking of another woman. No, it is because of that hair, those eyes, those lips, that voice. We are lost in rapt contemplation of the aesthetics of a woman's very womanness.

This may not be the sort of attention that women most welcome, but it can be the most rapt, the most engaged sort of attention we offer. It's the sort of attention only the best male novelists can reproduce. There's a story, for instance, by John Updike (a man notable, even let us say notorious, for his frank appreciation of women, and therefore far from being a feminist icon), in which a young man not pointedly in search of love wanders into a shop in a Massachusetts summer resort. One look at the shop girl, and he is instantly smitten by the arc of her splendid shoulders.

Updike's description of this earthly rapture was much on my mind one evening. At dinner with a group that included a moderately well known American novelist, I noticed a couple at the next table. Well, I noticed her; he remains a cipher. She had on one of those little black summer dresses that constitute significant evidence for the existence of God. Aware that instant dirty old manhood impended, I restrained my leering—at her perfect shoulders. And I noticed the novelist seated next to me doing the same. We exchanged glances: we knew. The usual trope is: women know these things. But there are things men know too.

Given that the company of women is so bracing, so enchanting, so engrossing, so entirely, winningly, compellingly other (that is, the not-me, the not boisterous, hairy, smelly, many-tentacled male), why then am I, why are so, so many men so, so reluctant, so talk-show famously reluctant, to commit? Why do we run from not just the act but the very thought, like a rabbit from a hungry fox?

Consider the male black widow spider. One tiny indiscretion, one microscopic orgasmic discharge, and his much larger and more powerful mate devours him; worse, in the process, she drains the tiny residue of the life fluid out of him. Many men see in this an apt metaphor for their own committed fates. Once mention love, once declare that the very sun rises and sets upon her countenance, or that you would venture to the highest Himalayan peak to pluck the last flower of a vanishing species for her, and you, my friend, are a goner. Love will suck you dry and leave you an empty husk to be scattered in the merest breeze.

■

I have been married twice, both times to lovely, remarkable, remarkably complex, but not remarkably easy, and not remarkably knowable, women. The first marriage lasted sixteen years to the day. I'd have said that shows a fair level of commitment, not to mention exquisite timing. Yet, as my first wife (or as my friend A. puts it of his own brace of brides, "my senior ex-wife") sometimes put it to me, as the years grew and we did not, I did not seem married, did not act married, did not look married. And thus, she suspected, I did not really want to be married.

I, of course, protested strenuously and, I then thought, sincerely. Was I not, despite the vast differences in our outlooks on life—she a hedgehog, I a fox, in Tolstoy's old formula—committed to her and the children? Did we not live together in mostly connubial calm, if not bliss? Was I not willing to accommodate her? Not, perhaps, entirely uncomplainingly, but accommodate nonetheless?

For instance, there was the time I had my eye on a lovely 1956 Jaguar XK saloon car, certain to be an automotive money pit, but super snazzy and a sure badge of the confident masculinity all men would like to project. Skeptical she suggested that, given our growing young family, perhaps a station wagon would be more the ticket. Of course, I recoiled in horror, as what man who aspires to red-bloodedness would not: the station wagon, signifier not of manhood but of suburbia, of tame domesticity, a sign that you, champ, have more or less given up. From now on, "woody" will refer only to panelling and not to activity in your nether regions. Eventually, we compromised on a boring, though mercifully not embarrassing, domestic sedan. (Later, single again, I indulged my mild chick-magnet-wannabe auto-eroticism with a yellow Checker cab: money pit.)

To do my senior ex some justice, I was bringing a guy's traditional armamentarium to what was essentially an emotional/psychological conflict. Responding to her perceptions about my lack of full commitment, I unloaded what I proudly thought of as my logico-skeptical *Weltanschauung*. "What," I asked, "does married *seem* like, *look* like, *act* like?" I think now that I knew, even then, that *au fond* (my slightly show-offy tendency to drop French, German and Latin expressions into emotional dust-ups was, I'm sure, an inducement to homicide—if she needed one), married is, looks, acts . . . married. If she, and her friends, perceived me as fundamentally uncommitted, could they have been entirely wrong? They were not. During the last half dozen slowly soluble years of the marriage, as her life choices veered off in ways completely unexpected, and to me unwelcome—if you think it's hard to compete with Brad Pitt, try God—I separated emotionally.

As for my "junior" ex, our less than year-long marriage was characterized by "commitment" on both sides that was at once provisional and blindingly intense, with an emotional temperature pitched so high I felt as if I were living in some absurdly theatrical, and permanent, psychodrama. Is this it? I wondered; does my life wind to a graceless end in mutual madness? The attraction may have been electric, but the desire for escape was cosmic. Fortunately, she made it clear that she always kept a packed suitcase—real or metaphorical—under the bed. So, though I loved her then and still do in my way, I hoped she'd packed her toothbrush too.

In the years since that marriage ended, I have noticed a mildly disturbing pattern in my behaviour. Let's say that I am standing in a line-up—at a supermarket, at a bank, at airport security, at a booth buying concert tickets. As I approach the presumed goal, that is, completion of task and liberation from line, I am overwhelmed not by a feeling of near-accomplishment, but by . . . panic is not the right word. Unease. The thing for which I have queued in the first place, even when the queue is self-selected, even when the object seems eminently desirable—a Springsteen concert ticket, a tub of Häagen-Dazs coffee ice cream, a trip to Paris—suddenly has come to be seen as not less desirable per se, but somehow almost frightening.

I put this down to an irrational fear of commitment, irrational because it is so short term, and so unilateral. Paris is indifferent to your charms; someone else will gladly fill your seat for The Boss. At first I thought this a question of fear of disappointment: what if the thing or event doesn't measure up to expectation? But it's more fundamental than that, more a question of limiting options, however trivial. Once you're somewhere, you can't be anywhere else, no matter what quantum physics tells us.

If even this puny level of commitment is a source of angst, what then of a woman, a living, breathing, hoping, expecting creature for whom commitment is more than licking the last drops from a half-litre tub of Häagen-Dazs and then chucking it in the recycling bin. No, with a woman, it's like this: as a relationship progresses from tentative explorations, complete with the sorts of prevarications designed to take you to that next step—"Oh, I get along famously with all my exes." "Why yes, Air Supply's one of my favourite bands, too." "Chihuahuas? Love them."—the sense of adventure proceeds hand in hand with a mounting sense of dread. What if she falls in love with me? Worse, what if I fall in love with her? What then? The easiest response: Flee, flee before you're trapped, run for your life. Run for her life, for you will betray her one way or another.

To make these complicated matters even more impossible, consider the Dawkins Factor. British geneticist, moralist and anti-religion polemicist Richard Dawkins wrote a famous book, *The Selfish Gene*, in which he turned evolutionary theory on its head. He argued that instead of thinking about how species use genes to replicate themselves, we should rather think that our (a word and concept now to be used with extreme caution) genes use us simply to make more genes.

The implication of this for men was that we could hardly be blamed for our nature, since sexual desire, and its formalization in courtship and marriage, could simply be seen as a displacement of, or corollary to, the commandment of the true god, the gene: "Lo, thou shalt spread thy seed widely and thus make more of me."

Flowing from Dawkins's Darwinian font were all manner of theories, including one suggesting that men instinctively seek out women with a waist-to-hip ratio of 7 to 10. Sure, things like a big-breast fetish or an appreciation of Rubenesque versus Kate-Mossy women may be culturally determined, but the survival of the species depends on that 1.43:1 ratio, and we men, though we don't know it, are universally driven by our master genes to seek it out. Hipsters *malgré nous-mêmes.*

Which is where younger women come in. Commitment eventually makes them unavailable, unless your commitment is to philandering.

Early in the film *About Schmidt*, Jack Nicholson has just retired from an executive position at an insurance company. Tucked into bed with his wife of many years, he wonders: "Who's that old woman lying next to me?" Indeed. There's a reason men like to invoke the fabled French formula for wives/lovers/mistresses: they should be half our age plus seven years. We have our own biological clock, only it never runs out until we do, just ticks a little faster. I'd say we begin to acquire a taste for younger women precisely at the same time as they begin to fail to notice us. No more admiring, smiley, possibly come-hither glances tossed our way as our bellies distend and our hair migrates.

I could argue that biology is destiny, that the male sperm simply wants to find the most likely source to replicate, and that's younger women, who have that crucial waist-hips ratio we're helplessly, blindly driven to seek. But of course, all those middle-aged executives who dump their mates for pneumatic young trophy wives already have families. Replication is not the first thing on their minds.

No, younger women offer us something more: hope, and the illusion that their presence in our life continues to make us the man we were, or thought we were. And, as Richard Wright's novel *The Age of Longing*—about a pathetically fading small-town hockey hero—has it, "Are we ever as happy as when we are on the threshold of hope?" I think that's not only why CEOs suddenly appear with arm candy thirty years younger than they are, but why Mick Jagger at sixty stills thinks he's twenty, why Hugh Hefner needs three twentyish identikit girlfriends, why Woody Allen's über-nebbishy characters seem always to be getting it on with the likes of Charlize

Theron, oblivious to the why-is-that-man-kissing-his-daughter-on-the-lips stares they arouse.

Back in the early 1970s, the American novelist and essayist William Gass wrote a powerful essay about the stylization of desire, about civilization as a process of ritualizing basic survival instincts. Thus, hunger gets civilized into gastronomy and $250 restaurant meals, while sexual desire and gene-driven lust are transformed into love and cloaked in all the rituals of courtship. For hard-line Dawkinians, love is merely the displacement of the propagation drive: simple genetic lust. When function is emptied out, form remains.

All this notwithstanding, I think the truth is that men want commitment, fear it, want it, fear it. We joke about it, mock it, wrestle with it, all signs that it sits ungentle on our minds. But it's just as true that we middle-class, protected, safe, coddled men—even we still want to be cowboys, pirates, James Bond, athletes, explorers, geniuses. In other words we want at least the illusion of being unfettered. Commitment to wife or lover means no going off with our pals to battle dragons (or, in my case, Nazis), no linking of arms and other appendages with that luscious Rita Hayworth clone draped over our tuxedoed self at a lavish Monte Carlo gaming house. (It is a measure of the power of fantasy that it is unchanged even by the certain knowledge that what you get in most casinos is saggingly unappealing women in pedal pushers and badly hennaed hair mindlessly stoking the slots. Of course, they're accompanied by paunchy men in gawdawful orange and green acrylic jackets—where *do* they get them?—looking sheepish and confused.)

There's another thorn in commitment's crown: Does its promise last? When my first marriage ended (actually, she fled; I, noble or—more likely—stupid or delusional, might have stayed indefinitely), I lived for several months in the apartment of a friend. Young, handsome, sexually confident, he collected bedpost notches as if they were hockey cards. This naturally gave him locker-room bragging rights, which he exercised only fitfully since he was also ruefully open about his commitment to conquest overriding any prospect of commitment to other. The conflict gave him genuine pain, but two opposing notions of manhood were at war: the angel on one shoulder, Dependable Dick; the devil on the other, Phallic Phil.

■

Which brings me back to that dread of line-ups, or at least of nearing the thing anticipated. I console myself that my phobia is earned: two fraught marriages and several other relationships doomed by my hypersensitive flight-response-triggering system. I tell myself that I do not want to be the guy who ties his shoes and picks up his car keys, or who, panicked by the interest of a woman, says he's just remembered that he needs to buy pencils and that the only shop that sells the kind he likes is in Kuala Lumpur. Or who tells a befuddled woman who thought he was enamoured of her that Saturday night is out because he has to perfect a guitar riff he's just learned.

This backhanded attempt at gentlemanliness may seem arrogant rather than considerate, may seem as if I believe that, given the choice, women will always accept men who want them. On the contrary, women are much more discriminating than men. After we separated, my junior ex and I once sat on a restaurant patio on a busy Toronto street—committed, at least, to friendship—and decided to spend an hour counting desirable prospects who passed by. She came up with at very most a half dozen, while I lost count, and the use of my salivary glands, somewhere in the hundreds.

Still, despite a sequence of what I always thought of as failures, I believed that I was a good guy in matters romantic, adopting as a motto the medical credo: first, do no harm; be the leavee, not the leaver. Short of telling her that you have a communicable fatal disease, or that there is a run of serial killers in your family, extrication isn't always that easy. One of my friends offers his simple solution: "I just treat her badly until she leaves me."

At the time I thought this a form of sexual cowardice. Not now, given my own less than exemplary post-marital behaviour. For one, there was J., a funny, smart woman. We'd been seeing each other for a couple of months in a relaxed way. Not even an undertone of pressure for anything more, yet when she went on a brief vacation,

I "neglected" to call her when she returned, or even to explain myself. Then there was S., an effervescent, good-natured, earthy younger woman. By then, I'd mastered the "I like you almost to distraction, but I'm not ready to get involved" shtick. Nonetheless, patient she and a slightly terrified creature that I recognized as a hall-of-mirrors version of myself went on for a couple of years in an off-on tussle that must have been terribly frustrating for her. Her view: love should be unquenchable, unconquerable, omnipotent. Mine: hmm. It is largely to her credit that we remain friends.

None of this is a matter of running up a sexual life list. This is not about Alfie, or the lines from old pop star Dion's "The Wanderer": "And when I find myself falling for some girl / I hop right into that car of mine and I drive around the world." That may be an appealing archetype for a wannabe Lothario, a guy who'd prefer to think of himself as a master seducer—love 'em and leave 'em, but show them a good time, leave them wanting more, and on no account fall for them. Nice credo, but really, who's kidding whom? Dion was a pop/rock star (the whole purpose of becoming one is access to women), while I'm a middle-aged man with thinning hair and a respectable little paunch, hardly the stuff of which Casanovas are made.

And, although the historical Casanova was, I was surprised to learn, a champion of an early form of women's lib, the line between Casanova and cad is a fuzzy one. (Canadian expat Rick Marin wrote a whole memoir called *Cad*, about his mistreatment of women— but really, girls, he's nothing special to look at.) No commitment-phobe wants to be thought a cad. Rather, our approach to women is a compound of a vestigial, partial, unrealized chivalric impulse, with a bit of "That's What You Get for Loving Me" tossed in, but not in a cruel or celebratory way, as it is in the Lightfoot song. Rather, it's rueful, wistful, sheepish, accompanied by the sense that perhaps things could have gone another way, if only . . . Except, mostly, they couldn't have.

It's not that we don't want women; we want them very much indeed. But what we may want even more than unfettered bed-wandering is unfettered boyness—the option of staying up all night watching old horror movies, of leaving discarded pizza boxes on the floor for days, of decorating the house entirely with baseball caps—as I confess I did not so long ago. We are afraid not so much of commitment, as of being deformed, reformed, conformed by it.

These days, though, the flight path runs in two directions: women are free to shun commitment as easily as men do. They have careers, friends, a choice of partners; no need for a protective hubby to bring home the tofu. Anyway, doctors don't marry nurses now; they marry other doctors. Though there are still women who go gaga over a guy in prison, or a biker, or man-babies who need serious looking after, women doctors aren't looking for perpetual frat boys who want to drink themselves into a stupor with their buds, throw up on the floor—a circle heave—and ravish the nearest barmaid. Huns at heart: a former girlfriend used to call me "hon"—little did she know.

And don't forget clods who can't remember a birthday, don't notice a new haircut, rarely bathe and, given their druthers, never, ever clean or cook. Even should the man in question be a cooking/cleaning/grooming/shopping metrosexual—a category I believe to contain no members, although sophisticated women have assured me they know heterosexual men quite conversant with the desirable thread counts of bed sheets—there are, as I have discovered once and twice to either my joy or sorrow, women who, though neither doctors nor CEOs, are themselves firmly non-committal.

I have more than the requisite number of regrets/guilt feelings about the way my various relationships/*amours* ended, but the truth is that when I let go/was let go, the most overpowering sense was usually relief, relief that this particular battle in the endocrine wars was over, relief that I could return to my idiosyncrasies for the moment without fear of critical scrutiny. Return to my own self, the one vehicle that—even if all the others fail—is sure to transport me from one darkness to the other.

You might think this a Peter-Pannish positioning of romantic partners as disapproving minders in waiting. But Peter had his reasons—and so do I. Boyhood—unless it's of the nightmarish Dickensian child-labour sort—is all rough energy and discovery and promise. I loved boyhood, and what survives of it in me, even at this long remove, is still more flame than ember. Why should I want it snuffed out?

Anyway, I see no absolute disconnect between boy and man, no definite time to put away childish things, no reason boy and man can't happily co-exist. To love, as I do, baseball, grade-z movies and rock 'n' roll, to be indifferent to most domestic tasks, is not in necessary conflict with being a responsible, loving father, a loyal and considerate friend to both men and women, a relatively engaged citizen and a man devoted to his work. These are all forms of commitment I've tried hard to keep—with varying degrees of success; it's only that love thing that's been sticky. Well, except for those damn line-ups, but I now understand that particular neurosis as a metaphor for the ambivalence of all desire, and not just my own male version.

In the end, I think, of all the impediments that stand in the way of commitment, the sturdiest is one half of the human soul itself. There must be fifty ways to fear your lover. There's fear of entrapment, fear of abandonment, fear of being s/mothered, fear of emotional pain (and sometimes physical), fear of failure, fear of intimacy, fear of not measuring up, fear of betrayal, fear of being unmanned by devotion. Some might say that these are all subspecies of gynephobia, the fear of women. (Beautiful women get their own phobia: venustraphobia.)

Of course, there's also the possibility of love, security, companionship and less-complicated-than-usual sex. I have even observed on occasion loving relationships in which neither partner is deformed or controlled, in which expectations are reasonable, in which respect for the independence of the other is allied with whatever one chooses to call that most primal need.

In his classic study *Love in the Western World*, the French philosopher-critic Denis de Rougemont explores the history and psychology of love, and the inescapable conflict between commitment and passion—the first associated with social and religious responsibility and the second with anarchic, unappeasable love. The male avatar of the first is Tristan, with his obsessive, singular love for Isolde; the model of the second is Don Juan, unable/unwilling to settle for a single source of love. There's something of both in all us men. We are fools for both love and lust—fictional constructs I've somehow reified by sheer endurance over the years, a straw man who acts as a convenient repository for those warring factions that sit uneasily but at least evenly on each shoulder. The never-will-die, relentlessly logical *homme moyen sensuel* co-exists with a (sort of) grown-up capable of committing to the plenitudes of passion. At least I hope so.

That realization leaves me still stranded at the commitment crossroads. Trouble is, there are no reliable directional signposts, and neither devil nor angel is offering a deal for my soul. Nor am I sure whether one road in this garden of forking paths leads to bliss everlasting, and the other to death by long starvation—physical and emotional. I can see the obituary headline now: "World's oldest adolescent dies—alone—at 84."

*Russell Smith*

■

SURRENDER

I knew, pretty well, that things weren't going to work out between me and V. when she first saw me wearing the leather cuffs.

I don't normally wear leather cuffs: I put them on other people. But this was a special night, a dress-up night: I was giving a reading in a bar crowded with women, and I wanted to stand out on stage. I was reading some sexy material, I was performing a bit. So I had my black leather trousers and my shiny shirt and my leather cuffs. Now, these aren't your ordinary rock 'n' roll wristbands; these are not costume cuffs. They are stiff and heavy, and each bears four metal D-rings. They will support your body weight if you some-how get hung from a ceiling or a huge wooden cross in them. They cost about a hundred dollars. They are the real thing. And if you can recognize them as the real thing, and not mere gothy fashion, then I have something in common with you. You and I should talk.

V. knew right away what they were. Not that she had a lot of experience, but she had heard these rumours about me. She had heard me talk about dark parties where people walk around naked, about ex-girlfriends who wanted to be tied up in public. And she wasn't keen to know much more. Not that I had done anything to frighten her: we had been dating for about a month, and I hadn't once been anything but tenderly romantic; I had not once pushed her over a dining-room table, not once even suggested an outfit. But I could tell she was bracing herself for my eventual depravity.

You can't really tell this, though, to be honest, after only a couple of weeks—I mean you can't tell what potential anyone's sex drive holds. I thought I would eventually turn her on. You never know.

I learned a lot about my women friends on the night I gave that reading in my leather cuffs. I was popular that night: I got off the stage and hardly made it to the bar before I was besieged by well-wishers, women who wanted to tell me I was just fabulous and they loved my work and where did I get my cuffs?

Not that they all wanted to be signing up for flogging work-shops. Most of them were just reacting to the rock 'n' roll heroism of the very skinny guy on a stage giving off some sign of heroin addiction. (I wasn't doing heroin, but I had lost an awful lot of weight, largely consequent to the stresses of constantly trying to seduce V.) But some were reacting to the fact that they knew something about those cuffs. They asked to touch them, or even to put them on.

Women all do the same thing when they put on leather cuffs with tough buckles: they stretch their arms out in front of them, their wrists together, to admire them, and to ensure that you admire them too. There is much to admire: chunky metal makes the slender forearm look even more fragile, and there is something inherently exciting to most women about the idea of constraint. I'm not sure why this is; perhaps it's because of a nostalgia for ancient gender roles, in which men were raptors and women helpless, or perhaps it's because one's dark sexual fantasies are not quite so guilt-making when one can claim passivity. The urge to submit to fate is age-old and universal—it is less effortful than being in control. It is the same urge that makes us read novels, so that we can be led somewhere surprising and exciting.

At any rate, they want you to see those tender limbs outstretched like that; they want you to think about them.

Surprisingly, the woman who most wanted to put on the cuffs was V.'s best friend, T. (It's funny that girlfriends' best friends can often be more flirtatious than girlfriends themselves are, but I'm not even going to begin to analyze that.) I willingly strapped the cuffs on T.'s tiny little wrists, and she did the arms-out thing and said, definitively, "Nice."

I could feel more than polite curiosity coming off T.; she was intrigued. This was a surprise: I had figured T. as a no-nonsense business type. And here she was standing too close to me and arching her back and grinning and almost, I swear, winking. She was giving off badness. She would do more than wear these cuffs, I thought. Too bad she was the wrong girl.

I was a bit turned on by the whole evening, by my general popularity. I couldn't wait to get V. out of there. We went back to her place. We sat in front of the fire and she opened a bottle of wine and I fingered the cuffs suggestively. "Okay," she said, rolling her eyes. "Put them on me."

I did. She did the arms-out admiration thing. But with a grimace. They looked lovely to me, but she wasn't impressed.

Then I pushed it too far. "There's a little clip that comes with them," I said, fishing it out of my pocket. "Just put your hands behind your back."

V. stiffened like a cat in the path of a vacuum cleaner. "That's okay," she said, uncuffing herself. "Let's have some more wine."

And that was that. Not for the whole relationship: I hung in there for another month of another kind of sadomasochism—the waiting-for-phone-calls kind. The cuffs didn't have much to do with it. They were just another item in a list of incompatibilities.

I don't mean to say that V. was a prude. She wasn't. And I don't mean to suggest that she failed me in some way, that the relationship ended because I was disappointed in her. In fact, it was quite the opposite: it was I who didn't excite her. She just wasn't that into me.

I'm guessing she found these accoutrements to be merely silly, as most people do. I quite understand this scorn. Most people don't think the erotic should ever be ritualized, as the libido is not subject to scheduling, and even though I chafe a little against that received thought, as it sounds a little all-natural-goody-goody to me, I accept it. I am not trying to convert anybody. I am not writing a paean to slavery, or even to the Internet clichés of plastic dungeons and over-weight "Mistresses" with vampire-novel names.

What I really want to talk about is appearances, because appearances constitute a language of desire. I write often about appearance, men's and women's, and it appears that I am obsessed with it. I am indeed obsessed with it, but probably because I am obsessed with sex and its stimuli, and I am obsessed with sex because I am idiotically romantic about it. Sex is emotion: it feeds our egos more than it fills a physical need. To be desired is more powerful than being admired: it is what we all want. I am trying to connect the superficial with the deepest, darkest drives and insecurities that we have. I am trying to say that sexy shoes are so much more than superficial: sexy shoes are the flashpoint of sex and theatre; they are the fulcrum between power and powerlessness; they are bondage and role-playing already. Sexy shoes, if you will forgive my voodoo metaphor, are the wormhole to the roiling interior.

And this is the thing: everybody has a roiling interior.

To be honest, I'm not really into S&M myself, not the way true fetishists are. I like the clothes, and I like the parties at which everyone is wearing the clothes and I get to stand around and look at a lot of naked breasts and buttocks. I get bored watching endless floggings, and I'm not much of a spanker myself. Fetish parties are for most of their participants simply foreplay for regular, old-fashioned sex. When I go with D., who enjoys it too, we giggle a bit. In fact, we spend the whole night on the verge of giggling. It's not something we take with embarrassing seriousness. We know it's silly.

Probably because we know we are not true fetishists. The true fetishist doesn't even need to have sex in the conventional sense; he can be satisfied by a night of humiliation or a lot of close contact with shoes. And true fetishists make up maybe 5 percent of the scene. I don't even know any. Fetishism has no appeal for me.

So what do I like about these superficial and goofy accessories? What do I like about this extremely uncool, unhip scene—and its often cheesy theatricality? Lots of things, not least of which is an opportunity to indulge my own exhibitionism. I want to be on a stage, too, in sex as in art. (If I weren't an exhibitionist, I wouldn't participate in the humiliating exercise of writing confessional essays such as these.) But I keep coming back to clothes. I like clothes because they are visually beautiful and sensual. And I like the clothes that are the physical markers of a dark side; I like a woman in an elegant dress that allows a glimpse of tattoo at her neck. I like a woman who is not afraid to wear a tight top without a bra; this mild exhibitionism seems to me to be a sign of a certain defiance. A penchant for abandon.

I am often wrong in these first impressions. The woman in the black leather skirt can turn out to be prudish and tense in bed; the horsey prep in the turtleneck can supposedly turn into a tigress once you get her out of her Gore-Tex jacket. (I wouldn't know, never having approached a woman in a turtleneck. Turtlenecks, with their deliberate and criminal obfuscation of the neck, the most beautiful body part to be regularly displayed, are, to me, the uniforms of the modern-day Anti-Sex League, and I don't care if I am right or wrong about that; I am so numbed by their anti-sensuality that I am exhausted before I even begin my inquiry.) Still, I am relentlessly drawn to these outward signs of inward subversion. I lust for women who show signs of intensity. Who are not afraid of extremes. The submission thing works like this: I want a woman who wants me, and my attention and my care, in an intense way. Maybe even in an extreme way. I want a woman who wants—who really actively wants, without any pressure—to tell me that she wants to give herself up to me, to do whatever I want her to do, dress however I want her to dress. It's not serious; it's not really about giving up power— in fact submissives have a great deal of power, maybe more than their partners, in ways that I will explain further on. It's just a game, a gesture, like a card with a sexy note written on it. I want these gestures because I want to feel and see her desire. I want to explore desire, desire and abandon, mine and hers, together.

Let me tell you about D. The first time I got her into bed, it was a bad scene. She was living with her boyfriend. (I didn't know, at the time, that at that very moment he was in a rage in their apartment, smashing her artwork, defacing her computer.) We were drunk. I promised there would be no sex—at least until the boyfriend thing was worked out. She put on my green silk pajamas. And then she asked me what was in the chest at the foot of the bed. I knew that she already knew what was in there. I said go ahead, have a look. She rummaged, giggling, in the toy box, and fished out a pair of cuffs. She was putting them on herself before I even made a move. She found the ropes tied to the bedposts, and clipped herself on.

This was the first time we had ever been even partly naked together, and already she wanted to be strapped to the bed, stretched and vulnerable. She wanted to be taken.

I have been with D. now off and on for two years. It has been blissful and hellish. We have broken up maybe five times. There have been screaming arguments on street corners, running out into the snow in tears with no coat; there have been falls down stairs and delusional accusations. And there have been whole naked weekends of raw passion, of sex without respite. There have been nude beaches and fetish parties and sweaty ecstasy-fuelled techno-furies; there have been euphoric silent sunrises after clubs, days of weeping, tender love. We have certainly known abandon.

I remember one night, at the height of our mutual self-destruction, when we got home late and we were too wired to sleep. I had scored an orange Clonazepam at a party, off a famous writer. I thought we could use it to come down. While D. was in the bathroom, I crushed it up and cut it into four bright lines. She came into the bedroom, drying her face, watching me prepare this obviously unnatural pharmaceutical—its orange luminescence looked just fantastically toxic—and didn't ask a question. Without a word, she took the rolled-up bill and snorted two lines. Then, wiping her nose, grimacing a little, she said, "What was that?"

This was what I loved about her. She would follow me anywhere. She trusted me to do for her—and to her—whatever I thought she would like. She knew that she would like it too. It was the greatest trust I had ever felt. She was surrendering herself to me. It was helium for the ego.

Yes, this sounds unhealthy. It had its unhealthy side. I am not going to gloss over the damage I did to D. Two years on, we are still together. But she does not touch booze, or powders or pills. I am guiltily aware of the hell she went through to get to this place, and that her slide would not have been so rapid or so tortured if I had not introduced her to these things.

Was it sick, a game of control with a dark side? No, it wasn't sick. Every relationship has its power games. People who have not played these games consciously often don't realize that submissives are not powerless. Their power is in creating your desire. Submissives are the centre of attention: they are on display. They are looked at, admired, adored. They are teased and pampered and cosseted. They are cared for.

It is easy to understand why many people who play these games are "switches"—they switch easily from one role to another. Being submissive is the exact and equal flip side of being dominant. Both partners in these games are always giving up control, both always in control.

Most submissives are exhibitionists. D. is, for sure. Like all beautiful people, male or female, she is a narcissist. She has been beautiful since she was a child, and so has grown up knowing the value of beauty, knowing how to use it, what it can get her. She has a conflicted relationship with her beauty: she cares for it, cultivates it and sometimes is at pains to hide it. Sometimes she hates her body, and has starved it and cut it out of spite. She watches other women with a connoisseur's eye; she looks at photos of naked beauties with a competitiveness that is at once detached and passionate. It is something not unlike lust.

She can destroy a room's social balance by walking into it in certain clothes; she can distract its attention, make it edgy and upset. She knows this and uses it. (I encourage her in this; it turns me on.) And yet she can be destroyed by sudden inadequacy; she can burst into tears on glimpsing herself in a mirror, refuse to go outside because of some perceived but invisible flaw.

Beauty is destructive. Beauty is convulsive, manic, cataclysmic. It flickers from light to dark. It is dangerous.

Women do not often ask men what they, men, find attractive. Women already know. It is easy to dress for men. Men like the conventionally feminine: they like long hair and high heels; they like gauzy dresses and clingy tops and cleavage. They like skirts, they like glimpses of bra strap, they like stockings and garters. This is too easy. Women don't dress for men, on the whole, just as men don't dress for women: we all dress irremediably conscious of the reaction of our own gender.

Women are much harsher judges of each other's clothes than men are. They set up strict rules and boundaries for each social occasion: the woman who breaches these is in for trouble. Sure, you could get a lot of male attention with that see-through top, but do you want to have to deal with the punishment you will incur from wrathful wives and girlfriends and single women in the room? They will tear you to pieces. It's not worth it.

Conversely, if you want admiration and appreciation for a piece of high fashion—for some black and gray rag dress with unfinished edges that has to be Kawakubo or Yamamoto, obviously—then you are not going to get it from men. You wear it for other women—not just to impress them, but to enter into a conversation with them, a dialogue of surfaces, a kind of play.

I am an atypical man in this regard, for I will get choked up over the beauty of the asymmetrical Yamamoto hemline. I am half girl, I suppose.

But I am probably not alone in always looking for that other thing, too, that element of subversion: the bright blue stiletto heels, the wide felt hat, the bizarre grey-gold lipstick. Natural beauty only goes so far with me. I am not going to go near the wholesome beauty who wears her fleece jacket over her turtleneck to the party, no matter how blue her eyes, how blond her hair, how athletic her figure. I just know there's no hope for me there: she's going to want to spend her weekends snowboarding or scuba diving. I'm going to be too hungover for that. I'm going to want to spend my weekends hoovering espresso and excoriating Canadian novelists. That's what I find relaxing. Basically, she is not going to be interested in me. So I don't risk the inevitable rejection.

On the other hand, the woman with the crooked teeth or the wide hips who decks herself out in fishnet stockings and some heavy black motorcycle boots is going to agitate me. I will gravitate to her. I will be charmed by her big nose or her flat chest.

(A digression about breasts: a lot of women still seem to believe that men want them to have large breasts. This is twaddle. Men want breasts of any kind. We love large breasts, and small ones and long ones and pointy ones and saggy ones and shallow ones. Small-breasted women have one huge sexual advantage: they can wear tight T-shirts and dresses with no bra. A woman with tiny breasts who passes by you in the clingy tank top with the spaghetti straps and her nipples on display, well, that's just electrifying, it's stupefying, it saps you of all speech, all detachment, all education and sophistication—your framed diplomas fall off your wall, smash! But then women actually do already know this—they know, really, that they, women, only want the perfect 34Cs because those breasts would match certain clothes they've always wanted to wear—so that they can look like other women or photos of women they admire. Again, it's about other women, not men.)

But back to my big-nosed motorcycle-boots girl. I watch her because I know what to talk to her about: she is going to know about punk rock and techno, she is likely to read erotica or even watch porn. I will start by asking her if she goes to art galleries and end by asking her about the porn. It's all part of the same continuum to me.

She is signalling with those boots, boots like a secret handshake, that she has a tough side, a boy side. (Just as I signal to her, when I ask her where she got those boots, that I have a girl side.) And I care more about a woman's style than about her body. She did not choose her body; she won it in the monstrously unfair lottery of genes. Her clothes and her hair are like her record collection: she can control them. They are better reflections of who she is than her body is.

(And God knows, I certainly want her to do the same, to choose me for my choices, for my expressive self, rather than for my degree of physical perfection. I wouldn't do too terribly well on that score. But then women have long understood this: they have always been more attracted to what men do and say than to what they look like.)

The secret sign could be anything, even a small thing. Red streaks in her hair—their suggestion of defiance. A glimpse of green silk camisole—its promise of sensuality. A glittering black choker around the neck—its suggestion of confinement. A Hooters T-shirt—its parody of wantonness. A piercing—its suggestion of aggression. A visible thong—its suggestion of exhibitionism.

I have known alcoholics who gave up liquor and found themselves craving shopping. They started pouring their money into clothes, as if they could replace the corporeal stimulation with an aesthetic one. They needed a high; they found it in the visual and the sexual. I am like this. I crave intensity.

It's not that I want to dress a woman like a toy girl. It's not that I want to control her. I want what everyone wants: to share tastes and interests. I want to encourage her exhibitionism and her wantonness. This is encouraging her to indulge herself, her own power. I want her to want me, and to want me to desire her. This kind of mutual possession—call it a mutual submission, a mutual ceding—is pretty much what I call love.

Nor do I need a woman to be mad. I would rather she wasn't mad, in fact. She doesn't have to do drugs, and she doesn't have to want to be whipped. She just has to be able to surrender—to anything, to me, to an aesthetic experience, to sex itself. Who does not relish surrender? Who does not associate it with love? What is love without surrender?

And love, like beauty, has its dark side. I want to touch that dark side, feel its hot and quivering surface, be afraid of it. If it's not volatile and dangerous, it doesn't feel passionate enough. What good drug is not dangerous?

I know that D. and I may never reach a state of steady contentment together. We are not out of trouble: we will fight and hurt each other in the future; we will cry and promise and reconcile. Sometimes it feels like a kind of freefall. But all I can think about right now is this morning. I woke up with her and pinned her to the bed. She whispered a lewd desire to me and I indulged her; I was merciless. She came. Then we had breakfast together, reading the paper. I drove her to work. All day we have been sending tender coded e-mails to each other. Just now she called from work and whispered, in the non-privacy of her cubicle, "When I get home this evening, this is what I want you to do to me." It was a love letter like no other. I am thrilled by our secret subversions, by the speed and roaring of this flight, this soaring, plummeting love. And this afternoon, I am going to slip out and buy her some shoes.

# David Hayes

■

## MY FATHER'S SECRET

First the snapshots. In this one, my father, then twenty-eight years old, is sitting in a 1932 Plymouth roadster convertible, beige with a red pinstripe along the side. It has red leather upholstery, including the rumble seat. My father was, according to my mother, a rakish bachelor who lived with a gang of fellows in a house in St. Catharines, nicknamed "the homestead." His friends called him "Hurry-Up Hayes" because he walked purposefully, with short, quick steps, as though there were important things ahead. My mother was a tall, leggy brunette with an angular face who looked like a great, noble, wading bird. She had her pick of eligible men, and chose my father. Later, when he infuriated or disappointed me, I would remind myself of this past life of his, the easy grace with which he carried himself, defining for me the idea of unforced masculinity. I believe to this day that he was more self-possessed, more relaxed with who he was than I was at his age, or, for that matter, later.

Here he's sitting, obviously posed but looking most at ease, every inch the successful executive: the double-breasted chalk-stripe suit, the dark tie with bold diagonals, the half-Windsor knot. It's the mid-50s and he is now in senior management at Abitibi's head office on University Avenue in Toronto. Look at his steady gaze into the camera, as if to say, *I am a man both comfortable and successful in this masculine world.* Sometimes, on a Saturday morning when he had work to catch up on, he took me downtown with him, setting me up at a desk in the office next to his with a pad and pencil. It all seemed rather grand, this world of men and work—his big mahogany desk, the important-looking typed pages, the wooden paper trays, his black dial phone with the Empire exchange, the leather office chairs that smelled like a baseball glove. My father's working life seemed dignified and important, having risen from a young chemical engineer to mill manager to Toronto executive.

Look at this, the perfect nuclear family, circa 1961. That's the year my father and mother took their younger daughter and me to Nassau. I'm eight years old, clutching Rabbit, one of my favourite stuffed animals. My father and mother are both dressed in North American tourist finery. Even in the summer, going out for a casual dinner, my father wore polo shirts and dressy Bermuda shorts, as well constructed as a good pair of trousers, with knee-length Bermuda socks. He was a stylish if conservative dresser, his presentation natty but without fanfare. He was what women would have described as "well turned out," although I don't remember him discussing this with me, except to declare angrily, around the time I was twelve or thirteen, that I couldn't wear all black, like a delinquent, nor grow my hair below the ears, in the style of the Beatles and the Rolling Stones. I rebelled against that, of course, but absorbed the idea that men put thought into what they wore, and that understatement was superior to flamboyance.

In this picture, taken around the same time, my father is standing with my mother in the living room of the house in which I grew up in north Toronto. It's evening. He and my mother are on their way out to a party or formal dinner. He's wearing another smart dark suit, one of many in his closet; my mother is wearing her stylish and elegant black Persian lamb jacket. In the mornings, or on evenings like this one, I often watched him standing in the bathroom shaving, then pulling on a starched white dress shirt that made a sound like a page ripped from a pad. I always thought my parents looked rather stiff in this picture. Maybe it was because my father loved living in small towns close to nature but, like most people, hadn't been able to resist a major promotion to the big city that would mean a dramatic jump in income and status. Or maybe it's that time when so many marriages stiffen, decades on. Or maybe I'm imagining it. Still, something had changed, and I'm sure I can see it in photos like this one.

Today I know that at this time the secret was out, or at least shared privately between the two of them. Is that what I see, a development around this time that became a hidden current unsettling the placid surface of their lives?

■

Our earliest understanding of masculinity comes from our fathers, although it's easier to absorb than explain. When I was small, I eagerly waited for my father to come home from work, change into casual clothes and roughhouse with me on the living room rug. I imagined this is what a powerful bear must be like playing with a cub. What impressed me as a child was his mastery over a physical strength that could hurt, but never did. I remember the smell of a sweet aftershave. Unless he was going out, most evenings he took me for a walk in the wooded area across the street. There, walking along a rough trail amidst the fir, spruce and pine trees, he extemporaneously spun his own versions of my favourite childhood reading— Thornton W. Burgess's woodland tales, featuring Peter Rabbit, Reddy Fox, Jerry Otter, Billy Mink, Hooty Owl, Jumper the Hare, Shadow the Weasel and others.

"Father Brown's boy went to the edge of the farm and looked out in the distance, and there was Bowser the Hound going *ow-whooo, ow-whooo*, because he couldn't see Peter the Rabbit, because Peter's fur, which was brown in the summertime, had turned white and it blended into the snow on the ground. And Bowser hoped that his *bow-wow-wowww* sound would startle Peter the Rabbit into running and then he'd catch him for sure."

My father paused, lit his pipe. A plume of smoke rose into the half-light. From our spot in a cluster of spruce trees, I stood spellbound, alternately staring at him or into the forest where I was fairly sure Peter would soon appear. His voice grew quieter, conspiratorial. "So Peter the Rabbit sat still as the deuce, even his eyes closed, so Bowser couldn't see the black of his eyes. Peter wished he'd obeyed the warning of Mrs. Peter and stayed in the safety of the old Briar Patch…"

These were among our most intimate moments, and I remember them with much fondness. My father didn't talk about emotions. He was born not that long after the Victorian era ended and came from solid Ontario stock. His father was a blacksmith in the town of Cannington, Ontario, who managed to make the transition from horse-drawn wagons to repairing motorized "Tin Lizzies," while maintaining a sideline shoeing race horses. His mother was sickly. His siblings, with the exception of his eldest sister who had religion and was energized by it, always seemed melancholy to me.

My father loved hockey. Our ritual was going to Leafs games at Maple Leaf Gardens on company tickets. He told me about how, when he'd finished high school, he'd spent a year working at a paper mill in Iroquois Falls, 300 kilometres northwest of North Bay, to earn money for university but also because he wanted to play hockey with the highly ranked Iroquois Falls junior team. Later he was a scrappy left-winger for the University of Toronto Varsity Blues.

He taught me to skate, with a tiny hockey stick in hand, when I could barely walk. I played organized hockey with my church team until I was fourteen. The coach believed in teaching children the principles of equity and fair play. He alternated his three lines every few minutes, so every boy had an equal chance. Even if, in the final minutes of a close game, the third, and weakest, line came around in the order, he would play it rather than substitute the stars in a ruthless bid to win. A handful of overbearing fathers—the type who bully coaches to favour their son and, in some cases, top up their snack-bar soda pop from a small flask—would hurl abuse, call him a fool, a pansy. My father always supported him. Driving me and a few of my teammates home in the car, en route to the ritual stop at Harvey's Charcoal-Broiled, he would have a compliment for each kid, no matter how badly he'd played. About the fathers, he would quietly remark that people "shouldn't behave that way," adding that the coach was "a good man."

And, in my eyes, so was my father. There was a time, of course, when I suddenly saw his faults. With all the self-absorbed arrogance of a pampered middle-class teenager—adolescence was a period of life my father was utterly unable to understand, as my sisters could attest—I decided he was cautious, uncomfortable with spontaneity, overly concerned with his reputation in the community. He was always an avid reader, a gift he passed along to me, but for a time I was tragically disappointed that his tastes were so middlebrow. (He had the classics in his library but spent more time reading Arthur Hailey, Ian Fleming and Nicholas Monserrat.) He committed a sin in the eyes of a child of the '60s—he was *conventional.*

I was aware that he could behave insensitively toward people, although I seldom saw this in his relationship with me. In reaction to a household dominated by women—my mother, my maternal grandmother and my two sisters (until my eldest sister married when I was four)—he adopted a defensive posture. He would sit in his red leather club chair in his den, the door half-shut, smoking his pipe behind *The Toronto Star*, looking like a *New Yorker* cartoon waiting for a caption. We argued about politics or the length of my hair. He loved me but had little time for my fool ideas. Once, though, when I was about nineteen, he listened patiently while I ranted about the immorality of his career with Abitibi, a company that in my eyes raped forests and polluted rivers. Then he disarmed me by disclosing that he chose the Abitibi job in Toronto over another, higher-paying offer from Hooker Chemical, the company responsible for Love Canal, a chemical landfill under a fifteen-acre neighbourhood in Niagara Falls that had become, around that time, the biggest man-made environmental disaster in the world. The tension evaporated and we both laughed.

Once I became an adult, our bickering was never poisonous but we were often at loggerheads, mainly because I wanted him to be someone he wasn't. Foolish as it sounds, I wanted him to share intimacies, tell me about the things he'd felt when he was young, about the dynamics of his courtship with my mother, about fear, about lust. My father would have no part of it. Whenever I tried to steer our conversation in this direction, he would change the subject to the weather or the Leafs or one of his favourite tales—the train derailing at night in the Rockies or the time Buddy the beagle got the porcupine quills in his nose.

Much later, I became intrigued by the ways he had shaped who I am. Perhaps it was my father who taught me that masculinity is a shell that we learn to wear from an early age. Perhaps he subtly taught me something more complicated and valuable, too—how to wear the shell, and how to slip it off.

I am described by friends as a straight man in touch with his feminine side. Like my father, I paid attention to how I dressed—although he didn't always think so, especially during my hippie cowboy period. I liked buying clothes and when shopping with women I could offer competent advice on fabrics and patterns that worked together. I've always put the toilet seat down. In the company of stereotypically macho guys, I feel either vaguely uncomfortable or bored. Men who adopt the pose of being unable to operate a washing machine or cook a meal seem infantile to me.

Are we born the way we are? Are we shaped by our environment, our culture? Am I who I am because I grew up in a houseful of women? Or because of my close relationship with my good-humoured, curious, tolerant and adoring mother?

And where did my father fit into all this? One day, in one of those curiously weightless free-association sessions with a therapist, I started talking about how, on a sunny summer weekend, my father would go into the backyard wearing a standard issue, early-60s-style man's blue-and-white-striped bathing suit. He'd unfurl a blanket, lie face down and bake in the sun for hours. He would also fold down the bathing suit until the crack of his ass was visible, until it was little more than one of those European bikini affairs that I think of as a pouch with a pair of side straps for stability. It was always just my father's backyard ritual, something I didn't think a lot about, but as I described it I realized it sounded odd.

"So, he was vain?" the therapist said. "Even though you describe him as so conventional a man, he also had a sensual, hedonistic side?"

I hadn't thought of it that way before, but said, "Yes, I guess that was true."

"Do you think he was in touch with feminine qualities himself, maybe ones you hadn't realized?"

I guess he was. By then, at the time of the conversation he was in his eighties, a frail old man supporting himself with a cane, all but blind from glaucoma. He dressed in the uniform of the twenty-first century elderly male as seen in malls everywhere—sweats or casual pants with a drawstring waist and runners with Velcro straps—but still proudly donned a sports jacket and ascot for special occasions. He was dependent on others and that made him either passive or cantankerous, especially around my mother. He was probably suffering from some kind of depression familiar to geriatric specialists, but he wouldn't go for counselling. Fiercely private, he brushed aside my suggestion that he might like to "talk to someone," and turned further inward. None of this was especially unusual for men of my father's generation.

By forty, I had found balance in my relationship with my father. He loved nothing more than when I would read to him a work-in-progress from a magazine article or one of my books. He was inordinately proud of my writing career. As a younger man, returning home from business trips to the *Chicago Tribune* or *New York Daily News* where he spent his time troubleshooting glitches in Abitibi's newsprint shipments, he would tell me excitedly about walking through the newsroom on his way to lunch or to his hotel late at night, after the final press run. The reporters pounding out stories on typewriters and working the phones, the editors barking out orders, the urgency in the air—it all seemed impossibly romantic to him.

For many men, being male is a private and lonely world. They bury their doubts and wrestle with their demons internally, often frustrating the women close to them who want them to share their emotional lives. And the deeper and more private the secret, the further down they burrow.

By this time, I mostly resisted badgering my father about his innermost feelings. Then it no longer mattered. He arose from bed very late one night, probably felt a dizziness sweep over him and called out to my mother. Later, the doctors assured us that the stroke that killed him probably did so painlessly before he hit the floor.

About a year after the funeral, I visited my mother, who had sold their house and moved into a comfortable apartment in a quiet neighbourhood. She was, by then, seventy-nine, a grey-haired, regal presence with a sharp mind and a laugh that, in full throat, sounded like a goose honking and compelled anyone nearby to laugh with her. She also has a habit of shifting conversational gears without warning from a lighthearted anecdote to a staggering revelation. We were casually reminiscing when she told me a story about a Saturday evening in the late 1950s when she and my father were entertaining their best friends in the recreation room. It was a common ritual: watching the hockey game and playing bridge. Suddenly my mother saw something that startled her. Excusing herself to get the food she'd prepared, she paused at the top of the stairs.

"I called your dad to come and help me," she said. "When he came up, I told him, 'I don't know what you're wearing under your pants, but get upstairs and take them off!'"

What she had seen was this: something black and ruffled and unmistakably feminine sticking out the bottom of his trousers. I knew before she told me what my father's reaction would have been. Looking away, he hummed uncomfortably under his breath before murmuring an assent and walking upstairs to their bedroom. Later, when pressed, he shrugged and said, "Oh, it's nothing."

My mother looked stricken. "Do you think I was living my entire marriage with a homosexual?"

I was flabbergasted myself, and still digesting the revelation. I explained to her that today we understand that a taste for women's underwear is a not uncommon heterosexual man's fetish. Like having an obsession with women's feet or… well, I thought it better not to enumerate all the varied, and sometimes alarming, fetishes out there. She looked relieved.

"Did you ask him about it later?"

"Yes. I asked him what this was all about. He just chuckled and brushed it aside. He always said, 'Oh, nothing.'" My mother paused and shook her head. "You know your father. He wouldn't talk about something like this."

Then she explained that one day, while putting away clothes in their shared walk-in closet, she noticed a lump in the sleeve of one of my father's suits. Assuming it was a stray shirt that hadn't made it to the wash, she pulled out some women's underwear.

"Was it yours?" I asked.

"No," said my mother.

"What did it look like?"

She looked thoughtful. "Black, like pantyhose. Fancy stuff, with a pattern."

"Did you think he might be having an affair?"

"No," she said firmly. "Besides, other times I found *my* underwear." A serious look crossed her face, and she added: "Not my good things, they were beautiful. I had a moss green set, really lovely. But this was my everyday beige stuff. I had lots of it and wouldn't have noticed an item or two missing."

"There were other times? How many?"

After thinking about it, she guessed eight or ten times, maybe more, over perhaps as many years. Each time the underwear was in the sleeve of a suit.

"What would you do?"

"I was confused and angry," said my mother. "I didn't understand it, and I didn't like it. Every time I found something and showed it to him, he'd look embarrassed but he wouldn't talk about it. He'd just say it's nothing. I told him that under no circumstances should you kids find out about this."

My poor mother had been forced by my father to confront something that had been misunderstood and demonized throughout her life, something that has only relatively recently become less taboo and, in some quarters, accepted. Depending whom you ask, a fetish is a mere preference or a miserable compulsion. The word (*fétiche* in French; *feitiço* in Portuguese; *facticius* in Latin) originally referred to a natural or man-made object believed to have supernatural powers over people. The term was coined by a French scholar to characterize the early stages of religion, but since the nineteenth century it's been the common term for a psychosexual obsession with a body part (like breasts or feet), object (like shoes, fur or women's lingerie) or practice (like spanking or exhibitionism). In most cases, the obsession takes root in childhood and is inextricably linked to masturbation. Experts can't explain why the vast majority of fetishists are men (although every woman I've mentioned this to has simply nodded, as though it came as no surprise).

My father's fascination with women's underwear was, on the scale of things, quite mild—especially when we consider that the scale includes *coitus à cheval* (a fetish for having sex on the back of an animal), emetophilia (arousal from vomit) and formicophilia, which involves ants and a jar of honey.

Today, studies suggest that somehow a body part, object or practice can become imprinted on what is known as an individual's "love map," usually in early childhood, then associated with pleasure and orgasm by puberty and reinforced through repetition.

Learning that my father had a fetish didn't disturb me. For one thing, it made him more human, as though after his death he had let me glimpse some of that intimate emotional territory that he'd denied me during his life. And, I thought, finally I see that he was, in at least one rather dramatic way, an *un*conventional man.

But there was another thing; my father and I had more in common that I'd ever imagined. While I didn't share his interest in women's underwear, I did have my own fetish, one that for many years I hid as carefully as my father had his. From the time I'd reached puberty my erotic fantasies included bondage and spanking, and for years they were uncomfortably at odds with my view of myself as a progressive, modern "feminist man."

∎

An early memory: I am a child of perhaps four or five, sitting under the dining-room table tying my bare feet with kitchen twine. When my mother lifted the tablecloth and said, "What are you doing under there?" I experienced a frisson of excitement and shame, as though I suspected what I was doing was naughty. It's a great story, except it probably didn't happen, at least not in that way. If I didn't invent the memory, my mother was probably just shooing me out from under the table because dinner was ready.

I remember feeling a tremor of excitement when I saw a woman spanked on a TV western and thrilling to the bondage-related scenes in my parents' James Bond novels. In 1963, I bought a copy of a newly published book, *The Velvet Underground*, a dubiously "academic report" on the "sexual twilight zone" of swingers, sado-maschists and pornographers in modern America, now most famous because its title was appropriated by Lou Reed for his seminal New York band. (What the clerk was thinking when he sold it to a ten-year-old still puzzles me.)

But how could I express the fascinations to anyone? They were hardly topics to bring up among my male teenaged friends. Suggest to the sweet-faced teenaged girls I was dating that I wanted to spank them? It seemed unthinkable. As the author and *New Yorker* staff writer Daphne Merkin put it in her famous essay exploring her own fetish for spanking, these urges created "feelings of embarrassment nestled inside shame nestled inside excitement," like those wooden matryoshka dolls from Russia. Merkin also pointed out that the 1970s and '80s launched a postfeminist world of equal sexual opportunity, where women could ask for whatever they wanted. But if women could ask for the previously unmentionable, all this made it seem even less appropriate for a modern man to admit to retrogressive thoughts of dominance and submission, symbolizing exactly what women had broken free of. So my desires remained private, although they threatened to bubble to the surface at any moment.

I was in my thirties when a girlfriend with whom I'd been living for a number of years discovered my fetish. She was exactly the kind of woman I had never imagined admitting it to—an intelligent, sophisticated feminist who shared with me distaste for traditional machismo. Yet she was scarcely fazed at all. She admired *Story of O*, the masterpiece of literary S&M that had been written by a woman, and she thought everyone should be free to enjoy his or her fantasies, whatever they were. In fact, we were both aware of friends who incorporated bondage into their sex play and she had freely admitted to being attracted to the fantasy of the "demon lover."

I'd so carefully nurtured my image as the sensitive man that I'd put myself in the same prison my father had been in, and by that point in our relationship my girlfriend had trouble casting me in this new role. When we talked about my unwillingness to reveal my interests when I was younger, she matter-of-factly said: "All kinds of women would have been attracted to a nice, sensitive guy with a dark side."

After this, I decided to fess up to future partners. For the past five years I've been in a relationship with a woman—yes, a smart, no-nonsense feminist with an adventurous spirit—who happily shares many of my tastes, but my good fortune also makes me sad. It reminds me that my father had experienced a kind of psychic bondage—the worst kind, the kind that seldom lets up, that never has a safe word. Many women believe that men enjoy the privilege of patriarchy, and when it comes to jobs and income in today's culture they often do. But the inner world of men can be a profoundly lonely, enslaved place, in my father's case causing him to repress an important element of who he was. What a delicious irony that where my father felt restrained from openly expressing his erotic life, his son found liberation in bondage.

But was that true about my father? There were a few things I didn't completely understand. Did my father merely have a fetish for the feel of women's underwear, or was he a cross-dresser, a man who liked to dress in women's clothing, to impersonate a woman? Or might he even have been a transsexual, a man who felt he was a woman trapped in a man's body? And another thing: why did he repeatedly hide his underwear in the sleeves of his suits where my mother was going to find it?

■

My curiosity led me to a faux Irish pub in Toronto's Riverdale neighbourhood where I met Michael A. Gilbert. He's a stocky, clean-shaven, bespectacled man of medium height with a mop of salt-and-pepper hair, and a father of five as a result of a blended family from two marriages previous to his present one. ("Divorced once and widowed once," he said with a grin. "So I'm not a two-time loser.") In his peach-coloured, short-sleeved polo shirt and black shorts, he could be any middle-aged dad living in this middle-class neigh-bourhood. He has an engaging, slightly distracted manner, like that of a tenured professor of philosophy at a university, which he is.

But Michael is also a cross-dresser, and his closet contains only his clothes of both genders, not himself. As a nine- or ten-year-old growing up in Brooklyn he remembers raiding the clothes hamper and putting on his mother's panties or panty girdle. Later, he would masturbate wearing women's underwear and eventually began dress-ing as a woman. Although he's comfortable with his life today, he tells me about the practice of "purging," where fetishists throw away all their paraphernalia with the intention of escaping their fetish. But if you're hard-wired from childhood, the purge is not likely to last.

"Transvestite is the old term for cross-dresser," he explains. "I use the term 'transgender' to mean anyone who plays with, or is uncom-fortable with, their birth gender. I'm a male with male equipment and happy with that, but sometimes I like to present as a woman, or as my interpretation of a woman."

Later that week, I drove to York University's main campus to sit in on a workshop put on by the Centre for Human Rights and Equity, which is responsible for addressing issues of sexual and gender diversity in the university. Michael was one of the facilitators at the session, except for this occasion he appeared as his alter ego, Miqqi Alicia Gilbert. She was carrying a black purse and was dressed in black flats with a small buckle, burgundy pants, grey jersey and a shell necklace. Her hair was curlier today, and combed out to appear more feminine than it had the first time we met. It's often said that cross-dressers look more authentic the older they get. Miqqi looked and dressed the way you might imagine any middle-aged, female tenured professor might look and dress.

Addressing the group, Miqqi told them there is a profound difference between a transsexual, who feels trapped in the body of the wrong sex, and cross-dressers. "Cross-dressers wear women's clothing because they like women's clothing. Transexuals wear women's clothing because they feel like they are women."

Over lunch we discussed my father. Miqqi agreed there wasn't much evidence that he was a cross-dresser unless he was very deeply in the closet. That's possible, she says, since the subject was so illicit in his generation that it was hard to even get information. He might have found his way into the cross-dressing subculture while travelling on business, although getting caught would have been a powerful inhibition. For most of his adult life, though, he would have been aware that the prevailing opinion was that he suffered from a perversion and needed psychiatric help.

If he had been a cross-dresser, I asked, if he'd been hiding so much, wouldn't there have been more evidence as he aged that he was profoundly tormented?

Miqqi said she thought so, then suggested I contact Xpressions, a non-profit support and social group for the transgendered community in Ontario. When I did, I talked to Keith Green, a software developer and designer living in Guelph. Keith, who is married with two children, is an active cross-dresser who attends monthly dinners in which a group of men go out to restaurants dressed as women. During a long conversation, Keith asked me if my mother ever found a stash of women's clothing—not just underwear—

either while my father was alive or hidden somewhere after he died? What about clues among his personal effects—magazines, phone numbers, a post office box to receive materials without having it delivered to the home or workplace? No, I said, nothing had ever been found.

About my mother repeatedly finding his stash, Keith pointed out that most people want to get caught. Sometimes it's a way to finally live authentically, regardless of consequences. It relieves the burden of harbouring a secret. Sometimes the act of getting caught is exciting, or as Keith put it: "Since he kept putting it in the same place, it sounds like he was playing, having some fun."

Either way, my parents had tacitly come to an understanding. "Your mother got angry at him and wouldn't discuss it," said Keith. "But maybe he didn't want to discuss it himself. Maybe he was happy doing what he was doing. He knew how far she would go. She wouldn't leave the marriage, and he could have the thrill of being caught time after time.

"Based on the evidence," Keith concluded, "I would say he just had a fetish for women's underwear."

■

One last snapshot. It's June 13, 1986 and my mother and father are celebrating their fiftieth wedding anniversary, a milestone for any married couple. They're toasting each other and the pleasure on their faces is genuine. They've already outlived a number of their peers, not to mention too many collapsed marriages to count (including two within the family). They'd produced three children and one of them, God bless her, had given them grandchildren, one of whom in turn gave them great-grandchildren. My father is 81, just nine years away from his death. The glaucoma that would rob him of his eyesight is rapidly advancing.

After retiring, he occasionally did a little part-time consulting but a few times I arrived for a visit to find him looking decidedly awkward as he vacuumed the living room to keep busy. As he grew frailer, the demands on my mother grew, too. I often overheard snippy exchanges.

Within any enduring marriage, there are more than enough reasons to drive a couple apart but presumably enough reasons to stay together that they do. For the children's sake is one common excuse, but once the children are grown other reasons include habit, laziness and fear, but also genuine fondness, even passion. If the reasons to stay are the right ones, or appearances are well-constructed, the couple is described as "happy." That's easy enough to say, but when you consider that life, in general, is a complex muddle that fuels a vast therapeutic industry ranging from self-help books to psychoanalysts, it's not easy sorting out the true dynamics governing the relationships of elderly parents. But like any married couple, my parents had dealt with irritations, conflicts and disappointments, and one wild card: the matter of those women's underthings. (The term "unmentionables" is poetically appropriate in this case.)

I find myself thinking about what Keith Green had said ("I would say he *just* had a fetish for women's underwear," as though my father had been a mere dilettante in the world of outside-the-mainstream erotica) and I feel a powerful need to defend him. I realize that in today's world, to hardcore cross-dressers like Keith and Michael Gilbert, my father's preoccupation seems pretty vanilla. But I see him as a pioneer, making his way as best he could through profoundly alien territory. If anything, I now think of him as an even more wonderful father, one who had symbolized masculinity balanced with grace, and grace under pressure.

It brought to mind something the psychotherapist and author Amy Bloom had written in her 2002 book, *Normal: Transsexual CEOs, Crossdressing Cops and Hermaphrodites with Attitude.* "The high-heeled, Chanel-clad lesbian and the football-playing, beer-swigging gay man perplex us, as if surely some norm is violated... Presented with nature's bouquet of possibilities, a wild assortment of gender and erotic preferences and a vast array of personalities, we throw it to the ground."

To my surprise and delight, my father was part of that bouquet, and he showed me, in ways both obvious and, I'd discovered, so subtle I'd never realized they were there, that a man is both masculine and feminine, strong and vulnerable, noble and foolish, dignified and pathetic, an infinitely more complex being than our culture's simple-minded male stereotypes.

*Ted Bishop*

■

JUST A TOUCH

When I was twelve, old enough to know something was going on but too geeky to do anything about it, I unscrewed my ballpoint pen and took out the slender translucent ink tube and the little spring surrounding it and placed both carefully in the pen groove at the top of my wooden desk. Both parts were equally important because without the spring the little silver knob on top flopped use-lessly, and the ball point, which hung down tantalizingly, would slip back into the plastic cylinder like a turtle into its shell the moment you touched the pen to the page. You couldn't even make a period. Nothing. There was no force. I was twelve and so read nothing at all phallic into this the way some of you are doing. I just knew I had to keep the spring and the ink tube together. It would be years before I knew or cared that the ballpoint pen had been invented by a Hungarian journalist named Ladislo Biro, who fig-ured out that printer's ink, that gooey, rubbery stuff that you have to mash with a putty knife and smush around before you put it on the rollers of a press the same way you have to mash up lard or butter when you're making a cake, did not dry out the way foun-tain-pen ink did, forcing you to put the cap back on every time you stopped to search for a word, or, if you forgot, obliging you to put the pen nib into your open mouth and breathe *haaaaah* warm air over the nib to humidify it again. No. The little rotating ball would do what the putty knife did: provide enough friction to liquefy the ink for an instant, not so much that it would run, but just enough that the rotating ball could lay the ink down on the page, like the roller of the press on to the type, leaving your warm breath free for other things. Such as the neck of Shirley Bassani.

Shirley Bassani sat in front of me in math and in retrospect I think she was probably beautiful, though at that time I was still being socialized by *Playboy* and the other magazines we tried to look at at the drugstore to desire pouffy blonds like the ones on the cheerleading squad, and it would be years before I came to acknowledge my hard-wired attachment to olive or almond skin and dark hair, so I didn't really see Shirley as an object of desire, I just kind of liked her.

She always had a warm laugh (as opposed to the cold, metallic, junior-high sardonic laugh), and when I unscrewed the pen and took the empty bottom half, placed it to my lips and blew a jet of warm air onto Shirley's neck, she laughed and shook her head slightly. I blew again and the jet of air parted the strands of her dark hair that fell just to her shoulders before it curled, and activated what I now suspect were the Meissner's corpuscles in her neck.

I blew again, angling my little plastic blowgun so that the jet of air swept an arc from the little hairs of the back of her neck just below the hairline down to the smooth skin where the slope of her neck levelled out onto the flat plain of her shoulder. "T-ed!" she said, giving my name a two-note tone it had never had before and squirming in her seat, half-turning around, and with a little laugh I had also never heard before, said, "What are you doing?"

My kingdom for a time machine. I had no idea then what I was doing.

Actually that's not true. I had, I swear, a glimmer, I wasn't that dumb, I knew something was happening, but I couldn't be *sure* and I always wanted to be sure (and so missed a million opportunities). Years later at a party a friend and notorious flirt came up to me as I stood with my beer in the kitchen and said, "Don't move," and leaned in, not touching me with her body, and kissed, no, hardly that, *grazed* me with her lips low down on the side of my neck. As the current flashed through me she was already drifting past into the crowd, and I wondered, What was *that*?—what nerve, what searing meridian? And was it this that I had stumbled upon with Shirley Bassani so many years before?

■

What is it about touch?

I consulted my philosopher friend Dianne. She's always reading those French philosophers whose names I can never remember. I told her it was the one whose name sounded like a wine.

"Bourdieu?" she said. "My students always pronounce it 'Bordeaux.'"

"No, it's not one of the 'B's."

"Baudrillard, Blanchot, Barthes," she rattled off helpfully.

"No."

"Bachelard, Benjamin, Bataille . . ."

"I said it *wasn't* one of the 'B's."

"Zizek is close to Zinfandel but he's not French, he's Slovenian. . . ."

"Dianne!"

"Sorry."

"Merlot."

"What?"

"The wine: it was Merlot."

"Merlot? Ah, yes! Merleau-Ponty."

"That's the guy."

"Yes, yes, you must read him! I read his *Phenomenology of Perception* when I was seventeen and it changed my thinking forever afterward." I felt sad for her. At seventeen I read all the James Bond novels. Still, philosophy could be useful. I borrowed her heavily annotated copy of *PP* and took it home. I read the underlined bits for a while, and then I read the bits between the underlines (they were smaller), not finding much that was helpful. As Merleau-Ponty was arguing that empiricism hides us from the cultural world I thought I might go make a sandwich, but then he began to talk about "a mode of perception distinct from objective perception, a kind of significance distinct from intellectual significance . . . erotic comprehension." Now we were cooking.

"Erotic comprehension is not a *cogitatio* which aims at a *cogitatum*." Exactly what I was thinking. It is "not of the order of understanding, *since understanding subsumes an experience, once perceived, under some idea*, while desire comprehends blindly by linking body to body." That's it. You don't want to think about it, you just want to think it.

And, "We are concerned, not with a peripheral involuntary action, but with an intentionality which follows the general flow of existence." That's right. I am not a compulsive lecher, I'm following the general flow of existence. Thank you, Merleau.

When he got to passive and knowing touch we parted company. "Passive touch (for example touch inside the ear or nose, and generally in all parts of the body ordinarily covered) tells us hardly anything but the state of our own body and almost nothing about the object." On the other hand, "like the exploratory gaze of true vision, the "knowing touch" projects us outside our body through movement. When one of my hands touches the other, the hand that moves functions as subject and the other as object." (I would learn that this is a famous example. Commentators take it up and they never talk about masturbation, but it's hard not to think about it. "The hand is," says Merleau quoting Kant, "an outer brain of man." To which the cynical will reply that maybe it's his only brain, used constantly to drain the blood from the cerebellum to the organ in the deep south.)

I liked Merleau-Ponty's distinction but wanted to collapse it: passive touch can do more than tell us about the state of our own body; it can also be an exploratory touch—and ultimately a knowing touch.

■

Touch gets a bad rap. Western philosophic tradition privileges sight and light: we want to acquire "insight"; possibly even have a "vision"; at the very least, "see." We value "lucidity." Saying "I feel . . ." is an admission of, not failure exactly, but approximation, qualification; touch is dark and dubious.

Dianne had also lent me *Textures of Light*, a commentary on Merleau-Ponty by Cathryn Vasseleu, who taught philosophy at the University of Technology (which sounded like a tough gig) in Sydney, Australia. She said wonderful things such as "Eroticism is the ex-static dissolution of corporeality, rather than the fecundity of incarnation," and "Voluptuousness is time out, an interruption in the time of being." I didn't know what she meant but the language made my knees buckle—voluptuousness, fecundity, eroticism.

I like cruising the dictionary (the online ones just don't do it for me; I like the heft of a book, and the digital search doesn't give you the chance encounters in the same way). Fingers tingling, I turned the pages to learn that *voluptuous* comes from the Latin for pleasure and delight, the Greek for hope, expectation. I checked out *touch*: to bring a bodily part briefly into contact with so as to feel; to meet without overlapping or penetrating. And then, Merleau-Ponty forgotten, I decided to look up the word I've always found so voluptuous I can't believe they haven't banned it, that they let you utter it in the supermarket: *succulent*. Just listen to the Oxford: full of juice, juicy, having fleshy and juicy tissues. If that weren't enough, they quote Crooke (1615) on human bodies: "Some [parts] are dense, others rare and succulent or juicy." Succulent has links to the Latin *sugere*: to suck; there's *succulency*, and *succulence*, and Webster gives us the *succulometer*: an instrument for measuring the moisture content of a fresh vegetable. Lower down on the page is *succumb*, to give way, yield; and above is *succubus*, a demon in female form supposed to have carnal intercourse with men in their sleep.

Words, too, have texture.

I turned back to Vasseleu, who was talking about the caress. Caress is the threshold—the opposite of groping. For her favourite critic, the Belgian feminist Luce Irigaray, "the caress is not so much a touch as it is the gesture of touch . . . a never-to-be-grasped beginning, an attraction without consummation, always on the threshold of appetite . . ." That's it. Always on the threshold.

∎

What men angle in for is the triangle. We'll dislocate our necks or feign shoulder tics to grab a glimpse through that three-sided gap that opens up on a blouse between the second and third buttons from the top, where the breasts force the fabric open. You have to be at right angles to see in, which is why checkout lines are good—you have a legitimate reason for being there, for lingering, and you can pretend to be watching the cashier's screen or just idly gazing into space when in fact you're compacting your whole being into your eyeballs and sending their beams forth into the Triangle, like in those science fiction movies where they shrink a crew down to the size of atomic particles and put them in a miniature submarine or spaceship and send them into the body, which becomes enormous and terrifying, with blot clots like The Blob That Ate Chicago, but here it's not like that, you're sending your eye beams into the land of lace and breast, homing in on that contact zone of cool fabric, crisp white—or black! Oh god, she's wearing a black bra under her uniform, that irresistible combination of the lascivious temptress and the demure clerk; like the librarian who will toss aside her thick-rimmed glasses and unpin her bunned hair and shake it loose in one flowing motion, it's the contrast, the disjunction . . . travelling from cool fabric to warm flesh, the hint of a curve, like the earth seen from an airplane at thiry thousand feet where you can just discern a bend in the horizon line, this bosom curve becomes the promise of a whole world, a lush hemisphere . . .

"That will be forty-seven fifteen please."

*Snap!* Your eye beams zot back into your head like bungee cords off a roof rack and you dig in your pockets for your cash. (Guys often look startled in completely ordinary situations, as if they've suddenly returned from outer space. This is because we have. We have just returned from the Triangle Galaxy and we're taking a moment to adjust to re-entry.) Cash is best because it allows for more contact. (The other pleasure of cash is intellectual and political—you're a subversive, they can't track you, "they" the marketeers who know how many bananas you buy at a time and what kind of razor blades you like.) You don't swipe your own debit card. You hand the cash across and the way she takes it will tell you everything.

The everything you want to know is, *Will she touch?* Will she, as she takes the bills, extend her fingers underneath so that her fingertips touch yours? There's that brief charge if she does, and also the emotional pleasure of knowing you've been deemed touch-worthy. She has been aware, weighing the broccoli, swiping the cans of tuna, of your presence (I have been told that, subtle as men are, women can sense when we're zeroing in on the Triangle Galaxy) and so has made the decision whether or not to allow your eager fingers that *frisson* of contact. So she hands you back your change. Avoid Safeway because they have those machines where the coins come banging down a chute, like a waterslide into a pool, and you have to scrabble with one hand to pick up the change while you reach across with the other to get the bills. It's awkward, it breaks your concentration and it minimizes contact. You do not, in fact, want any bills at all.

You want change because then if you are lucky, if she has decided to grant you the next favour beyond the fingertip brush, you will get the caress. No, I don't mean she'll leap across the counter and fondle you. I mean her hand, holding the coins, will come down in your hand like one of those little diggers at the Exhibition, those little mechanical steam shovels that you use to try to pick up a prize and drop it in the slot, and her fingers will open like the scoop of the digger, letting the coins fall into your hand.

There are three ways she can do this.

1. She can drop the coins into your hand from above, forcing you to cup your hand so the pennies don't bounce off onto the counter. This is crushing, a denial of contact, and you go away feeling rejected and scumbagulous, exposed as a leering voyeur.
2. She can touch down with the ends of her fingernails, open up, and allow the coins to slide into your palm. Did her fingertips graze your skin as she opened up? Yes. Maybe. You're not sure. It's ambiguous. Or she's left it ambiguous. There's no

eye contact, and she's already reaching for the plastic divider to begin ringing up the next customer's cat food, but you go away feeling good.

3. She can go all the way. She says, "That's two ninety-three change," looking you right in the eye, and you know already it's going to be a lot, two loonies and three quarters, a dime, a nickel, three pennies, and she places her hand in yours and her fingers, right up to the first knuckle, against the fleshy lobe at the base of your thumb, her thumb with its wide soft knuckle against the base of your little finger and you can feel the warmth of her, and then she opens to you, slightly at first, fingertips moving across your hot palm, compressing the coins up into a column and letting them start to flow into your hand, and then she opens all the way and the coins rush down and there's a last brush at the edges of your fingers and she's gone.

The re-entry is worse than from the Triangle Galaxy and you have a responsibility not to stand there flat-footed. You're in this together. You have to respect her. The woman with the cat food is on the verge of harrumphing. She knows what's going on, but if you're cool she can't prove anything. You smile and say thank you, and move on.

I liked what Merleau-Ponty said about memory: "We can, in recollection, touch an object with parts of our body which have never actually been in contact with it." On the street we are like hunters, we bag the flash or the graze. For the instant we fix all of our sensory powers on it so that it is imprinted, incised, branded on our brain, and then we take it home, to recollect in tranquillity. Toward the end of his book, Merleau-Ponty nails it: "My gaze, my touch and all my other senses are together the powers of one and the same body integrated into one and the same action."

From Diane Ackerman's *A Natural History of the Senses* I learned about Meissner's corpuscles, capsules just below the surface of the skin that enclose "branching, looping nerve endings" that are "like the many filaments inside a light bulb." These corpuscles are amazingly sensitive because each area can respond independently, like the separate coils of an innerspring mattress. I pictured my skin as a tiny mattress full of flexible plastic light bulbs with blond filaments. The Meissner's "seem to specialize in hairless parts of the body—the soles of the feet, fingertips (which have 9,000 per square inch), clitoris, penis, nipples, palms, and tongue—and they respond fast to the lightest stimulation." Like your palm to the cashier's caress. Or Shirley's neck to the pen-channelled breath.

There are also thick, onion-shaped Pacinian corpuscles that respond quickly to changes in pressure. Or, for those more sustained moments, the saucer-shaped Merkel's disks, near the surface, and the deeper Ruffini endings, both of which respond to continuous, constant pressure.

■

"Does that hurt?" she said.

"Uhh."

"I'll go a little slower."

"Um."

"How's this?" she said, and moved in closer. I could feel her thigh through the thin cotton against my upper arm, and then as she leaned over, against my shoulder. Her eyes met mine over her mask.

"You've been bad," she said. Her arm rested lightly on my chest. "You know that every day, *every day*, you must floss."

Dental hygienists. They have you pinned, they're opening one of your most sensitive orifices, probing soft flesh. Agreed, some of them trained at the Nurse Ratchet Academy, where they learned to starch their scrubs and use disinfectant for deodorant. They're the ones who like doing the deep scaling and say with no apology, "Now this is going to hurt." The unspoken words being, "And you deserve it, you flossless slacker." So you find another one, one who treats you right, and every six months (oftener if you're lucky enough to have gum disease) she'll tilt you back, adjust the light, and slide in next to you. "Open wide . . ."

Each time it's different. Sometimes she's friendly, conversational. Other times she's all efficiency, hovering above you, attacking your gums with the swiftness of a sushi chef, not deigning to touch you. It's a game she plays. She's showing you that she's in control, that she can reach every point she needs to without touching you. So that when, near the end, she swivels her stool around to the top of your head and comes in from above with a quick twirl of her steel probe to lay into that buildup behind the lower incisors, and she slows down now, works carefully, leans in, and you feel the cotton and then the heat behind it, and you're willing your scalp to register everything, everything because now you feel pressure, touch and release—it's her breathing, you can feel her breathing and that's her what? her rib cage and belly against you, the pressure soft but firm, in and out, and she says, "This is built up here, we'll have to go slowly," yes, and your breathing quickens and you feel, yes, hers quickens too you're not imagining it, you're breathing in unison and you forgive her her standoffishness with the molars, her coolness as she worked the bicuspids, yes, because she's here now and you're breathing together, and you remember the first time in the back of a car when you slid your fingers down her cheek her neck her hardly daring to touch to press her breast and now you feel with follicles rather than fingers that same soft pressure so evanescent it's hardly there but it is there, yes, her breast is that possible it must be, yes, the soft underside of her small breasts and she says, "We'll get all this tartar out, you must be a mouth breather when you sleep," oh yes I am, take it all out, and on and on and on she works and there is no body now only your mouth and your hair her breasts and the breathing the rhythm the almost throb eyes closed on the verge of a swoon and a voice cries,

"Hey! How about those crowns? Your insurance gave us the go-ahead—we can do them both for five thousand!"

Christ. You feel like Harker in *Dracula* when he's being enveloped by the succubae and then the vampire count flings open the door and says, "He belongs to me!" The succubae slink away; the hygienist slides back. Your dentist owns you both at the moment, and he slaps some X-rays on a screen—they could be of licorice nibs and white corn for all you know, but they give him authority—and as he rattles on about how this is a superior product with carbon-fibre reinforcements to meet your oral needs, your hygienist's eyes meet yours and you don't care about the crowns, you'll do them of course, why not, your share is only $2,500. But she's pushed her chair back and peeled off her gloves. When she thinks you're not watching she massages her wrists. Carpal tunnel? She may not be here next time.

■

But I digress. The point is that these encounters are unspoken, unacknowledged, unconsummated. That's what makes them so delicious. I remember meeting some friends for drinks at a club with an outside patio on a warm spring night, and I'd been riding my motorcycle and so was dressed down for this trendy new bar—motorcycle boots and jeans, a black leather jacket that I hung over the back of the chair, and the heavy cotton work shirt I always used for riding. The others were all in light linen. When the waitress came—poised, aloof, immaculate, like she was doing us a huge favour by coming at all—I felt even seedier. But she came to my side of the table, and as she leaned forward to light the candle I felt her miniskirted thigh press against my shoulder. "Can this really be happening?" I wondered—not wondering, *Is she touching me*? because in fact it was a full-flank press, but wondering, *Can she be doing this to ME*? (I realized later that of course it was not me—it was the black leather, the zippers, the Spanish boots. In a seersucker jacket I would have been chopped liver, but that's a whole other essay.)

The Server Touch is like the Professional Smile. It's about money, not pleasure. Ackerman reports on an experiment at a restaurant where servers unobtrusively touched diners on the hand or shoulder. The customers who were touched did not necessarily rate the food or the restaurant better, but they consistently tipped higher. I knew a young woman who put herself through university by working Friday nights in a pizza trailer outside a bar. She'd put on her black push-up bra and say, "These babies are going to make mama some big tips tonight." She'd lean way over to hand out the change and she usually got most of it back. Enticing as such moments are (we're hardly going to look the other way), they're a titch overt, they lack romance, they can slide toward the sleazy. Like the time at the hairdressers' where I once had a great sweaty boob dangled in my face for most of the procedure and experienced that *Gulliver's Travels* gross-out, that moment when Gulliver is in the land of the giants where not only are the mammaries mammoth but the attendant warts and pimples are as well, and he decides there can in fact be too much of a good thing. I left a 9 percent tip.

It, the real encounter, always begins with your body responding instantly but your mind holding back. Part of the delight is the uncertainty. You're not quite sure it's happening. You can't ask. You have to feel your way into it. And you have to enjoy it for its own sake, for its own duration. Seek to fix it and it evaporates. Push it and it turns into a clumsy come-on.

■

Yet it can be more potent than wild, unbridled sex. I have a friend who has a radically incompatible girlfriend. I mean "radically" in its original sense: base, root. They don't like the same books or movies, they have different circles of friends, they have warring conceptions of interior design, their internal clocks and bio-thermostats are so different they joke about living together in different hemispheres, and when it comes to money they complement each other the way a banker does a bank robber. What started it all was they travelled well together, and the sex was fabulous (he said, "It's true what they say about Asian women," but didn't elaborate) and they both loved Thai food. He suspected this was probably not enough to build a relationship on.

When he was younger he would have dumped her after two months. Except that she would have dumped him after one because he would have been so obnoxious. He wasn't obnoxious (or was considerably less so) because he'd reached the point in his life where he decided not to sweat the small stuff, also not the medium and a considerable portion of the big stuff. Actually what he'd discovered was that the things he thought mattered didn't, or, rather, that he didn't have a choice.

It was a warm day and they were taking a nap in the afternoon in Rome, and they hadn't been making love, hadn't been intimate on any level, hadn't even been crabbing at each other: rather, it was one of those mornings when the discordance of their sensibilities had made them not angry but sad. They were so far apart they had become civil. They knew there was no point in fighting because they knew they were just running out the clock, waiting to get back to Canada to break up. In that truce they found a kind of comradeship, a shared acknowledgement of the impossibility (racial, financial, aesthetic) of it all, and it was in this multiple exhaustion that they lay down on the bed to sleep.

She turned on her side, away from him, and before turning away to his side he leaned over and touched her between the shoulder blades, just above the line of her halter top, and then kissed her there, one light kiss, and then rolled back. "God damn it," he thought, now wide awake. For he knew in that instant he would never leave her. She fell asleep in seconds (another thing he resented about her), and he lay awake and stewed in the heat and in his mind, staring at the coarse wooden beams in the ceiling and going over her many faults, imagining the horror of their life together, how the simplest transactions from buying yogourt to washing socks would be fraught with contention. But it was no use, it was the feel of her skin that had hooked him. Skin to skin, subject and object dissolving while the intellect and emotions danced around saying, *What are you, crazy? Let's get out of here!* and his body, content, oblivious, refused to budge.

That was twelve years ago. Every day since has been a struggle. Sometimes he swears she has been placed on earth solely to drive him mad. Yet he has only to feel her skin to know he's home. The knowing touch. It settles everything.

# Ian Pearson

■

## JONI'S DIARY
## (A FANTASY)

*March* 14, 1970

Willy just got back from Marrakech bearing striped *djellabas* we can wear at home. We had a wonderful homecoming. I spent all day making *tajine* and he brought *arak* when he showed up for dinner. Lovely man, he feels like a child and a father to me. He played me a new song he's written for the Crosby, Stills, Nash and Young album called "Our House." I played him "Woodstock" and we had a blissful evening of lovemaking. But there's something wrong, and I feel too embarrassed to bring it up. Willy gave me an out as we lay overlooking the canyon—he said he couldn't live with me because of an ancient injury. It lets me off the hook because I just couldn't tell him my heart belongs to someone else. I feel ashamed, because it's someone I've never met and who's completely out of reach for me.

But I'm totally obsessed with him and his very existence makes relationships impossible. I'm just like a schoolgirl penning this in my diary, but there's no denying it. I am in love with Ian Pearson.

*March* 15, 1970

It's impossible falling for a celebrity, but the press has revealed so much of his inner life that I *know* he's my soulmate. Of course, Ian Pearson wouldn't appear to be my match. Five foot seven, pudgy, sixteen years old. A little short, bespectacled and young perhaps.

He's no James Taylor, he's not even David Crosby. But I know he's my type in so many more important ways. His poem "I Am a Child" stirred me so deeply: "I am a child who has been stoned and scorned, fondled and loved, beaten and praised. In my own subtle way I want to save the world. Alas, I am a child." Remarkable that someone so young carries the wisdom of the ages. (Must remember to give Neil Young a copy of the poem.) His essay on alienation in *Hamlet* illuminated more of the modern condition for me than Sartre. And, my heart be still, when *Rolling Stone* ran a list of his record collection (93 albums!), he had *Song to a Seagull* and *Clouds*! I also know he grew up in Alberta, so we share a defining landscape. I know I could reach him if I could get to him, but there's always an impenetrable wall around a star like that.

## *April* 3, 1970

Ran into Licorice of the Incredible String Band. She told me how thrilled she was to see in the *Rolling Stone* list that Ian Pearson owned three of her recordings. One more than *moi*, but surely he isn't attracted to flowery chicks in granny dresses (and it definitely wouldn't be her singing or hand cymbals). I couldn't believe how jealous I felt. My third album comes out next week—that should even the score. At least his proclivity is toward Likky and Judy Collins and me. If Led Zep or the Stooges ever started dominating his record collection I'd feel my chances diminishing.

## *June* 8, 1970

Sure enough, *Ladies of the Canyon* made it into his record collection (*Rolling Stone* is now running biweekly updates of his collection—more important than *Billboard* they say). Ian told an interviewer how an oafish friend of his stained the pristine white album cover orange. He was cutting up a vitamin C tablet with a razor blade in hopes of passing it off as acid. Oh, if I could only be there as he listened to it. Could Ian ever know that I wrote, "Sometime in the evening/ he would read to her,/ roll her in his arms/ And give his seed to her" fantasizing about him?

I picture him in his basement bedroom with his *Clouds* poster on his bulletin board (*moi* holding a lily against Saskatoon's river valley, though he likes to think it's his home of Edmonton). His copies of *Sometimes a Great Notion* and *Be Here Now* rest on his bedside table. He's lying on the bed in his Stanfield pyjamas—robin blue with navy blue elastic cuffs. (INSPIRATION: how about a song and album title called "Blue"?) He stares longingly at the poster and his hand moves down the pyjamas . . . I MUST STOP!!! I need a long break.

### *February* 4, 1971

My hiatus is over. The break from touring and recording did wonders for me and I came back from Europe with some killer songs. But I am still not "cured" of Ian Pearson. Under the Matalla moon in the Mediterranean, I threw myself at a lusty old devil just because he was so exactly not Ian. Last night, I drew a map of Canada on a coaster with Ian's face sketched on it twice. The news (it was front page on the *Herald Tribune*) that he got 61 in his grade 12 trigonometry exam fills me with awe and admiration. Talk about sticking it to the man—just enough to pass, but otherwise pure civil disobedience. There's a little of Gandhi in my *petit Rimbaud*.

### *October* 10, 1971

Rhymes with Ian: being, seeing, FREEING!

### *October* 12, 1972

The newscasts are full of Ian Pearson's first days at university. I should be ready to cut loose from my fantasy, but my heart gets tugged with every tidbit of gossip. There's his first college infatuation—a beautiful, willowy blond. Is that a hint or what? Warners Canada called me excitedly to report that Pearson had gone to Sam's to buy the 8-track of *For the Roses* so he could get it a week early (and he doesn't even own an 8-track). They want to milk this for all it's worth, but I told them to play it cool—I wouldn't want to give myself away. The signs are all there—if only there was some way of getting at him. I daydream about surreptitiously enrolling in first-year English at the University of Toronto and then—what? Drop a pencil? Hi, my name is Joni and what courses are you taking? Easier to indulge in full fantasy: he's sitting in his dorm with a friend and they open the gatefold of *For the Roses*. In the photograph, I'm standing naked (butt to camera) on a rock in the Pacific. His friend ogles the shot and says, "Wouldn't you like to be on that rock?" In my dream, Ian says, "Yes, more than anything in the world." But I mustn't let myself go there.

## *December* 1, 1975

Dylan calls, and I hop on the Rolling Thunder tour in time for the Maple Leaf Gardens show. I know in my bones that *he* will be in the audience. I ask Dylan what to do. Should I brazenly introduce "Woman of Heart and Mind" and say, "This one's for Ian"? Get Neuwirth to invite him backstage? Dylan gives me a dismissive stare and drawls, "Nobody can talk to that dude. He scares the shit out of me. What are you going to ask him? Open your mouth in front of him and he'll make you a fool." I sing my four songs to my difficult muse who's out there somewhere.

Then I slink back to the Hyatt. The bed becomes vast with the thought that he is sleeping (or lying there not sleeping—aaargh!) only a couple of blocks from here. His plaid shirt and jeans would be thrown on the floor (he's so brave in his fashion resistance). Maybe he's lulling himself to sleep with side two of *The Hissing of Summer Lawns*. And Ian enters the dreamscape of "Sweet Bird" and he and I glide airborne through the prairie sky.

*November* 19, 1977

He is losing himself in noise. I read how he likes to hop mindlessly while listening to The Clash and Elvis Costello. I know he needs to be out there on the edge, but I quietly hope he's pulling out *Don Juan's Reckless Daughter* for contemplative late-night listening. Look fella, that's me as the soul man on the cover. I did the black-face routine for you, hoping I'd get some cred in light of your recent George Clinton fixation. And "Paprika Plains" is in honour of your favourite dish at the Blue Cellar.

*March* 28, 1978

Intense writing sessions with Mingus. He doesn't have much time left as his debilitating disease takes its toll. But my great jazz mentor manages to cut to the core of everything I do and say. He nails my melancholy. It's not just a white chick's repression, I protest, it's a guy. What kind of cat? he asks. I show him a picture of Ian Pearson. He is now bearded and looks like one of those cute Smith brothers on the cough drop package, and he has the sexiest aviator glasses. Huge convulsions overcome Mingus. He drops the photograph, turns blue, and rolls on the floor, short gasps of breath. I'm so worried because of his horrible illness, but when he gets up he's smiling, with tears of laughter rolling down his face. "Thanks, babe," he says. "Needed a laugh."

*September* 2, 1980

Sometimes Ian's work makes me feel so small. He's writing for magazines and tackling important issues like airline deregulation in Canada or the loss of shuffleboard tables in Toronto bars. And here's little Joni, stuck mapping and remapping the confines of her own puny heart. I know my ditties aren't very important, but wed me to his concern and what we could do together! But then I read something like his *Maclean's* article about the shortage of nurses in Canada and I am cowed. Even Jaco, the king of all bass players, could never match the wild pulse of the rhythm of his prose. For my part, I'm not going to think about it for a while.

## November 21, 1982

My wedding day—this time it's personal! Larry is the most wonderful guy. We commune like instruments—my weird chords and his steady rhythm. What I've always needed. I like to think that I've put away childish things, i.e., my obsession with Ian. But then the worst fear hit me as we were standing together taking our vows: "This is lovely, but it isn't Ian." Earth to Joni: get real.

## March 3, 1991

Ian's list—which has moved to MOJO since it's too boomer and retro for *Rolling Stone*—reveals he bought *Night Ride Home* on cassette instead of CD since he "didn't want to take too much of a chance." What the hell does that mean? I spend three years forging songs from the depths of my soul and he's afraid to fork out an extra five bucks in case he doesn't like it? I note the preponderance of sensitive chick singer-songwriters on his list: Lucinda, Mary Margaret, Rosanne, Shawn. No Joni, no them. (But no Ian, no Joni?)

## October 29, 1998

Lost a fine husband in Larry, gained a fine man in Don. Same old, same old. But I found my daughter!!! Even though I'd lost her for more than three decades, Kilauren completes me in ways I could never imagine. She's given me the life force to tour again, and here I am once more in Maple Leaf Gardens with Dylan. I'm singing every song to Killer—here's my life, my art, and it's only for my own flesh and blood. Not for anyone else. Not a thought of who else could be in the audience. Nope. No way. (But I did watch from the wings during Dylan's set, and HE was there in row five. That baseball cap and that red Eddie Bauer fleece jacket—I still love his sense of anti-style.)

## October 30, 1998

Breakfast with the Warners rep. He tells me Ian Pearson sold his copy of *Taming the Tiger* the day after he bought it. Too wordy, he told the clerk in the used record store. He walked out with discs by the Sonics and the Thirteenth Floor Elevators. A ridiculous spectacle: a forty-four-year-old man trying to reinvent his teen years with all the garage fuzz he hated at the time—because the lyrics weren't serious! I was the one who nurtured him musically and now he tries to hide it.

What's the point of going on? Six more dates on this bloody tour—I can't back out now. But in my mind I've quit. If I can't reach Ian, there's no point to my music. If it's too wordy, maybe I should just shut up.

## June 21, 2000

The abandonment is now complete, and he has piled scorn upon rejection. The news arrives that he has started his own record label to put out the work of Eleni Mandell. I can accept the fact that his personal life is happy and he's found the perfect mate (though I notice she's short and dark—maybe he's secretly pining for me and can't risk being near a tall blond). But to devote himself to another singer-songwriter. A woman. From Los Angeles! I can't deal with this.

I've made a formal announcement that I've given up songwriting. The ostensible reasons I've given to the press are true, but the truth is when I lost Ian's ears, I lost my heart. But I've learned, I guess. Don't make anyone into a hero because they're certain to disappoint you. Then again, maybe you can only know what you haven't got when it's gone.

## October 10, 2001

Rhymes with Ian: simian, peon, plebeian.

# Jake MacDonald

■

## CARS AND CAROL

Around the time of my forty-fifth birthday I decided I needed a convertible.

I've never really been the convertible type. In fact for most of my life I wouldn't have taken a ragtop if you gave me one. They're cold in the winter, brutally hot in the midday sun and, on the highway, they produce so much wind noise you can't listen to the radio or conduct a conversation. But one summer evening I went for a drive in a new convertible and that did the trick.

The weather was particularly lush and beautiful that summer, and my father was in the hospital with a stroke. He was staying in a dark and cavernous Winnipeg hospital that dated back to the Victorian era, and it was no fun going to see him. He'd always been a tall and almost brawny man, with sloping shoulders and a natural athlete's easy saunter, but the stroke had dropped him like a tree. His arms were thin and pale, and he lay on the bed with his eyes open. He didn't know where he was and his face was creased with fear. A window in the corner of the room was open, and through the screened slot came the sounds of the evening—the rattle of an idling ambulance's diesel, and the festive burble of robins.

One evening my little sister Mary Kate showed up during my visit and I caught a ride home with her afterwards. She's a judge, but resists the drudgery of her occupation by keeping fit and driving saucy automobiles. Her new car was a teal-green Chevy convertible with cockpit seating, rumbling exhaust pipes and a sound system that knocked up your heart rate when she slipped Dwight Yoakum into the CD player. As we drove down the street, the music, the sweet air of evening and the canopy of leafy elms parading overhead produced a conviction in me, however illogical, that enclosed spaces represent death, and open spaces represent greenery and life. Smelling the new-mown grass, holding the door frame, which under my fingertips still held the heat of the day's sun, I realized that life affords few opportunities to make a *beau geste*. A convertible was a vote against practicality, a nose thumbed at the inevitable. It revived the old Gaelic definition of *carr*—"a chariot of war or triumph; a vehicle of dignity and splendour." Driving a convertible was not just an option but a duty. Turning to my sister, I said, "I think I'm going to buy one of these."

It took a while before I located one that I both liked and could afford. The summer passed. My father came home from the hospital one weekend and refused to go back. My brother Peter tried to persuade him, but he gripped the arms of the recliner chair from which he'd watched *Hockey Night in Canada* for decades and simply refused to get up. Peter is a surgeon and he knows about hospitals. "I don't blame him," Peter said. So my dad stayed home, crawling up and down the stairs like a 200-pound toddler, sitting by the window and watching the birds at the feeder. Sometimes on Sunday afternoons I took him for rides in the country. We'd drive out through the autumn woods on the edge of town and look for deer. I was driving a Bronco at the time, a sturdy little 4x4 that worked well for towing boats, hauling stuff and getting through snowed-in roads at the lake. I couldn't afford to buy a new vehicle, so I decided to look for an older convertible that I could fix up and use as a summer car.

Everyone says that the best time to get a good price on a car is in the winter, and that's probably doubly true when you're shopping for a convertible. So when the bitter winds of winter descended on Winnipeg, I began perusing the *Auto Trader*, looking for an older-model Chrysler product that needed a new home. I liked the Chryslers because throughout the '60s and '70s their designers stood firm against the adoption of the baguette-shaped fuselage that was Europe's contribution to global motoring thought. Dodges, Plymouths and Valiants were cut with cubist, masculine lines that I agreed with; oblong tail lights and angular fins and hoods as broad and flat as a dining room table.

I was living, at the time, in a rambling old third-floor apartment at the corner of Stafford and Grosvenor. It was a large seven-room suite, with oak woodwork, an ornate fireplace, screened veranda and spacious dining room. The rent was peanuts. I'd acquired it thanks to a friendship with the writer Carol Shields. I had met Carol years before. She was a demure Winnipeg housewife who'd moved here from Chicago, where she'd grown up in the same neighbourhood as Ernest Hemingway. (Carol once asserted that her main claim to fame was that her mother had once boarded with the Hemingway family.) Carol had written a couple of novels and short stories that nobody read, and I had written several books of fiction that were even less popular than hers. She was keen on connecting with other writers, and attended nearly all the local literary events and readings, most of which in those days were so sparsely attended that the entire crowd would fit comfortably into a medium-sized living room.

One day I ran into her on the street, and she urged me to come to a poetry reading. Her husband, Don, who taught engineering at the University of Manitoba, was out of town on business, and Carol seemed to be looking for moral support. (On the other hand, I had just gotten divorced, so maybe Carol thought it was I who needed a night out.) Fiction and poetry, at the time, were considered to be hipster art forms, and Carol, a forty-five-year-old mom who'd spent most of her adult life cooking, cleaning and shopping for five kids, never quite fit in with the Bohemian types that frequented these literary events. (Her most recent novel, for example, was *A Fairly Conventional Woman*, the story of a married woman who goes to a quilting convention where she is tempted to have an affair, but thinks better of it.) Her husband usually came with her, and was certainly a good sport about it. But when Carol came by herself, I often felt a bit sorry for her (that's a good one) so we would stand in the corner, discussing books and social issues, about which, in most cases, we amiably disagreed.

That night at the poetry reading our host was Don Bailey, a reformed bank robber who'd learned to write short stories under the tutelage of Margaret Laurence. Don was doing well. He'd come to realize that it was easier to get money out of the Canada Council than the Bank of Montreal. He always seemed to have lots of projects on the go and a nice place to live. His apartment was a beauty, with high ceilings and a hearty fireplace and large windows overlooking the treed avenue. Being on my own again, I needed a place that was large enough for my daughter and me, and Carol took a maternal interest in my situation. "You need a large place like this," she said. She buttonholed Don as he was going by, and asked him if there were any upcoming vacancies in the building.

"Everybody asks me that," he said. "But there's a long waiting list." She instructed him to call me if anything came up. About a month later, I was working late in my office when the phone rang. I was trying to finish a paragraph and didn't want to lose it, so I let the phone ring. It rang about fifteen times, then I finally picked it up.

It was Don Bailey. "I'm moving," he said. "Do you want my apartment or not?"

My daughter and I moved into the apartment and fixed it up, painted the walls eggshell white and refinished the oak floors. It was a great neighbourhood. Caitlin's school was two blocks away. My favourite restaurant happened to be right across the street, my bank was next door, and the best food store in the city was on the main floor of the building. I could do all my day's errands in my slippers. I maintained a country place in Minaki, Ontario, three hours from the city, and I commuted back and forth. I called Carol and thanked her for taking an interest in my situation and supplying the necessary twist of fate. We kept in touch that way, by phone, and ran into each other at parties, dinners or readings. Sometimes we'd go for lunch. It was during one of those lunches that I realized her life was changing.

We were sitting in the Mozart Café, the place across the street from my apartment. Carol had just published a novel called *The Republic of Love*, and she'd brought me a copy. While she was powdering her nose, I flipped through the book. Not only was it set in

Winnipeg, but one of the scenes in the book took place right at this restaurant. Carol had always insisted on locating her novels in her hometown. She believed in the magic that resides in everyday lives. Many people go through their entire lives without experiencing betrayal, violence, adultery and so on, and she believed that writing about those things was equivalent to being dishonest with your readers. I thought it was quaint that she was sticking to her literary guns and achieving some degree of success by doing so. But what startled me were the reviews on the dust jacket of *The Republic of Love*. Apparently she was not only developing a readership in Los Angeles and New York and London and Sydney, but international critics were raving about her work. When she sat down, I raised my glass to hers, and congratulated her. But it was like saluting her across a sudden gap. Carol's career, with banners snapping, was pulling away from the quay, and mine was staying behind. Much of our friendship was based on intuition, on things inferred but not said. I understood, now, that this luncheon was a sort of farewell.

When someone is departing, you have to make your peace and let them go. I wasn't upset about Carol's success. I had my own life to live. But Carol still made a point of staying in touch. She called to congratulate me if I happened to win some rinky-dink writing award, and I called to congratulate her when she won the Pulitzer Prize for *The Stone Diaries*, a book which I regret to say I haven't yet read. She sent me a note of sympathy when my father had his first stroke. She brought Don to Minaki one wintry weekend in March to see my place, after first ascertaining that the bears would still be in hibernation. (Carol's Canada didn't include bears.) And she even asked my advice about writing projects.

"Now Jake," she said (this was how she always began our telephone conversations). "I wonder if you would talk to me about cars."

Hmm, I thought. Was she stalled somewhere? Was Don off at some asphalt symposium and her battery was dead?

The last time I'd seen her, she'd been having car trouble. She told me she'd been on her way home from the University of Manitoba on a stormy winter night, when a passing motorist waved at her and shouted that her tire was going flat. She pulled into a service station and asked the man at the gas pump if he could fix her tire. He agreed, and got the air hose and started filling up the tire, but she said, "No, no, it has to be changed." She opened the trunk, gave him the keys, and went into the garage to stay warm.

Standing at the door, she watched him through the gusts of sleet as he fumbled with the jack, crawled around in the slush and struggled with the tire iron, trying to get the lug nuts off. She kept glancing at her watch, worried that she was late for dinner. He seemed rather incompetent, but finally got the wheel on. She hurried out into the storm and opened her purse. "How much do I owe you?"

"I beg your pardon?" he said. "I don't work here."

She laughed when I reminded her of this story. This time, she said, there was no car trouble. She was working on a new novel and was trying to decide what kind of car the main character drove. I had already heard a bit about her new novel. My writer pal Larry Krotz had run into her on the street and Carol told him she was writing about a flustered, well-intentioned Winnipeg man who was twice divorced and trying to sort his way through the complex maze of his life. She said she wanted to call it "Larry's Party," but since the details of her character's woes more or less perfectly matched Larry's issues, she was concerned that people might think she'd filched elements of the plot from the real Larry's life. "I could change his name to Barry," she offered. "But the title 'Barry's Party' doesn't sound quite as appealing. Don't you think?"

Larry told her not to worry. "It's the closest I'll ever come to having my name on a book by a Pulitzer Prize–winning author."

She asked Larry another favour—could she take him out to lunch sometime and interview him about men? Carol was by now an international superstar. It wasn't even fame. It was a sort of mass psychosis. My sister had gone to one of her readings at a bookstore in England and was utterly unprepared for what she saw. Squads of police were there, holding back the mob, and when she saw Carol she said the crowd was jostling her and pulling at her as if she were a rock 'n' roll goddess. She said that Carol looked frightened, and of course they never even had a chance to say hello. Juxtapose that level of literary charisma if you will with the rather comic image of Carol going around Winnipeg and asking her boneheaded male friends for advice. She told me she'd already interviewed Larry Krotz, David Arnason and Dr. Ray Singer, and now she was getting around to her old pal, me. She asked, "What kind of car are you driving these days?"

I had, by now, acquired a convertible. It was a black 1981 Chrysler LeBaron with two hundred thousand clicks on the odometer. There was a player's pass for the Winnipeg Blue Bombers applied to the windshield. The former owner, whoever he was, had apparently been in the habit of leaving it with the roof down while he was taking care of business because the floor had been rotted through by rain. Foam rubber bulged from rips in the bucket seats, and there was a hole in the dash where the stereo had once been. When you started the car, the engine climbed into a smoky, chattering idle so quickly that when you shifted into "D" it was like getting hit from behind. Once upon a time it had no doubt been a nice car, but it needed work, and I was slowly getting it back into shape when Carol called.

She was interested in both the effort I'd devoted to finding the so-called right car, and the apparently non-ironic enthusiasm with which I was restoring it. "Now Jake, what is this business of men and cars, exactly?"

Hmm, I thought. Men and cars.

"Can we discuss it over lunch?" she asked. "My treat." I had had hip surgery recently. I knew that Carol's ulterior motive was to make sure that I was okay and to get me out of the house.

"I would love to have lunch," I said. "But I'm still on crutches. I'm not sure I can fit in your car."

"Oh dear."

"What kind of car is it?"

There was a moment of hesitation at the other end of the line— the same awkward hesitation you get when you're talking on the phone and you ask the female clerk if you have to drive "east" or "west" to get to her store.

"It's a blue car," Carol finally said.

"Carol, are you saying you don't know what kind of car you drive?"

"It's small and it's blue."

"Maybe that's a good place to begin our discussion."

We solved the crutches issue by going to the restaurant across the street. It was the sort of place where a lot of people would recognize her, so it wasn't the best place to have a quiet conversation, but we gave it a shot. During lunch we talked about cars. Like most women, Carol didn't care much about automobiles. She didn't understand why anyone would spend more than a few seconds of their precious life thinking about cars. She regarded a car as a mechanical contrivance designed to get you from one place to another. She knew the location of the ignition, the wipers, the gas pedal and the brake, and that was it. She believed that most women shared her disinterest, and she wanted to know why men invest so much importance in their vehicles.

I told her I couldn't really speak for all men. Some of my male friends didn't even drive. But the younger a man is, the more he values his car, and the various things his car represents. When I was twenty-one years old, I bought a 1954 Chevrolet for $80, and drove it all over the United States, studying maps and getting the lay of the land. It only had a 6-volt electrical system, so I put a 12-volt battery on the floor of the back seat and used it to power my tape deck. A fully powered battery was necessary for any outing, because like most young men, I suffered from a wild need for independence and a pathetic sense of loneliness. These two emotions pulled at me from opposite directions and with equal force. Rolling down the highway with an Eagles soundtrack in the background encouraged me to imagine that I was not in fact a complete loser but a cool dude on my way from one adventure to another. It was all a waste of time, of course, but I needed to circle the continent anyway, like a young dog sniffing the fence posts.

Eventually I settled down and got married, bought a house and began raising a daughter. In those days I drove an apple-red Jeep Cherokee; a sporty outfit with four-wheel drive and a roof rack.

Sports utility vehicles are big and practical, and they're comfortable to drive. But for a young man, they send the same message that young women convey with high heels and a sexy dress. The SUV says, yes, I may be married, and yes, I may be en route to the all-night pharmacy to buy another bale of medium-sized Huggies, but in my own imagination I'm still a footloose dude on my way from one adventure to another. I told her that, in my view, that's why so many social commentators don't like SUVs. It's true they're gas-guzzling road hogs that dwarf other cars. But family vans are even worse. Most vans, in fact, are bigger than the average SUV, get equally lousy gas mileage and are just as dangerous in a collision. But nobody fumes about them. Nobody writes scathing editorials about all those lumbering Voyageur vans with "Baby on Board" decals. SUVs are considered anti-social not because they get poor gas mileage, but because they symbolize a man's refusal to be domesticated.

Carol rolled her eyes in amusement. As always, she was per-plexed by the contrariness of the male outlook. Whenever we had lunch, we would always get into these little debates. Carol would tell me what the world looked like from a woman's point of view, and I would tell her what the world looked like from a man's per-spective. We disagreed about most things, even books. She thought most of my favourite writers were grown-up juvenile delinquents, and I thought her favourite writers were bores. But we tolerated each other's questionable judgment, because our association wasn't based on literary admiration, but on something higher, that is to say, friendship. In fact, we seldom talked about books anymore, other than to clear up the issue with a few dutiful questions. (So what are you working on?) What we did was talk about the human species, and in those conversations, we rarely looked at things the same way. It wasn't a matter of arguing; of quarrelling over who was right or wrong. It was more a matter of comparing notes, and being surprised that we each saw things so differently.

She wanted to know why men have such a fear of domestica-tion. After all, isn't the institution of marriage mainly to their bene-fit? In a traditional marriage, men go to work in the morning, and they come home at night to a neat house and a balanced meal. They lounge around in the evening and play with the children or read the paper while their wife washes the dishes. If the wife gets fed up and asks for a divorce, the husband goes into a tailspin. He moves into a bachelor flat and sleeps on the floor. He skulks around in sweat pants with liquor on his breath. The wife joins a yoga class and drops twenty pounds. She buys a new home and uses her reduced income to make it bright and comfortable and airy. She looks good, but her social life is a bust because the men of her generation are all either married or living in basement apartments and drinking too much. "How reasonable is it," she asked, "for men to organize marriage for their own benefit, and then carry on as if women are dragging them into it?"

"I didn't say it was reasonable. I'm just saying it's what men think."

She said that Larry, her main character, was going through something of a mid-life crisis, and perhaps he might buy a convertible as an expression of that. She wanted to know if I drove a convertible as a way of hanging on to my long-lost youth. I told her I'd outgrown all that, and had no interest in pretending to be young again. I just liked the openness of a convertible, being able to smell the grass, look overhead at the trees and the puffy skies of summer. I told her that the next time we went for lunch, I'd pick her up in the convertible and we'd go find a picnic bench by the river, which would also afford the possibility of a normal conversation. Having lunch with Carol was like having lunch with Gordie Howe. Every few minutes someone came over to the table. They told her they loved her books; and what was she writing now? Carol was determinedly polite, which encouraged them. They'd stand by the table and yak at great length. We'd no sooner be rid of one book-lover than another would appear. We finally gave up on our meeting, and reiterated the plan to go for a ride when the convertible was finally fixed up.

By the time I recovered sufficiently to discard the crutches and get my car back on the road, Carol had gone away for the summer. And, for one reason or another, we never got the chance to go for that long pleasant ride in the park with the top down. When her book *Larry's Party* was finally published, it was amusing to see that Larry drove cars that suited his personality. Larry was a bland guy and he drove bland cars. His automotive resume consisted of "two Toyotas, an old tan Corolla that he traded in for a semi-new Camry. After the Camry came the deep silver Audi, and now the two-door Honda Accord. These cars are the clothes he puts on after he puts on his primary clothes. That's it in the wheels department."

Then Carol got cancer, and I saw her only sporadically. One Christmas I gave her and Don a special edition of Handel's *Messiah*, a stripped-down period-authentic version performed on the original instruments. When I called them on Christmas Eve to say hello I could hear it playing in the background.

The last time I saw Carol was at a house party in Winnipeg. Her friends had gathered to celebrate another of her literary honours. My girlfriend, Ann, and I drove over to the house with the top down. It was high summer, verdant and warm, and everyone was dressed in white. It was hard to accept that cancer could exist on a summer night like this.

Carol was frail and weak. She sat in a straight-back chair in the corner, and people took turns talking to her. When I sat beside her, she draped her small hand on my forearm and asked me to tell her a story.

At the end of the evening, Don and Carol made a point of walking everyone out to their cars. I'd waxed the old convertible and it looked pretty good, parked there beside the lilac bushes in the streetlight's glow. "So this is the car," she smiled.

Ann and I told her we'd come out and visit her in Victoria. We hugged and fussed and made promises. Carol tended to be businesslike about taking her leave. There was, after all, a proper way of doing these things. "Drive safely," she said, dismissing us with a little wave. I honestly thought I'd see her again, but was wrong. The last image I have of her is on that boulevard, holding Don's arm, lifting her hand to wave goodbye as we drove away.

# David Eddie

■

## HOT-zzt-L

Deep down, all men are dogs: bad dogs, junkyard dogs. All of us. Understand that, and you've got most of the picture.

Doesn't matter who you are. You could be a Nobel prizewinner, pillar of the community, married to a handsome wife, with children who are the apple of your eye; you could be a religious figure; you could earn your living crisscrossing the country lecturing on the evils of infidelity, preaching the virtues of the monogamous life—and a Sexy Young Thing could come along and knock over the whole house of cards with a single hair-flip.

Never underestimate the hair-flip. It can sweep aside whole civilizations.

■

I'm a dog, too. It's a simple syllogism: "All men are dogs. Dave is a man. Therefore, Dave is a dog."

I look inside my soul, and that's what I see: a bad dog, a very bad dog, growling and whimpering and thumping its tail. But unlike many of my fellow-mongrels, I've trained myself. I strain and bark and whine. But I don't have to be beaten or punched or kicked to realize I'm best kept collared.

I come from a long line of bad dogs. My sire was a very bad dog, indeed—"a hard dog," as they used to say of former U.S. president Bill Clinton, "to keep on the porch."

My father was one of the boldest and most audacious philanderers I've ever heard of. When he was living with my mother in a small southern town in the United States, he would have his lovers come and stay with them, in the house he shared with my mother. They came from Canada, and Europe, where he often went on (monkey) business, posing as "colleagues," or "friends" . . . and it burns my mother to this day to consider the fact she actually *put on an apron* and cooked and cleaned ("Three meals a day, Dave!") for women who turned out to be dad's mistresses.

Once, he went to the opera with my mother and his secretary, with whom he was sleeping at the time.

On another occasion, he invited the same secretary/mistress over to help move house. She sat on the stairs, in the way, while my mother humped boxes and furniture up and down the stairs.

My father was also a vintage-car buff. And during this time, he owned a block-long 1970-ish Cadillac with licence plates that read: OLD CAD.

I've had a lot of time—twenty years—to think about those plates. What was the deal with them? A cry for help? Plea to be caught? Proud boast to the world? That's what my mother thinks: "Oh, yes, your father was very proud of his swordsmanship," she says.

But I think she's wrong. Knowing my father, and his generation—the so-called "greatest" generation, who defeated "zee Germans," true, but who also seem curiously lacking in irony, subtlety, and self-knowledge (I snuck a peek at my father's diary once: it read like this: "I had a hamburger for lunch today. It was delicious, if a trifle overcooked." On and on, page after page.)—he probably didn't even make the connection. They weren't vanity plates. Those plates were lack-of-introspection plates.

Of course, for all we knew back then, all they referred to was the make and model of the car. The family's always the last to know. It's said that "a lie flies around the world while the truth is lacing up its boots." Well, the truth is very slow to put its boots on in cases of adultery. Only after his death, for example, was it discovered that folksy, "straight-shootin'" CBS correspondent Charles Kurault had secretly been meeting his mistress in a Montana hideaway *for 30 years*.

For my mother, suspicion began when my father started getting his mail delivered to his office rather than to their house. "*Why?*" she wondered. So one day, when he went away for the weekend, she searched it. And after five hours of painstakingly going through his stuff, replacing it exactly as she left it, the afternoon sun slanting through the blinds, she finally found a letter in the pages of a book. A raunchy love letter from the secretary, the first piece of a none-too-savoury puzzle she would slowly, with characteristic patience and meticulousness, put together over the next twenty or so years.

At first, she held back the details from my brother and sister and me, not wanting to prejudice us against our father. But I squeezed it out of her. She comes over to babysit my kids, now. After eight or nine years, and about a thousand cups of coffee, I got the story.

Looking back on it all now, I feel . . . I'm not sure there's a word in English for how I feel. Maybe the Germans have one, one of those formidable compounds—maybe something beginning with *schaden*, and meaning "shame in retrospect." Or maybe some word that means "the sense of puzzlement which remains, after all the pieces of the puzzle have been put into place."

If there is such a word, then that's how I feel, when I think back on my old man, already snowy-haired in his mid-forties (my age now), cheating on his wife like there's no tomorrow, riding around a small Southern town in a pimp's car with OLD CAD plates.

■

His generation got married too young, I think. (My only contemporary who married in his early 20s followed a similar trajectory.) My father married at twenty-three, to his first serious girlfriend (my mother). And he was left with all this . . . *curiosity.*

Not me. I was thirty-five by the time I finally got married, after . . . well, let's just say "a very active bachelorhood."

I hope that doesn't sound boastful. Viewed from the outside, I'm not even sure it was all that pretty a picture. My father's bad-dog blood burned hot in my veins. Even my most horrible friends were horrified, even my most scandalous friends were scandalized, by my incredibly high "BTL" (Bimbo Tolerance Level), my penchant for "low-hanging fruit," the sheer *amorality* of my erotic pursuits. I double-crossed friends, cheated on girlfriends, and filled the air with lies. Basically, I did whatever it took to persuade women to pop off their tops in my filthy, verminous little apartment (described as furnished in "early 80s crack house" style by one of my friends: "I thought there was something wrong with the enamel of your tub," my wife, Pam, says now of her first encounter with my bachelor bathroom. "I didn't think it could just be *dirt*."). I call this period of my life Bachelor Hell, though I have to admit I felt I was having fun at the time.

The point is: dog that I was, in that era, I got it all out of my system. I dated every sort of woman under the sun. So now, if, say, I were to run across a drunken Marilyn Monroe lookalike at a party—an outrageous blond dipso/nymphomaniac with a breathy, come-hither whisper, who would, pie-eyed, stick her tongue in my ear and rub up against me, her full, round, panty-clad buttocks grinding into my crotch area—I think I can honestly say my only reaction would be: "Yawn! Been there, done that."

Hyperbole? Maybe. But I've seen where that all leads: to madness, usually. To loads of dull dialogue in the middle of the night, crazy/boring drama-queen scenes in the street . . .

When Pam, the woman who is now my wife, finally came along, even I could see—even a blind man could see—she was head and shoulders above the women I'd been dating. She was Smart, Sexy, and Sane, the Three Ss Every Bachelor Seeks™. (Men have a terrible reputation for being obsessed with body parts, ladies, but ask any guy who's been around the block a few times and he'll tell you the sexiest body part in the long run is a sensible head on shoulders.) As a man who once considered himself a bad boy, a loner, and an outsider, who once vowed to be an eternal bachelor (marriage was for suckers, I felt, and would interfere with my writing) I surprised more than a few people when I was caught running to, not away from, the nearest church to take my vows.

Around the time of my wedding, so many people came up to me to tell me what a "lucky bastard" I was to be marrying her that it became kind of insulting. But I knew what they meant. She was a goddess, a queen bee. God sent her to save me, and she saves me every day. To cheat on her would be to spit in the face of God. My friends would turn their backs on me, mock me and not feel sorry for me as I trudged off with my little backpack full of dirty shirts, off to one of those fleabag roadside hotels featuring a neon sign and an eternally burnt-out letter buzzing through the night: HOT-zzt-L, HOT-zzt-L . . .

■

Which is not to say I've never been tempted, that I have never, along with former U.S. president Jimmy Carter, committed "adultery in my mind."

Fidelity-wise, I'm very lucky in my choice of profession. I spend my days alone, up here in my third-floor aerie, my sanctum sanctorum, double-doored against the screams (and laughter: equally distracting) of my family; triple-doored against the clamouring and Klaxons of the madding crowd. There's nothing up here but me, some books and some antique machines (fax, air-conditioner, stereo, radio, computer and an ancient, shuddering "bachelor" fridge). Not a lot of temptation, in other words.

But, a couple of years ago, for a number of reasons, all of them financial, I got a job in an office—my first in seven years—as a television producer. I was there for a year. And during the course of that year, I got a better sense of exactly what it was my father may have been up against in his day.

At that point, Pam and I had three little kids under the age of seven; we both had stressful, full-time jobs; and we'd been married seven years, preceded by four of living together. As we all know, in a long-term relationship, sex goes in cycles. Sometimes we'd go through a cycle where we had sex once a month.

Then, other times, we'd go through a cycle where we didn't have it nearly so often.

And outside, it was spring. You know, in high school, and college, I never used to understand what T.S. Eliot meant when he said

"April is the cruelest month." Why would April, lovely April, be the cruelest month? Now I think I understand. Eliot was married, after all. What he meant was: April is the cruelest month *for the married man*. Especially married men who live in cold climates—it's the month the parkas and heavy sweaters come off, it's the month the breasts come out of their cocoons. It's the month that great harbinger of spring, the belly button, makes its first appearance. And that spring, it was also the month that my boss hired a 23-year-old intern.

Let's call her "Vickie."

At first she flew under my radar, under everyone's radar. She wore crazy, nebbishy clothes and glasses. She was quiet and reserved. But as the weather grew warmer and she grew more comfortable in her job, the outer layer of her clothing came off. She started wearing tight, striped T-shirt dresses and filmy white shirts through which her black bra was clearly visible. She was built like a Playboy bunny—and not a modern Playboy bunny, either, one of those from the sixties, when the breasts were real.

Glasses and a Playboy body. . . . Now, earlier, when I said that during my Bachelor Hell era I dated "every kind of woman under the sun," that's not entirely true. There were a couple of types I, unfortunately, overlooked—hot-button types in my case: 1) the voluptuous redhead; 2) the naughty librarian.

And this girl, Vickie—who dyed her (blond) hair with crazy red streaks and wore big, owlish glasses, was, technically, *both*.

She was the "office hottie." She had all the (mostly middle-aged, mostly married or otherwise committed) men in the office drooling. They called it "Vickie Fever." Like malaria or dengue or beri-beri—something tropical, anyway: might go away for a while, but it's in your blood, and it always comes back.

Worse yet, the office hottie appeared to have the hots for me. She was very touchy-feely. If I told a joke, even a lame one, she put her hand, ha-ha-ha, on my arm. Once, we were sitting around talking, and she laughed, ha-ha-ha, and put her hand on my *thigh*. She was of that breed of women who profess, usually in the presence of older men, to like only older men, and to loudly lament, in the presence of mostly taken men: "Why are all the good men taken?"

Also, she was the type to get drunk after about half a beer. Once, we all went out for drinks after work. "You've been awfully quiet, Vicky," my boss said to her at one point. "What are you thinking about?"

"Oh, you don't want to know. I am thinking very, very bad thoughts . . ."

And she looked straight at me, with such naughty intensity I felt my mouth dry up and my father's blood, bad-dog blood, run hot in my veins.

She was Trouble, in other words, with a capital T, and that rhymes with D, and that stands for both Dave and Divorce. Dave in a cheap fleabag, HOT-zzt-L, HOT-zzt-L . . . I kept myself on a short leash around "Vickie." Not knowing how else to be, I acted all twinkly and avuncular around her. Donning my invisible sweater-vest, puffing on a metaphorical Meerschaum, I gave her career advice, told her what it was like to have kids, and so on. She became my friend, then my "special" friend—and we all know where that's heading, don't we? What a greasy, slippery slope it is from "special friend" to "secret friend." Next thing you know you're getting your ticket punched and heading to "the cheatin' side of town."

But I dodged that bullet, luckily. My contract came up and my boss sadly informed me that due to circumstances beyond his control, the vagaries of the marketplace, the fragmenting of the television market, the advent of the Internet, etc., etc., he could not renew it. I got the hell out of there and, with a vast sense of relief, returned to my little third-floor aerie with the fax and phone and shuddering fridge.

■

The best analogy I know for how to avoid adultery comes from a friend of mine, who says. "It's like the Air America days of cocaine smuggling." (He'd just been reading a book about the days when everyone was smuggling cocaine into the U.S., even the CIA on its

Air America jets.) "If you had a private jet, and you flew back and forth from Peru and Colombia, you'd have an experience where someone might come up to you and say, 'I'm going to put a gym bag on your plane and if you just look the other way you'll be $100,000 richer by sundown.' You had to know in advance you'd say no to an offer like that, or else the temptation would just be too powerful."

Precisely. And all men are metaphorically the pilots of private, light, low-flying, Bogotá-to-Miami aircraft: you have to know in advance exactly what you're going to say.

And then you have to stick to it.

You don't go straight from white to black: you move through ever-darkening shades of grey. Here's how a lot of guys get their fingers burned, as it seems to me: Okay, I'll go out for drinks with the sexy new intern at work, but not alone. Okay, I'll go out just the two of us for drinks, but not for dinner. Okay, I'll go out for dinner, but I'm not going up to her apartment. Okay, I'll go up to her apartment, but I won't have sex with her . . . .

But by the time you're in her apartment, it's too late. You're sunk, brother. Unbeknownst to your own higher functions, you made the decision sometime between the carpaccio and the swordfish. Or maybe even earlier: between the first and second martini. On your way out of the office. All that's left is just to play it out.

■

At this point, I don't even like to flirt.

Well, that's a lie. I *love* to flirt. Through flirtation, the married man is able to ascertain, without ever actually laying a finger on anyone, some kind of answer to the Third Most Dangerous Question a Married Man Can Ask Himself: "Have I still got it?" (the second is "What would it be like?" and the first is "Could I get away with it?").

I don't know why it's so important for men, especially married men "of a certain age," to have some sort of answer to this question.

Well, I have some idea. Gloria Steinem famously complained that women become "invisible" past a certain age, but what about us? In the sense she means it, we've been invisible our whole lives! No one's whistling at *us* as we sashay down the street; no one's trying to peek down our pants as we pour them a drink. Ladies, we don't like women looking right through us, anymore than you do. Especially if one is going through a period in which one's wife seems lukewarm to one's charms, one begins to wonder: "Does the rest of the female population share her lacklustre reviews of my attractiveness? Do I still interest women at all?"

(The good news is all on men's side in this arena, though, thank God, if you keep yourself in reasonably good shape: I recently overheard a gorgeous, blond thirty-five-year-old friend of mine describe a seventy-year-old man as "sexy.")

Before we go any further, there is a crucial distinction to be made, I believe, between two types of married-man flirtation: the Conditional, and the Declarative.

The Conditional Flirt says, in effect: "My 'sweet sorrow,' if things were to be different, would you. . . ?" Frankly, I don't know why women even respond to this type of flirtation. Perhaps they do it out of charity. Or maybe it's nice for them to feel wanted by a married man. Either way, I don't even care. I appreciate it.

The Declarative Flirt says: "*Pourquoi pas*, baby, my wife doesn't understand me, let's go back to your place and 'make love.'"

I always try to do the Conditional, never the Declarative. Partly, I'm afraid for my reputation. Married men who give out "the single vibe" are cheesy, and known to all the women of the community. Plus, women share that information, and I don't want to be known as an OLD CAD.

Partly, also, I'm concerned for Pam's reputation. You have to pay some attention to how things appear. Recently, getting together with some friends at a bar, I took note of a white-haired gentleman—I knew who he was; he didn't know me—sitting quietly in a corner, having an earnest conversation with an attractive woman about thirty, and I remember thinking: "There may well be a perfectly reasonable explanation for that, but it's still a tad unseemly."

Mostly, though, I'm frightened. I'm strong, but flirtation, like cocaine, is a powerful drug; you don't want to get hooked. My policy vis-à-vis flirtation is the same as my policy vis-à-vis cocaine, in fact: only once in a while, only a little, and I'll never seek it out. Only if it falls into my lap.

■

So how do you deal with temptation when it does fall into your lap? I'm not sure I know the answer. I'm not sure anyone does. Oscar Wilde said "the best way to get rid of a temptation is to yield to it"—and that was one of the few truly stupid things he ever said. (Later, from prison, he seemed to recant, and dropped a much darker, truer and ultimately much more useful observation, particularly for the would-be adulterer who thinks he might get away with it: "I forgot that every little action of the common day makes or unmakes character, and that therefore what one has done in the secret chamber one has some day to cry aloud on the housetop.")

In married life, you give in to temptation, and the next thing you know you're ringing the doorbell of the house you *used* to live in, asking your wife's new boyfriend (Pam's a babe, she'd have me replaced in a flash) in a timid little voice if you can see your own children for a pre-approved, court-ordered amount of time.

And that's just where it begins. I have an e-mail correspondent, a teacher and a single mother, who goes to war with her ex, an investment banker, every spring over who gets the kids when during the summer. Or, rather, their lawyers go to war (all of which sounds really pricey: don't tell Pam, but apart from everything else I'm too *cheap* to cheat on her). The children become pawns in their exhausting, never-ending battle. Sometimes, when the ex is dropping them off, he just opens the door of his enormous fucking SUV and lets them run to her house. Then he'll toss the car seat out the window, onto her lawn, and peel off down the street.

The car seat is the detail that gets me. The car seat symbolizes everything I don't want to become. I don't want to become a *car-seat tosser*.

Ultimately, I guess the only way to deal with temptation is to grit your teeth and take it. Because that's the lot of man, isn't it, from teenage years to old age: to perpetually have one's hat in one's hand, to be forever frying on the griddle of temptation and sexual frustration? Sophocles said he was looking forward to growing old because he would finally be free of "the fierce and savage master" of lust, but it's not working out like that for me. I seem to be getting hornier every year.

■

I don't know where that little "friendship" with "Vickie" the intern was heading, but I do know this: even if my contract had gone on for several more years, I would never have cheated on Pam. I am calm and firm in that knowledge. I would never have done it because I know I would get caught. In that knowledge, too, I am calm and firm.

Pam's like Sherlock Holmes's smarter sister. She can come home, look around the house, and tell me what I did all day: "Hmm, let's see now, for lunch you made a tuna fish sandwich with green onions, then you went for a walk and got a Blueberry Thrill at Fresh, half price, then you bought a secondhand copy of *Animal Farm* even though you already have one in your office," etc., etc. There's no way I'd try to slip something as duplicitous, subtle and devious as adultery past her.

She'd catch me, and that'd be it: HOT-zzt-L. . . . Ding-dong, "Uh, hi, Frank, I'm here to pick up J.J. and Nick and Adam. Uh, are they ready?" I'm not going out like that.

But it's not just fear of detection and a hot-on-its-heels divorce that keeps me on the straight and narrow. I love her. We started off as soulmates; now twelve years later it's as if we're the same person. I talk to her the way I would speak to myself. In her presence, I think aloud. If I were ever to do something I wasn't proud of—a massage with a "happy ending," say—I'd lose that closeness, that rapport. I'd have to edit everything I said to her.

"So what?" one of my last remaining bachelor friends said when I told him this. "I edit everything I say to chicks."

Which is fine. That's his path. . . . At this point in our marriage, I explained (to his amazement), it's possible for Pam and me to have an argument based on our *thoughts*. I might think something nasty about her and she'll actually *see* the thought cross my mind. And she'll say: "Hey, what's that? What are you thinking?"

"What? Me? Nothing," I'll protest.

"Come on, I know you better than that," she'll say. And she'll grill and cross-examine me until I crack and confess the uncharitable thought.

And we'll have an argument based on that! About a thought I didn't even want to tell her in the first place! Sometimes a bad argument: one thing will lead to another, everything will be called into question, our voices will rise in volume and pitch until, finally, they subside into silence, the silent treatment, and ultimately the dreaded, marital *omerta*. Which can last up to twenty-four hours until the sheer *hauteur* of her *froideur* will cause me to break down and apologize for everything.

"Jesus! Sounds like hell, dude," my bachelor friend said when I told him all this.

But he doesn't understand my way, the Way of Dave. My sire was one of the great hunting hounds of his day; when I was single, I was a naughty puppy; but now every time I'm "out there"—out on the town on a Thursday night, say—I think, "I'd hate to be back out here with all these dogs." It's looks exhausting, apart from everything else. I can concentrate on my work. When we do have sex, it's great, it's intimate, it's so . . . personal (if the kids don't come running in and wreck everything). What is hell to my bachelor friend is, to me, a best-case scenario: to be so completely and thoroughly *known* and still loved.

After twelve years together, I would say Pam's attitude toward me could be roughly summed up as follows: "Dave, I know you down to the ground, I know you better than you know yourself, all your quirks and faults and all your bullshit and all the dumb and annoying stuff you're capable of. But I love you anyway."

Need I add that is exactly how most men need to be loved? Am I going to trade that for a roll in the hay with some intern who's going to turn out to be crazy anyway?

I don't think so.

# Geoff Heinricks

■

## DRUNK AND
## DISTORTEDLY

I have been a winebiber of an almost Old Testament quality at times in my life, a Jameson-sodden guardsman, a foreboding lager-lout, and even—when treasure filled my pockets—an urbane Champagne Charlie. For the most part, as I test the waters of middle age, I have put away the amusements of youth. To retool a snippet by Saul of Tarsus: "When I was a child, I drank as a child, I uneasily stood as a child, I brought up as a child; but when I became a man, I put away childish things."

I can still get righteously, wickedly drunk, though the frequency and intensity no longer flirt with the unknowable boundaries of human capacity as they once did. I drink when I can, when the company encourages or requires it, and though, as a winegrower, I try to have a glass or two of wine most days at dinner, there are vast stretches of time when even that does not happen. And once, while at school, in a silly wager with a friend (which I won), I even laid aside all stiff and nurturing beverages for months, creating a wearied, joyless group of friends and inflicting undeserved financial punishment on many bars in Kingston.

Like most men, I have flushed majestic rivers of beer and other brownish liquids through my system, have opened and poured un-recorded cases of wine with women, and at mixed functions have cluttered up the kitchen to be close to the fridge or the table of bot-tles. Overall my drinking history is a remarkably unremarkable story—though varying in some parts, still a tale almost any man can recount. Yet the details and small ornaments of each man's almost interchangeable experience are the bedrock of literature, the plastic arts, film . . . and, above all, laughter.

Not many women will believe that drinking is tied to cultural achievement and interesting artistic expression, as that sounds like an anxious rationalization. (And to a degree they are right: but then, they should get a load of Miles and Jack in the movie *Sideways*, or better, follow them through Rex Pickett's novel.) My wife and I, when young and unfettered by the charming but dampening bonds of parenthood, often sat and laughed evenings away over a bottle or two of wine. No more. Explaining such behaviour to our twelve-year-old daughter, who already protests and hectors us as if she were Scottie Fitzgerald saddled with F. Scott and Zelda as parents, would be unprofitable.

So if I'm to reveal to blinking, uncomprehending women why men get drunk, I may as well do it for her too, as one day when she reads this she will be enraged, mortified, embarrassed . . . but maybe, ultimately, provided with some understanding.

■

I have to sneak back to my rationalization again, as I see need and opportunity to bolster it. It isn't my theory alone. The bizarre and amusing Hilaire Belloc wrote an essay in 1934 called "Advice to a Young Man in the Matter of Wine," and in it he stated that "Athens, august in the use of wine, is immortal gloriously, but who read or remembers Lacedemon? Where are its songs, its vision, its philosophy, its laughter, or its marbles? There are none known, for they had none. Lacking wine, the Spartans could not create, and their city was transformed into a squalid hamlet, which it remains to this day. So much for the Spartans."

When asked to justify why we drink, this particular answer comes up not only because it is fanciful and convenient, but because it is true.

As a truth, it unfortunately gets abused and is made absurd by a continuing parade of hard-drinking writers, artists, performers (I'd tuck lawyers in there, too) and athletes who believe the greater the cup, the greater the achievement and fame. That, of course, is crap, but a dry society is truly desolate and parched. I know enough about the Muslim world to recognize that many of their most lasting cultural achievements, especially in architecture and poetic language, date to the period when drinking was still a valued part of Muslim life, and that modern, alcohol-free Muslims continue to coast on those ancient wheels to this day.

Although I've unwisely picked a fight in getting to the point (and without a drop in me, too!), I'll immediately explain all, and offer the single reason, the ethereal magic key, as to why we lads get legless. It may come as a surprise to many other drunken men out there, but most of my brothers live unexamined lives, which are desolate and parched in their own way, and consist primarily in a lot of cutting the lawn and driving for milk. We get drunk for one reason, and one reason alone.

Change.

It is a deceptively simple, pure rubric, almost Eastern in its plain, beautiful honesty and craftsmanship. Actually it's more like Douglas Adams's answer to Life, the Universe and Everything—forty-two—in that it requires the ultimate question. And though this all-powerful question has a honed intellectual blade—this question is more of a statement, because a man simply will not ask himself *why* he's singing old rugby songs with his pants down while standing in a planter on University Avenue. He knew the course was plotted in advance, and just followed the pencilled line, using the perceptive equation of— and here you may want to get a notebook and pen: "I want X to change, and so I am potted."

The X, however, is a tricky little variable. The common and worst mistake a woman will make, knowing this male equation, is to inflate the variable to ridiculous, even ominous, proportions. Instead of assuming the X in the subject man's behaviour is something tragic and horrible, or (and this is the silliest and most dangerous assumption) in any way connected to his relationship with her, a woman, on finding her man full to the back teeth with drink, must learn that ninety-nine times out of a hundred the X is something rather trivial.

The variable is easily programmed and given content; it may be a chance meeting between a man and a friend, setting off the thoughts, "Gee, I haven't seen old Bill in ages." Correcting the Absence of Bill then becomes the order of the day. This, unfortunately, may then become a loop, and on realizing how funny Bill is, especially after a few beverages, the man's desire to change Time itself then takes form—and a few more rounds of beer effectively does that, too. Eventually, cabs must be found, and an explanation offered to a woman somewhere. Such an accounting rarely works out because the logic, so pristine to a man, is scoffed at by a woman. So a man learns to keep quiet, take his lumps, and mumble his apologies.

This altering of Time (which also *does* temporarily render all telephones inoperative), this changing of tiny bits of life, makes up the reason for almost all deeper social drinking and even good benders. As a force for good, this changing of the tempo of life helps isolate positive things—laughter and friendship, for the most part—and extend them tremendously .

Occasionally, this force works on sadness or even mourning, which exist in a different continuum of time and especially space, one that eventually snaps smartly back into place. That is a mature(r) man's drunkenness.

Younger men get drunk using a much quicker, result-oriented X variable. For example: "I haven't been laid in months; that has to change; I will go get drunk; something may happen." Or: "I have been doing nothing but essays and exams for three weeks solid; that must change; I will get drunk; something different will happen." With a younger man, the X is much easier to solve. Most common of all is the "Life is pretty boring; that must change; I will get blotto." The danker, darker side to this sort of youthful problem-solving goes to the stereotypical "That girl's sort of okay; that can change for the better, if I am drunk." Usually this is a sub-loop of the "I haven't been laid in months" equation, and can lead, at best, to much art and literature.

Unravelling and understanding a man's sports-related inebriation can be a bit confusing for a woman. This is a hybrid longing: either "I haven't seen X, Y, Z and good old A, B and C in eons; that

must change," etc., looping into temporal distortion; or "The Bru-
ins haven't won the Cup in ages; that has changed; I must get drunk"
rationale, which makes the latter a special line of unique, unused
code. It is not uncommon to see both of these rationales combined,
and of course they are subject to repetition if the subject male still
plays sports—because then equations such as "We never win; that
must change, etc." and "Hey, we won; our lives (for a few moments)
have changed; let's keep that feeling going" cycle up and into view.

Agreed, these are all reasonably thin excuses, at least in such a
vale of tears and misery as our world. But there is a genuine logic to
them, a logic that can be unravelled by a faultlessly patient, con-
summately understanding woman. It still isn't going to take that
ticked-off look from her face, but at least she'll know it's not about
her, or her and him (the lout), or anything remotely to do with
their relationship. I acknowledge a certain airy cellular structure to
what I've unveiled. However, that gauziness reflects merely what
I've always observed: that men will get drunk, more times than not,
for no reason (or at least for simple and trivial reasons). Whereas
women get drunk for a Purpose, and with Purpose.

When a woman is smashed, there is usually a traumatic cause
for it—break-up, divorce, some bad news or hairstyle, a deep subter-
ranean unhappiness. Occasionally women will try to imitate what
they believe is standard male behaviour, and overact and overdrink
in the company of a male stripper or two, though such a performance always plays out like a parody of what they think men are up
to all the time. (We hold women to higher standards, which is only
one reason we love them—for being capable of such heights.) There
is also a frightening quality to this sort of event that makes me
shudder for the poor stripper, a Pentheus substitute waiting to be
torn apart by Agave and the other furious maenads of Dionysus in
Euripides' play *The Bacchae*. Women on a romp are not to be trifled
with. They have an end post in view, and anyone between them and
the goal will become hamburger; they don't need or enjoy romps
for their own sakes.

A very few women do come to the glass using the same sound
equation as men, and these are usually the women that earn the

recognition (and the similar calm reverence) as "a guy's guy" gets. They also earn the undying enmity and scorn of other females. It's all in the approach and execution.

For both men and women, getting hammered for a Purpose is a pardonable and slight offence if it is done once or twice in a lifetime. Frequent repetitions are more worrying. One of the great literary examples of being forgivably stewed is presented by P.G. Wodehouse's newt-fancying Augustus Fink-Nottle, who is advised to tank up in order to get the courage to both become engaged and hand out prizes at Market Snodsbury School.

Although he earns the epithet 'Spink-Bottle' from one disapproving female patrician throughout the rest of the Wodehouse oeuvre, this purposeful (and to a degree accidental) alcoholic performance is not repeated. (Women really trying to understand male drinking should read Wodehouse, which I always cite as a trove of great and richly rewarding examples of responsible but hair-triggered male elbow-bending.)

Even extended periods of sottish antics work themselves out, provided a natural end to them comes. Poor old Mottie (Lord Pershore) from Wodehouse's *My Man Jeeves* is let loose in America from the confines of the English countryside and runs around crying, "I've got about a month of New York, and I mean to store up a few happy memories for the long winter evenings. This is my only chance to collect a past, and I'm going to do it." That's a fair enough reason to get blasted.

But compared to the above, persistent or hidden drunkenness is a problem, even a sickness as society defines it—and not what we're discussing here.

Sometimes the change equation is kidnapped and reprogrammed into an escape clause whose unfortunate grip is impossible, in turn, to loosen.

This is a definite breakdown: the "My life sucks; if I am drunk, it will change" equation, but caught in a severe and constant drinking and drying cycle. And, of course, any of the one-time purposeful picklings can devolve into this tragedy if the changes attempted are too ambitious, and the subject is physically vulnerable to this chemical crutch.

The worst occurrence of this phenomenon affected a greater part of men in the nineteenth century, when the greedy and powerful overturned the world, and, in pulling everyone out of the old rural social order, created a brutal urban, traditionless world of exploited labourers. The result was a pandemic of alcoholism set off by the entrenchment of the "My life sucks; if I am drunk, it will change" time warp. The freshest horror, just as the economic inequities were righted to a degree, was the female harridans of the temperance movement. They beat their tiny fists and hand axes upon the symptom, rather than the cause, though fortunately all the legislative silliness they built up eventually tumbled down. But it has left a deep and abiding distrust between the sexes, and to this day any man stumbling across the transom of home and getting the fish eye suspects he's about to be made a casualty of the neo-temperance movement; and any woman, on meeting same in the hallway, frying pan in hand, naturally begins to think great-grandma and her spinster aunts were onto something pretty inspired a hundred years ago.

I am here to assure you there is no need for such unpleasantness.

Armed—or at least acquainted—with the aforementioned psychological formulae, women may now effectively calculate why we may be sideways or squiffy at any moment; you certainly don't have to understand it, or celebrate it, and we'll still sleep on the couch to keep the snoring down.

# *Philip Preville*

∎

# SHOP LIKE A GIRL

Three years ago, my fiancée and I went out shopping at an upscale Canadian department store. We dressed up for the occasion at her insistence—not in formal evening wear or anything close, but stylishly enough to command the respect of the sales staff. We immediately headed to the women's wear section, and within seconds my fiancée was in that familiar shopper's trance I call The Zone. She was sifting through the racks, mesmerized by swaths of colour and neckline contours. She rubbed items of silk and cashmere between her fingers, letting the textured impulses shoot from her fingertips straight through to the deepest pleasure centres of her brain. I'd lost her. There is no gentle way to pull a woman out of The Zone. All you can do is wait it out.

Trouble is, I'm stuck in the women's wear department. Like most men, I can fake it for a little while, so I do: I go and poke my way through a rack of skirts, pretending to shop for her, but my behaviour quickly becomes awkward. I pull a couple of items off the rack and examine them at arm's length, clinically, the way a lab-coated scientist might hold a beaker of volatile chemicals. I become self-conscious to the point of paralysis, because—the shame is immobilizing—*I have no idea how to evaluate any item of women's wear off the rack*. Maybe this strappy thing I'm holding in the air like a mouse by its tail is really ugly. Maybe I am embarrassing my fiancée by putting my poor taste on display. Maybe I had better stop. So I put it down and do what most men do: tune into the muzak and walk amid the racks, as though surveying them for something particular, while in fact surveying the footwear of the other female customers.

That's when a large, well-dressed black man named Charles—so his name tag says—approaches me and says hello. I consider him a godsend. I am palpably relieved to be in the company of a man amid the women's wear. Am I looking for anything in particular? he asks. No, just along for the ride, I reply. He inquires if I have visited the men's wear department yet, and offers to take me down to the basement—men's wear is always in the basement, men are most at home in caves—to peruse the ties, once my fiancée is finished up here. His invitation strikes me as odd, so I turn the tables on him with some questions of my own. Does he work in men's wear? And if so, what's he doing here in the women's wear section?

It turns out that I am the victim of a sophisticated retail sting operation. Charles works in men's wear, but he keeps a station up in the women's wear department, waiting to spring himself on men just like me. He cites market research to justify his strategy: studies show men and women shop together more often than ever before, but also that most men get antsy if they're stuck in women's wear for more than a few minutes, and would give anything for another guy to come along and break the tension—even a guy who's trying to sell them something.

The market research profile fit me like a bespoke shirt. I appreciated Charles's honesty. But I was not at all happy to learn that I had the words SHOPPING SUCKER written across my forehead in that special ink visible only to customer service associates. I don't like anyone to know anything about me that I don't know myself. After all, I'm a man.

■

I began reading up on the market research to find out what else I was telegraphing, immersing myself in books such as *Why We Buy: The Science of Shopping* by "retail anthropologist" Paco Underhill and *I Want That! How We All Became Shoppers* by Thomas Hine.

And I was mortified to discover that, far from being the complicated man I imagine myself to be, I am completely and utterly predictable in any retail environment.

Polls show that almost three-quarters of all men say they do not enjoy shopping. I am one of these men. What's more, I exhibit all the typical North American male behaviours identified by surveys, videotapes and thousands of hours of in-store observation. Most notably:

- Men don't shop unless they have a need for a particular item, such as a pair of slacks.
- Men don't like to spend anymore time in a store than they absolutely have to. Even walking past the cosmetics counters raises their heart rates. All they want is the slacks.
- Men don't like to talk to sales staff. About anything. Not even to ask, "Where are the slacks?" As Underhill puts it, men shop like they drive.
- If men take a pair of slacks into the change room, those slacks are as good as sold. The only reason men won't buy them is if they really don't fit. They feel obligated to buy them, as though it were the duty borne of intimacy, like the phone call the day after the night before.
- Men panic easily, set off by the inability to find any of the following: the slacks department, the right pair of slacks, the change room, or the price tag on the slacks. In other words, if the predictability of the shopping experience breaks down at any point in the process, we're outta there.
- Nothing drives men to fury more than the unconvincingly fawning chit-chat of sales clerks—especially male sales clerks.

My sense of self-worth plummeted as I read, as each observation about how men shop was revealed to me. I routinely exhibited all of these behaviours. It was as though all those in-store researchers had been following *me* around for my entire adult life, recording my every move. What's more, I'd been observed while *shopping*, during the moments when I am essentially preening, checking myself out, and plotting new strategies to make myself attractive to friends, to colleagues, to women—in other words, when my vanity was on display. "All men are vain," said my fiancée when I told her of my indignation, "but they don't like to admit it and they don't like it pointed out to them." It's true. Shopping is a public activity, but we would prefer that everyone treat it as if it were private: we live every day as though our vanity were a secret. If I'm going to be secretly observed, I'd rather it happen while fucking than shopping.

Perhaps the best way to explain men's relationship to shopping is to compare it to the most male institution of all: the military. Signing up for service is a male shopping utopia, because there is no shopping—just standard issue boots, clothing and gear. We even get the same haircuts so we all look the same, and head-to-toe camouflage so we blend into the background.

But, for me, the most remarkable revelation in the research came from studies of female shopping behaviour, which actually confirm the existence of The Zone. As Underhill writes in his book *Why We Buy*: "Women can go into a kind of reverie when they shop—they become absorbed in the ritual of seeking and comparing, of imagining and envisioning merchandise in use."

For years I had watched enough women enter The Zone, lose themselves in it, and have a blast shopping. When you're in The Zone, sales staff work harder to please you. The Zone lets you play make-believe in full view of strangers, without embarrassment. In The Zone you can linger, look, feel, ask, try, consult, ponder, discuss, complain, act up, try some more and, even after all that, you can still say no and walk away free of guilt.

The conclusion is obvious: shopping in The Zone sure beats the macho modus operandi. So I set out to find The Zone. I decided to teach myself to shop like a girl.

■

No one knows exactly why men and women are such different shoppers, but the most popular theory is the hunter-gatherer hypothesis. In prehistoric times the men set out in unforgiving nature, hunted down a mammoth, killed it swiftly and skilfully, hauled it back and made it last as long as possible. Millions of years later we're still doing the same thing, with slacks. Meanwhile, prehistoric women set out daily seeking, sniffing and testing all sorts of berries, leaves and mushrooms. These responsibilities gradually evolved into a series of manual tasks—growing food, baking bread, preparing preserves, making candles, knitting clothes—then into a series of consumer choices. And those original gathering skills, deeply coded within female genes, are still usefully activated on shopping excursions.

Ergo, learning to shop like a girl will require me to reverse centuries of genetic programming. Must. Stop. Hunting. Mammoths. The transformation is made all the more difficult by the shopping environment itself. Most retail stores cater to women and are designed to help lure them into the comfortable psychic space of The Zone. But men's retailers, knowing that men aren't comfortable shopping in the first place, do everything they can to keep men out of The Zone: their phallocentrically designed shopping experiences are based on the shortest distance between two points. The real reason department stores keep the men's wear in the basement is to keep it easily accessible from underground walkways or from the street—no need to walk through the women's stuff or ask for directions, just a straight line from the street to the slacks and back again. In Canada, some department stores have even taken to building separate street entrances for men, a throwback to the days of sexual segregation, when schools had separate entrances for boys and girls. Because the terrible truth is this: if a man has to walk through an array of cosmetics counters to get to the men's wear, the sight of glass countertops and the scent of mixed perfumes will paralyze him, and he's just as likely to turn around and leave as to try and forge his way through.

There are a few stores that actively encourage men to enter their own trance, so to get acquainted with my gender's version of The Zone I head down to the greatest of them all: Home Depot. Gauge the heft of the cordless drill . . . listen to the clank of the toolbox lid as it closes . . . stroke the paintbrush along the rim of the shelf . . . feel the grain of the pine plank . . . heaven. But there's a reason why

The Zone comes so easily to men in stores like this. The tools we buy and the things we build from the raw materials will last months, if not years. At Home Depot, I'm still hunting mammoths.

The trick is to find that same sense of bliss amidst the twigs and berries, or the shirts and ties. Desperate for help, I actually placed a call to Harry Rosen, the most successful retailer of men's wear in Canadian history. Harry has spent thirty-five years trying to coax men into The Zone; surely he knows the obstacles better than anyone and can tell me how to overcome them. "The traditional way of displaying merchandise intimidates men," explains Harry. "In a rack of shirts, nothing stands out to them. They don't know what goes with what." Harry solved the problem with lifestyle displays: matchable shirts, pants and jackets grouped together in the store, often on a series of mannequins. "That way, men can understand whole wardrobe options at a glance." In other words, Harry arranges his stores based on the assumption that his customers can't find The Zone, and never will. This strikes me as clever, but also as cheating: Garanimals—you know, that mix 'n match line of kids' wear—for grown men.

■

Truth be told, the biggest obstacle standing between The Zone and me is no genetic riddle. It is actually one of my deepest secrets, and I have shared it only with my closest male friends, and it always elicits a me-too response: my wallet talks to me.

From the moment I step into any store and the sales staff say hello, I can feel my billfold sink deeper into my back pocket, clenching my ass. Don't let them get me, it says. Shhh, I reply. Don't make a fuss. These people are here to help us. But I don't believe a word of what I'm saying. I believe what Wallet believes, namely, that these people are here to sell me overpriced goods I don't need. But I tell Wallet lies, only to keep it from making a scene until I can get us both out unscathed.

Time and again, my wallet has thwarted my attempts to enter The Zone. If I found a beautiful shirt and tie combination that looked fabulous on me, my wallet shamed me. If anything was on sale, my wallet insisted it was poor quality. Shoes with rubber soles were too cheap; shoes with leather soles were too costly. Why do men refuse to buy new underwear until their old pairs have worn through? The silent shrieking of their back pocket.

Even wealthy men behave this way, and the reason is not because we're all cheap. The market research has a lot to say about the relationship between men and their money when they shop. In the retail consulting industry, men shopping with their partners or families are commonly called "the wallet." We get a kick out of paying, because our wallets represent another dimension of male vanity: breadwinning, and its accompanying shared conceit that we are the ones in control. We still have a lot of self-esteem tied up in the wallet; we can't help but *be* the wallet. Often, the wallet gets the better of us. Paco Underhill himself, the greatest shopping researcher of all, tells the story of his own revelation in the supermarket on the very day when he learned that, after years of struggling, his research company would be a success. "Standing in the imported goods aisle," he writes in *Why We Buy*, "it suddenly hit me that I could afford to buy anything there I wanted . . . even if it cost maybe *four or five bucks*. I no longer had to sweat over my food budget, I realized, and at that moment I began to cry."

We men like to think we know the value of a hard-earned dollar, and we're instinctively skeptical of anyone who wants to take it from us. To wit: sixty percent of men believe retailers are not as honest as they should be. In the retail consulting industry, sales clerks are also referred to, from the male shopper's perspective, as "the leeches." Which is what they are. They pretend to help by telling you what makes a product useful, or how good the clothes look on you, or what tie goes with what shirt. But as Wallet always says, they're lying.

■

Finally, after months of aborted missions in search of The Zone, success came one sunny weekend afternoon not long ago, when my fiancée and I found a small unisex clothing boutique stocked with the work of local designers. The stuff on the racks was clearly good quality. We both liked what we saw, and everything was on sale—minimum forty percent off. This is it, I thought. Now I'm going to do it right. I don't need to buy anything; I'm simply going to have fun. Shopping.

I sauntered over to the racks of men's wear, gingerly, so as to not draw the wallet's ire. I began feeling textures—wool, silk, cotton—and as I did I slipped sweetly, almost imperceptibly into The Zone. My pupils dilated, my heart rate slowed. I surveyed a rack of solid-coloured shirts like I never had before: slowly, down to the end, then back again. (Gold, orange, lime, lime, blue, grey; grey, blue, lime, lime, orange, gold. Cool.) I even found myself paying attention to the stitching detail on the pants, and as I did, time seemed to stand still.

Then came what was, for me, an unexpected crescendo. I chose the items I liked, at least eight—progress!—and commandeered a change room. Some items I tried once and discarded. Others I tried twice, in varying combinations. I asked the staff for information and opinions. I paraded myself through the store, gauging the reactions of strangers every time I emerged in a new ensemble. And from this extended foraging session came two gems, a pair of pants and a shirt. They were clothes that complemented me, pushed my personality out a bit. On sale too. Great clothes, great deal. Time for the shopping high: time to buy.

That's when my Wallet started acting up with its familiar resistance campaign. You don't need this stuff, it said. This wasn't part of the plan, it cried; you've been in here way too long. I was certain I could keep it at bay this time, but it put up more of a fight than I bargained for. I ground to a halt and slumped down on a small bench a mere two yards from the till. I won't be pulled from The Zone, I thought to myself. I'll just catch my breath a moment and steel my resolve for the final transaction. That's when the sales clerk saw me sitting there with a long look on my face, and made a terrible mistake.

"What's the matter?" she said aloud, so everyone in the store could hear.

"Just thinking it over," I said sheepishly.

"The clothes look great, right?"

I nodded.

"And the price is great, right?"

"   ."

"Well then, *what's your problem*?!"

In my mind's eye, she grew fangs.

"I told you so," said Wallet. "Get out. Now."

■

My fiancée sensed my turmoil and stepped in to save the day. She said more or less the same thing the sales clerk had said, but she whispered it into my ear in dulcet tones. "Those clothes look great on you," she said, knowing she's the only person allowed to say such things, because of course to the rest of the world my vanity is a secret. Then she turned one of my favourite expressions back on me: "Don't think—you'll hurt the team." What she was really saying was, Come back to The Zone. The Zone is a safe place. The Zone is Nice to Wallet. Wearing the clothes is fun. Soon you'll be able to wear them any day you want. She was about to offer to handle the financial transaction for me, but I sucked it up and paid. (The only thing Wallet likes less than buying clothes is having a woman buy them instead.)

I bought the clothes. I can wear them any day I want, though most of the time I wear various combinations of the many other clothes I have bought since then. I am married now. My wife and I are on a budget, one that earmarks a good chunk of money for clothes—a strategy that appeases Wallet (the money was allocated, so shut up back there) and lets my wife spoil herself. And as for me, I am well on my way to becoming a shoe bitch.

*Max Fawcett*

■

# ZEN AND THE ART OF
# HOME RENOVATIONS

Six months ago I embarked upon a spiritual journey, which is un-usual because I am and always have been an atheist. But this voyage didn't involve heading to a Buddhist monastery, casting off my worldly riches (which, sadly, wouldn't amount to much) or getting to know Jesus Christ; instead, I decided to renovate my apartment *by myself*. It was a Zen-like experience—at least if you share the Buddhist belief in Zen as "an assertion that enlightenment can come through meditation and intuition rather than faith." I had no faith upon which to rely. And I leaned more heavily on intuition than I probably should have.

It seemed, at the time, like a fairly innocuous decision. I'd paint a few walls, change a few sockets, and perhaps—if I was feeling ad-venturous—install a light or two. The sum total of my experience as a handyman involved erecting an IKEA bookcase, hammering a few nails, and building a misshapen key holder in my first, and not surprisingly only, high-school shop class. People, well-meaning people, tried to warn me against this course of action. "Hire some professionals," my roommate said. "Don't bother wasting your life," my mother argued. "Don't you have better things to do with your time?" my then girlfriend asked. I couldn't see what the fuss was about. I thought it would be an important exercise in practical self-determination.

The only person without an opinion was my father. In retrospect this should have triggered some alarm bells, as he's rarely without *some* opinion. But this time he was silent. Six months later, I know why. He understood the role that fathers and mothers play in the life of a son: mothers protect their children from potential dangers, while fathers encourage them to move forward, in the hope that they'll a) learn something, and b) survive. I did, and I did, barely.

The previous tenants had painted the apartment a hideous baby blue, electric yellow and what can only be described—though I'm sure the Behr colour chart refers to it as Café au Lait or Damascus Dream—as an inarguably shit brown. The entire apartment was more conducive to bad acid trips than everyday living or relaxation. I began the transformation by painting.

Painting is the handyperson's equivalent of a ski hill's easiest green run. Painting requires only nominal motor skills and sobriety. Picking a colour scheme requires more, so I farmed that decision out to my roommate, who ended up selecting a surprisingly pleasant combination of creams and green tones. But the painting—less a demonstration of skill than an act of endurance—I could handle, and after ten rolls of painter's tape, three brushes, four pots of coffee and a splitting paint-fume-induced headache, I had the job done. This isn't so hard, I thought.

I was wrong. Men, I rediscovered, are inherently susceptible to delusions of grandeur when it comes to their own prowess and talents. Apartment painted, I declared myself the second coming of Bob Vila and embarked upon a far more ambitious project: playing with electricity.

The wretched colour scheme left behind by the previous tenants was outdone, in terms of poor taste, by their choice in lighting. I mean nothing by it when I say the couple was from the former Yugoslavia: it simply appeared they had packed a few lighting fixtures from the local communist mental health facility before immigrating to Canada.

First, I had to find some suitable replacements. I went to my local big box home improvement store—to find the new fixtures. It's no secret men refuse to ask for directions, whether when behind the wheel of a car or the handle of a screwdriver. So it is for most men, as it was for me, at the home renovation store. There are always a number of aggressively helpful-looking people within earshot, but very few men are wise enough—that is to say, lack the vanity—to ask for help. For a man to ask for help is a sin unto itself; to ask for it in a hardware store is blasphemy. It is to admit incompetence and weakness, and most men would rather die horribly in an electrical fire of their own making than ask Mitch in lighting for instructions on how to rewire that faulty switch in the bathroom. Why? Because in our modern domesticated state, we long for our prehistoric undomesticated hunting selves, when we set out each day into an unknowable series of events. Refusing to ask for directions is simply another way of having an adventure with an unforeseeable outcome—no different from watching a football game on TV or taking on a home renovation project.

On the other hand, football is not electrical.

I arrived home with my new lighting fixtures and proceeded to rip the old fixtures out. That was easy. The rest wasn't. Not being monumentally stupid, I took the precaution of flipping the appropriate circuit breakers and cutting off the electricity. Not being smart enough to bother reading the instructions on the new fixtures, I forgot about the residual charges that were still resting, waiting to ground themselves somewhere, in the exposed wires. When I raised the base plate of the first new fixture and tried to pull the wires through, that residual charge grounded itself through my body, jolting me off the chair and onto the ground, knocking me unconscious for a few moments. I think it was only a few moments, but I was unconscious.

It has been said that females learn more effectively through vicarious education, whereas males respond to more direct forms of teaching. Electrical work, it turns out, is the most direct form of teaching I've ever encountered. If you make a mistake, you get immediate and painful feedback. I've never acquired a skill more quickly in my life than I did the ability to work safely with electricity. It was, in a literal sense, like a recreational form of shock therapy. My mistakes were magnified, my failures punished without remorse and my lessons consistent and uncompromising. I had wasted nothing. This is why men like to live rather than talk.

Success, on the other hand, is an exquisite feeling. Only good sex and great food can trigger the release of more endorphins than the male brain gets upon completing a difficult physical task for the first time. It took, in total, almost two days to finish a job I had budgeted half a day for, and I nearly killed myself in the process—but it was done! All men remember how they felt after they first had sex—a combination of pride and power along with an urgent need to spread the good news, possibly at a remove from the woman in question. What I felt at that moment was remarkably similar.

More significantly, the endorphic satisfaction of completing a dangerous and previously unimaginable task proved highly addictive. Rather than lick my wounds and quit—as the cliché so wisely has it—while I was ahead, I interpreted my success as a sign that I was ready for an unthinkable challenge.

The bathroom, another disaster in aesthetics, was my next target. The floor was linoleum turned a brownish yellow by years of wet towels, shower spray and missed targets around the toilet. But—chastened by my electrical handshake—I decided this time around to do some cursory planning. Seeking help in private was tolerable, I decided: it required only a private confession of incompetence.

I began my search for guidance on television, having observed at a distance the explosion of home renovation shows of every conceivable orientation, format and style. Since I don't own a television myself, I crashed the home of my most gadget-inclined friend. He happens to have a set with time-shifting technology, which allows you to watch a given show whenever you want to. I time-shifted my way through Debbie Travis, Mike Holmes and a litany of lesser home improvement gurus, trying to learn from these self-described masters.

What I learned is that it's impossible to learn anything from these shows. They're simply an extension of the reality television franchise, just some more high-voltage voyeurism with which to burn time. Trying to learn how to tile a floor by watching one of these shows is a lot like trying to learn how to build a warp drive by watching an episode of *Star Trek*—a self-defeating exercise and an expenditure, albeit an amusing one, of time. And then there's the fact that it's impossible.

But a man cannot survive adventure if he is diverted by uncertainty. The hell with it, I thought. If I can survive an encounter with electricity I hardly need to worry about a few ceramic tiles and some mortar. I carefully mixed the mortar per the instructions on the bag, spread it on the floor and began placing the tiles. So far, so good, I thought. I stepped outside for a quick—and I do mean quick, since it was minus eighteen degrees outside at the time—cigarette, and returned to find my roommate inspecting the three tiles I had already placed. They looked, he observed, like a horizontal version of the Leaning Tower of Pisa, and he was right. While I had mixed the mortar to correct specifications, I had ignored the instructions regarding the appropriate amount to place on the surface to be tiled. I fished the mortar bag out of the trash and discovered that half an inch of mortar was an ideal thickness. I had spread almost two full inches.

The tiles were bobbing uneasily on this ocean of mortar, angled like buoys in a rough sea. Worse still, the mortar was beginning to harden into concrete. I frantically, and successfully, removed the three tiles from the floor and tossed them in the trash. Realizing that the mortar in my bucket was also hardening, I haphazardly splashed the mortar across the entire floor, and spread it to the recommended half-inch depth. I quickly placed the tiles, one after the other, until the floor was almost entirely covered. Almost. In my haste to correct my previous mistake I forgot to work from the inside out—that is, from the toilet in the centre of the bathroom toward the edges of the room—and instead placed the tiles from the outside in.

I needed to act fast. Remembering that, like many young men, I sometimes struggle with my aim at the toilet, I improvised and filled the no-man's land I had created for myself in the middle of my bathroom with a "landing strip" made of thin white tiles that contrasted nicely—I thought—with the newly laid black tiles. Improvisation, in the world of home renovations, has little to do with the theatrical derivation of the word. There's nothing artistic about it, in fact. Instead, it's male jargon for "I screwed up, but I meant to screw up like this," a nifty way of rationalizing our own incompetence. "What the hell is this white strip?" my roommate, inspecting the completed job, asked. "It's a design feature. Meant to do it," I answered.

By now, of course, my reputation as a handyman par excellence was growing, if only because my ability to make mistakes was matched by my ability to keep those mistakes to myself. I had, over the course of the renovations and the dozens of trips I made to the home improvement store, acquired an impressive collection of tools. Friends began calling me to install their lights, to build their bookshelves, even to hang their pictures. I discovered to my delight that my skill set was a negotiable and profitable commodity. There are very few acts one can commit anymore that begin to subvert and circumvent the monetary economy, but being handy around the house is one of them. I acquired Mötley Crüe concert tickets in exchange for building a flower bed for one friend, and a substantial bar tab in return for the installation of an IKEA halogen light fixture for another.

A few of these friends, I regret to report, were men. I regret it because, despite the post-feminist/metrosexual revolution and the new, improved, more feminized man it has produced (I often count myself as one of them), there are—I am surprised to find myself saying this—few figures in male culture as sad as a man who can't or won't wield a hammer. Deep down, men understand this. The adventure with the unpredictable outcome is often undertaken alone, or in a small pack: there is no one to help you out if you get into trouble. You have to be able to cope. The tool belt, the hammer, the voltmeter: these are the modern vestiges of that ability, or at least of that hope. The calls for help I received from my hapless male friends were always conducted in hushed tones, at the ashamed and muted volume used by someone sharing a deeply embarrassing secret. Not even a biological dependence on little blue pills emasculates a man like being unable to *fix shit*—because at least the little blue pills work.

Having proven myself, the major renovation projects were then finished. I continued to *fix shit* over the next few weeks, making my share of mistakes along the way. I installed a set of mirrored sliding doors in the hallway in order to replace the folding doors that my psychotic black cat, Sid Vicious, ripped to shreds one night. I misplaced the glue-on handle on one side, putting it noticeably higher than the other. Another "design feature," I argued.

I removed a putrid-looking ceramic toilet-paper holder, only to discover that it was mounted in the wall and that removing it left me with a gaping hole that I subsequently covered with drywall. I replaced my rust-stained bathroom sink with no apparent errors, only to wake up the next day to find water spouting up through the seams of my hardwood floors. The entire project, for which I had budgeted what I thought was a wildly pessimistic one thousand dollars, ended up costing three times as much. Even so, I know it's not the last time I'll try to renovate something.

■

The obvious question is, Why? Why, after electrocuting myself, spending three times as much as I had budgeted, inflicting injury and experiencing as much failure as I did success, would I even think of doing this again?

Because, quite simply, I'm a guy. The relaxation of the standards of traditional masculinity—be tough, don't cry, and never express emotions—has been an unquestionably good thing for men, women and those who fall somewhere in between. But men still respond to, and are driven by, thousands of years of male behaviour, biological history and evolutionary clues that shape our instincts. Autarky, the condition of complete independence from other nations, is no longer possible in a globalized world. The last nation to try to achieve it was Nazi Germany, and we all know how that turned out. But home renovations are, for men, a step closer to *personal autarky*, a condition that satisfies our biological need (*and* responsibility) to provide shelter and safety for ourselves and our loved ones—without their help, if need be. If there's a broken pipe, a leak in the roof or a new bookshelf to be built, we can do it our-selves. For guys, in spite of modern comforts and technological de-velopments, not to mention the often significant measure of physical risk, this need to achieve autarky in our homes is a biolog-ical calling that we must heed.

So the next time your son, brother, husband, boyfriend or crazy uncle tries to fix something that's clearly beyond his limited expert-ise, cut him some slack. It is, for him—and I mean this from the bottom of my genes—a form of self-expression no less significant than an artist's painting or a musician's score, a call of the wild that he must answer. Just make sure you have plenty of Band-Aids and hydrogen peroxide on hand and 911 on the speed dial.

SOUL

# Don Gillmor

■

## A ROOM
## OF ONE'S OWN

My office is the third floor of my Toronto house. It has beautiful light; in winter when the sun is low, it comes in the sliding glass door that dominates the south wall and spreads across the floor. To the north, a picture window looks down onto placid neighbours and a bucolic street where tradesmen and police routinely pull over and sleep in their cars. I tore out the dull grey carpeting, painted the brown walls white, and ripped out the unused deck that blocked my light and housed a family of raccoons. I rented a hundred-pound floor sander and sanded and varnished the pine floors and found matching wood to replace damaged boards. I built shelves and installed cool lighting, a stereo and a leather reading chair. My wife would routinely come up, sit on the stairs like Natalie Wood in *West Side Story*, and sigh. "You have a great office," she'd say covetously. She'd linger. I'd stare at the computer.

It is a great office, but it has tragic flaws, chiefly the lack of a door. The acoustical configuration of the house is such that every sound from two floors down is magnified as it funnels upward. My wife's voice arrives at a concert pitch. When she is talking to her sister on the phone, I can occasionally hear both sides of the conversation. But it isn't just the intruding sound, it's the psychological burden of knowing I can't shut out the world. The space is not hermetic, but part of a larger whole. As a result I began to colonize the rest of the house, to see it as an extension of my office. I was nineteenth century England, and the other rooms were the pink countries that used to appear with such certitude on every school map.

This was fine when everyone was out of the house, my children at school, my wife at work. But she coveted not just my office: she coveted my freelance life. Her workplace was fraught with politics, she said, as well as outrageous parking fees, and she didn't have enough smart outfits. She looked at my world, my daily, unshaven walk up two flights of stairs, sipping espresso, not answering the phone after looking at call display, listening to Satie, staring out the window.

Tragically, she decided to freelance, to work on the family computer in an ersatz office between the living and dining rooms.

She was on the phone a lot and her voice and laugh invaded every hour. Satie was useless; I looked to Mahler, to Beethoven, to Hendrix. But it wasn't just the noise. In her quietest moments, I still resented her presence. She resented my resentment. My defence was only partly pragmatic. While it was certainly much more difficult to work, to concentrate, to goof off, there was something else, a larger, darker need for solitude that went beyond work. It was visceral, and difficult to explain. I tried to formulate an argument for masculine solitude as biological determinism, and she dismissed it as ridiculous. Professionally, she had been weaned in cubicles, a Dilbert existence where a dozen people were on the phone within hearing distance, chasing down stories, initiating divorce proceedings, threatening, flirting, weeping. Lives were on display. I had seen the cubicle life. Briefly, I had a cubicle, but never worked there, because it was impossible. I listened to other people's phone calls and was careful never to make any myself. When I actually had to produce something, I took a cab home to my office.

My wife couldn't grasp the professional argument, let alone the poorly articulated case that there was something innate, something larger at stake, that a clearly demarcated lair was fundamental to my happiness. My office had now become an extension of the house: I was one of the pink countries, having unfamiliar customs foisted upon me. I didn't need democracy shoved down my throat. It became an issue, then a dangerous gulf that eventually we both chose to ignore.

■

A door would have been the obvious solution, though an architecturally awkward one, and the construction would have been a blight in the office, and the door would have blocked off badly needed borrowed light that came in from the third floor. A better solution was an outside office, which had certain attractions. For one, staying at home is a passive act, and it means herding everyone out the door every morning, a frustrating experience that can go on for more than an hour. But leaving is active, and on those mornings when I wasn't taking the kids to school, I could simply grab my hat and say I had to be in early at the office. I'd pick up a coffee at the Starbucks, a copy of the *Times*, I'd nod knowingly to other men heading to their offices. I could work late, with all the wicked connotations that phrase holds. I'd be free. Even better, all the housework that inevitably falls to whomever is at home—the dishes, grocery buying, the laundry, parging the basement walls—would no longer be my jurisdiction. Doing these things wasn't the problem, it was the fact that they went unwitnessed, the work subsequently unrecognized (O housewives, rally around my cry). Now I was gloriously exempt.

I found an office in George Brown House, an elegant historic mansion that once belonged to the *Globe*'s irascible founder and had oddly affordable space. I took a small office there, a square unadorned room where the single window was situated too high up the wall to look out of, a monk's cell with no distractions. I moved minimal equipment into the space: table, chair, dictionary, a phone and a lamp. Great things would be accomplished.

But it was across town. It meant a commute. It meant getting dressed. I still hadn't disassembled my home office, and on rainy days, or humid days, or when it snowed or there was a parade, or when I was flu-ish, or I got a late start, I didn't go to my new office. Eventually, I told a friend he could use it, and eventually he, a famously unreliable man, came to inhabit it. "What if he burns down the building?" my wife asked. "A *heritage* building. And the lease is in your name. And tell him I want my goddamn chair back." I signed over the space, with great misgivings, and he in turn gave it to another writer, who works there diligently I'm told by a mutual friend. Was the door open? Did you actually see him writing? He may have been sleeping, or masturbating, two strong statistical possibilities. Even Hemingway, the twentieth century literary action figure, admitted to doing both on a regular basis.

Proximity, I learned, was an issue. The second outside office was a twenty-minute walk, an eight-minute cycle away. It was secluded, overlooking a ravine, almost pastoral, and it was affordable, in the way things are affordable when you've convinced yourself they're a necessity rather than a luxury. The only other tenant in the building was a psychiatrist. It was a short walk to five cafés, two bookstores, two legendary pubs and a really good restaurant. You could barely imagine an office this ideal. Three weeks into my tenure, the landlady called me at home in the evening, asking for the rent five days early.

"I wonder if you could pay it today. If you could bring a cheque around."

I said I couldn't bring it that night, but I'd have it for her the following week, when it was due.

"It's just that I'm going to the bank tomorrow. I mean, if I have to make another trip . . ."

The conversation began to take on the familiar illogic of breaking up with my Grade Twelve girlfriend over the phone, a minor detail escalating into nuclear winter over the course of fifteen minutes.

"I'll bring it next week."

Teenaged silence. "First my father's illness. And now this . . ."

"You know, I don't think the two are related."

"*Who's* saying they're related. *I'm* not saying . . ."

The cheque that isn't due isn't making your father sick, *you're* making him sick. This last thought, which would have been uttered, or possibly yelled, into the phone at my Grade Twelve girlfriend, remained unspoken. This is the wisdom that comes to a man in his maturity.

"Maybe I should just find a new *tenant*."

"Maybe I should find a new *office*."

"Fine."

"Fine."

Click. So, no prom date.

■

The fathers of many of my childhood friends were aloof, some to the point of coma, middle-aged men who, while not defeated, had passed the apex of their life's trajectory, whose final promotion had happened or failed to happen, whose days now had the feature-less quality of a sled dog's. They withdrew into ham radios, or alcohol, or affairs, and my memory of them, certainly exaggerated, is of Edvard-Munchian figures lurking in the shadows. But they had all carved out a space, a place apart. I remember a pristine study with leather-bound copies of *The Decline and Fall of the Roman Empire* and a blond oak desk unblemished by activity. Some had basement workrooms, some had only a chair, a La-Z-Boy, into which they re-treated behind newspapers. They all had somewhere to withdraw. The need for withdrawal is something resembling a gene, I suspect, that lurks in most men.

I saw it in my neighbour who sat on his porch for the last decade of his life, slowly, publicly dying of lung disease. In one of our daily skittish conversations, he told me that he hadn't had any real friends since he was fifty. The bowling league, tavern visits and poker games had all quietly withered, as everyone withdrew. For twenty years he had been isolated with his incredibly nutty, darkly pessimistic Irish wife, who almost never came out of the house, hence his porch-sitting. This, I realized with time, was *his* office. He gave me an electric hedge clipper, a gift that pretty much ensured that I would cut our mutual hedge and all the rest of his hedges while I was at it, so he wouldn't be entirely cut off, so he could at least see a small piece of the world that he wasn't connected to. His Beckettian funeral, which featured a handful of mourners and a priest who hadn't met him, depressed the hell out of me. Most of the people were there out of obligation, and I was reminded that the view from our offices was almost identical.

Why is solitude a necessity? What do we do with it? Writers need a place in which to invent stories, but also to invent themselves. It is this need for self-invention, or at least revision, I think, that is behind the need for masculine solitude as well. I once interviewed the author Martin Amis, who said he thought women were more provident than men, that they took a pragmatic view of the future, while men held to fantasy. He suggested that Margaret Thatcher, with her blithe environmental policies and disregard for the planet's well-being, would eventually be revealed as a man. Like other men—professors, writers, day labourers—she wasn't interested in the burdensome realities that would come to pass only too soon; she was busy thinking about what to do with the cash prize that comes with the Nobel. The masculine habit of reimagining our lives extends far past adolescence. We can tinker with our persona well into middle age, but it helps to be alone.

There is something more prosaic and weaselly about solitude of course. David Mamet wrote that he used his writing cabin as a way to get out of things, telling family or visitors he had to work. The only time he didn't use it as an excuse was when he actually had to work. Once in the cabin, he would play darts, smoke cigars, check the paper supply, stare out the window. The need to disengage recurs often in the limited literature on offices (just as male disengagement is a staple of women's magazines). Inaccessible cabins, as actual offices or objects of fantasy, are a common theme. They tend to be spartan, without much material comfort, a perfect illustration of the Calvinist conflict: I will be alone but I will be uncomfortable.

In her 1929 book, *A Room of One's Own*, a book so seminal that the title has been adopted by half the feminist bookstores, magazines and chat rooms on the continent, Virginia Woolf wrote that "a woman must have money and a room of her own if she is going to write." Her essay explored the dominance of male scholarship and literature. Women, she argued, lacked the opportunity, and the "room of one's own" was both metaphorical and literal. There were other conditions that needed to be in place, but at the root there was that space. There was the need to disengage from the roles that we find ourselves in, and to engage in the selfish act of writing. For a man, the act of being is equally selfish, equally solitary.

Which is why what constitutes an office is so eminently flexible. Thomas Wolfe wrote standing up, with the top of a refrigerator as his desk. Erskine Caldwell wrote on ferry boats that ran at night between Boston and New York, lulled by the waves and insulated by the featureless dark. Mark Twain, Truman Capote and Paul Bowles all wrote in bed. Blaise Cendrars said, "Like Saint Jerome, a writer should work in his cell. Turn the back." Allen Ginsberg could write poems anywhere: planes, subways, cafés, walking along 34th Street. Norman Mailer likes a room with a view, "preferably a long view. I dislike looking out at gardens." William Faulkner was once the landlord of a brothel, which he felt was the perfect milieu to work in. It was quiet in the mornings, it offered drama in the evenings and the bootleggers all called him "sir." "The only environment the artist needs," he wrote, "is whatever peace, whatever solitude, and whatever pleasure he can get at not too high a cost."

■

So I'm back in my home office. My wife is downstairs. There is a kind of pissing match that goes on. I tell her of a friend, a writer who lives alone at the end of a dead-end street in a house that borders a park, who routinely rents a house in another city to be free of distractions. "What about J.K. Rowling?" comes the counter punch. "She wrote *Harry Potter* in a café with a baby attached to her." I saw the café she wrote in. It was in a documentary on her fabled success. It was a great café, huge and unpopulated. I should be so lucky.

There are new distractions. A clinically depressed Russian cleaning lady comes on Wednesdays, bringing an outlook so bleak that the entire house darkens for three hours. I tell her not to bother cleaning my office but she comes up anyway, standing behind me with her Buster Keaton face, breathing loudly until I move. But there are new pleasures too. My ten-year-old daughter moved her electronic piano up to my office, where it sits in the window.

Occasionally she comes up to practise, the sun shining on her hair, the peaceful, hesitant notes of *Au Claire de la Lune* filling the room.

The perfect office is, of course, a trap. What excuse would be left then? Much of the literature I prize has to do with singular male protagonists who are in an entertaining descent. Fitzgerald, Richard Ford, Joseph Heller's *Something Happened*, Guy Vanderhaeghe's *My Present Age*, most of Thomas McGuane's oeuvre. Paul Auster, Martin Amis, Julian Barnes, John Cheever have all contributed. There is a vast body of work that describes the diminishing worlds of men, most of it written by men in small rooms, tracing their trajectories, both real and imagined.

# Chris Koentges

■

# ON WINGS

## THATCHED OF

### MOUSTACHE

+ will you get a dog?
– you're allergic to dogs.
+ i think they make allergy-free dogs now.
– oh.

We have travelled far. Probably we have come all this way through Greece and Cyprus and Istanbul merely to say what we could not that starry white night before Christmas when we were relegated to the non-smoking fishbowl section at Hooters restaurant in the industrial end of Calgary just after my mom/his wife died following eight months inside what they called the "Yellow Wheat Room" on the second floor of The Salvation Army's Agapé Hospice along the northwest corner of Riley Park. Which is a mouthful, I know. My memory of the time is clogged with these oddly mixed mouthfuls. My hope is that this account will keep the flavours straight when I am his age, and am thrown for such a loop.

It was simpler in the beginning, like your own memory, maybe too hell bent on deciding which of them would have to go first. Which has nothing to do with whom you love more—only who has to die first. My mind had trouble with this selection. It would not allow itself to picture them apart. Over and over it would say *fuck it*, they will die together at exactly the same moment of premature old age—perhaps with your parents (all our parents, actually)—just as the bomb goes off between the tusks of Salvador Dalí elephants jostling for position in the locked trunk of a Trans-Am that is skidding through the icy cargo hold of a 747 with broken wings, piloted to the bottom of a hurricane by ninjas whom I—whom *we*—would spend the rest of eternity tracking down.

Always they returned, though.

And always I thanked God when they did. But always I was baffled that they had. That the universe kept misfiring gave me hope that the path of life had not already been pre-carved by Him and His filthy head ninja.

The mind thus unhinged began exploring the which-one-first question in more specific terms. Terribly specific terms. Boyishly specific terms. Dad was a better provider, mom would be capable of soldiering on. He hit sharp ground balls at me, she stuck my hands in raw ground beef and said my little chef. He would X, but she might Y, him and her, on and on, and never did one actually separate in my mind from the other. Only once. As we drove home from school in her orange Chevette in one of those full blown mom/son moments, before the son is too self-conscious and ironic. We're laughing so hard about something, and I love her so much, turning off 24th onto Crowchild Trail, with McMahon Stadium in the rear view mirror, a Friday afternoon in spring, a tumour growing in the frontal temporal lobe of her brain that had not being growing before we turned. Slowly. Slowly—

For years, slowly. Biding its time, gaining pace until twenty years from the turn, it created such immense pressure in her brain that the normal electricity which allows cells to communicate became too erratic and her body seized violently, convulsing, breaking, a neurosurgeon drilling through her dark hair, then the olive flesh beneath, the skull, into the left lobe, my dad's mind bartering with God's, trading away the proverbial farm, just to get her through this one craniotomy. And the next. And the next after. And all the treatments and experiments, what-nows and what-ifs that followed. He stopped drinking (even though he never really did in the first place), he sponsored starving kids in Mali, he stopped caring about the Flames and Stampeders, he pretended to like vegetables—just give us this, his mind said. Neither he nor I would hope for anything but this.

He was careful and conscientious, and the three-month prognosis was pushed back and back. But at some point in those extra years he finagled, it became impossible to keep the promises straight, and with one innocent misstep on some unseen crack, the miracle of her survival—

Cancer does work this way. Don't believe differently.

So in the glow of tinsel and Nina Simone, three years after the bargaining began, I stroked her left arm, whispering Frost and the psalms and Italo Calvino in her ear, while he held her right. She drew a good breath after some hours of crooked ones, turned her head slightly towards him, opened her eyes, smiled, and never drew another.

The look, frozen for an instant and then in our psyches forever, said my sweet dear, you have done more for me than any other man would be capable of. I have put you through—

Go live now.

We were even with God. Or maybe it was that God now wanted us to get even.

■

+ you like olives now.
– yes.
+ and red onions.
– yes.
+ and cucumber.
– yes.
+ you didn't like these things last year.
– well.
+ she liked these things, you ATE them, but didn't like them.
– no.
+ i wonder what that means.

We are between Rhodes and Damascus, four months later. It is spring. We have purged guilt in a way that eases it deeper into our bones. He has treated our journey with reverence, and I with bemusement because I am too ironic to believe in sacred journeys, just as I am too ironic to talk sacredly with my dad. Irony is the great overlooked filial affliction. It is maybe at the heart of all a young man's misdealings with the modern world. It is the ADD of 2005.

Going to Hooters, that was ironic. All the smokers whose moms and wives hadn't just died, dudes who don't dick up and get wasted at a real peeler bar, or even a bikini bar, glared at us, alone in the fishbowl. We oozed something wounded, tentative, we appeared to have vital matters to discuss. Nobody who has something important to discuss goes to Hooters.

My inheritance—ironic. One half of one fifth of three quarters of one other fifth of her father's ancestral land in a small village on a remote island located between the Ionian and Aegean seas. She always dreamed of visiting, but had never laid eyes upon it. This crumbling stone peasant hovel being appropriated by a distant cousin named Demetrius, at the same time squatted in by an Albanian deserter named Armando. On a January afternoon that was the equivalent of frozen cud a name, "Rob Kerr," materialized in my Yahoo Mail inbox. I had been aimlessly clicking "check mail" several times a minute for several days in a row then, trying to gnaw the cud back into flavour. I knew this name. Rob Kerr. This was my best friend from age four until about thirteen, in fact he could very well have been in the orange Chevette the day—

Rob's message—also ironic. We had not spoken in a decade. He was sorry to hear the news. He was sorry we had lost touch. "If you happen to be in Cyprus in June," he PSed, "you should come to my wedding."

*As it so happens,* I wrote back to Rob, *I will be in Cyprus in June.* I took a deep breath, then tried to bite down hard on all the irony. Carefully, I proposed a journey to my dad. We would visit her ancestral island, we would go to my old friend's wedding. For good measure, we would knock off Istanbul too. We would do it with backpacks. We would smoke a water pipe. Climb remote gorges.

Sleep on buses and not shave. Move backward and forward through time. Just like the vague civilizations that send their dads and sons away, and don't let them back until they've figured out how to proceed without their women.

The plan concerned my dad, a meticulous planner, who had grown conservative in middle age. To my surprise, however—and my own deep trepidation—Istanbul clinched it for him. He vetoed nothing. I overheard him talking excitedly with a friend on the phone.

– No, I don't know where we'll stay.
– No, I bought a BACKPACK.
– No, I don't know how to "work it."
– No—YES, there ARE fifteen million people in Istanbul.
– That's right, NO plan.
– I KNOW I always have a plan.

She would have scrunched her brow, trying to read one of us (me) for signs of a put on. She would have said, "What do you mean you went to Hooters to talk about my funeral?" And if I didn't crack up giggling, I would have scrunched my face up like hers and replied, "Actually, we talked about the Flames' new backup goalie," Miikka-something-or-rather—even then we had near-biblical trust in their new coach, Darryl Sutter. Actually, she would have loved going to Hooters. It would have been—

She craved experiences.

After the neuro-oncologist told her there was nothing left to do, I remember that she sighed a couple of times, took us for chai at her favourite café The Double Mo (because brandy would have interfered with the steroids and anti-seizure meds), then she went home, phoned the university and signed up for Level I Spanish. Because there is always something left to do.

Before she got sick, he'd been abruptly pushed out of his job at the university by some second-rate figurehead. He had not known what to do with the rest of his life; her illness gave him the proverbial grand and noble mission, it gave him a million details to take care of, it put his mid-life decision of what now on hold. I am over-conscious to the point of blissful detachment—nothing, as you already know, is not an ironic gag served up by the universe for my amusement—but his over-consciousness works inward. They'd had their retirement all plotted, a complex set of road trips, long walks in the hills, hours in the garden. Once, he confided to my sister that there would be nothing left to live for once she was—

I wanted to know if he would remarry—or rather, would he consider another lady. Would he give her nighties to Interfaith? Would he get involved in local politics now? Had we found Jesus in all this?

+ you cried when Pal died.
– yes.
+ i laughed at you.
– oh.
+ i didn't know dads cried then.

I got drunk alone in a lounge off 6th Street drawing matrices with his strengths and weaknesses. He was in his fifties. I believed he could actually blossom from this. With enough spin, this could be an opportunity. He'd been given a chance at life as an individual rather than part of a couple. I'd pitch him these opportunities, awkwardly, at Knossos, at Ephesus, in the Blue Mosque. We need to establish some new protocols! I even bought a blue notebook I named "notes for the conversation," but never put anything in it other than "need to have a conversation." We had two months to have the conversation, there was no hurry. I saved the final version of the matrix on my PowerBook, but never printed it.

Plan for Dad Matrix

+ take courses at the university
+ volunteer
+ run for council
+ co-write gritty pilot about hospices for HBO

There are some things about this matrix. It bites, yes. And technically, no, it is maybe not a real matrix. And also the term "dad" is used instead of "father." In my presence she only referred to him as dad. Never Barry, never father. The difference between the words is the difference between died and passed away. Passing away is accidentally letting out flatulence until you've deflated to nothing. She died. He was my dad.

■

We arrived in Athens, hoping to track down a film director I had to interview for a documentary about the Cyprus problem, a project I'd undertaken at the last minute in order to take pressure off the conversation. The director was a wild spirit. After our first rounds of ouzo, he infused in us the sense that we had come to the right place. We hopped between tavernas, feasting and drinking from tin ewers. In the terminal years, there was a constant buzz. Our hearts stopped in the moments before each MRI result, our minds never stopped spinning at the gravity. We made big complicated last meals of cassoulet and timpano, we went to the mountains, we listened to Miles Davis. We put her through all the final requests and experiences one should check off before they go. The intensity of flavour spilled out of our mouths, down our chins. And with that urgency gone, our own had evaporated. But now feral street dogs were howling at the foot of the Acropolis, and the director was howling, and my dad was beaming, we hadn't slept in a couple of days of flights and trains and buses, and in a couple of hours we'd be hurtling down the peninsula, then on a rickety boat towards the island. Life was suddenly so distracting, there was so much to taste, that you couldn't stand to miss even one moment with something so insignificant as sleep.

+ she would have loved this place.
– oh god—

Where she would come out and demand to know what was up, he sparred. He spoke through fungos and jump shots, half-nelsons on the rumpus-room floor. Always we tried to elude each other to make our points. In these moves, pure acts stripped of language, we communicated what was necessary. He monitored how I was growing based on the distance I could hit a ball. He gauged my mental progress by my capacity to find open ice and analyze Stampeders drives. He made sure I wasn't a drug addict with his special spin Ping-Pong serve. We still fake jab at one another when there is an important point to make, and even now, my tendency is to karate chop the neck of a girl I love when I really mean to whisper the words in her ear. Because the words are too banal for me. Our language of elusion, on the other hand, is perfect; nothing could suit my irony better.

+ we did all we could.
– i want to feel guilty about this.
+ so do i.
– you don't show it.
+ i'm forgetting that i am guilty.
– how?
+ i am distracting myself with work and wandering and women and wine and other "withs" until I die.

The Albanian is adrift, alone and sad in my grandfather's house, his woman living in poverty outside Tiranë. Demetrius is too sick to see us. Suddenly the land is not so important. Finding small, remote unlocked stone churches teetering at the edges of cliffs is important. We light candles for whoever might need a candle lit for them that day, we light candles for her. We sit beside each other. Silently. Imagining what the other is thinking. Wherever we go, people are adrift. The whole world has been cut loose from itself. She had to die first, I decided in the orange Chevette, because he would need to realize that the world was adrift. She had already understood it.

+ do you want to do some spanish classes with me?
– i don't have the capacity for that sort of thing.

+ there are equivalent things.

—

The great Reverend Victor Kim conducted her service, he addressed each of us—dad, sister, me—separately from the pulpit. At my turn, he used Hemingway. The world breaks everyone, Reverend Kim quoted, and afterwards many are strong at the broken places. But those that will not break it kills. It kills the very good and the very gentle and the very brave impartially. If you are none of these you can be sure that it will kill you too but there will be no special hurry. It is a perfect reference. But I am far too ironic for Hemingway.

On the island we chill out with a composer named Panayotis, a thoughtful man, a wise man, perhaps a bonafide wise man, midway between my dad and me in age. We drink mountain tea one crisp afternoon in a white and blue cube-shaped stone house he has converted to a studio on the plain outside a derelict village, the wind howling outside, pounding through the soundproofed walls. Panayotis has been thinking about my dad for a while. He is sad. "Live a long time," he eventually says, his sadness turning to a smile. "So you can remember." My dad tilts his neck. The way he does when he is accepting a new idea.

■

With enough time, perpetual stubble can be classified as a beard. I have a beard because I think shaving is a waste of time. My dad has a moustache because he won a bet in the 1960s—or else he is still trying to win the bet (I think he has forgotten which). Our faces look the way they look by such defaults. Moustaches and beards have served us well on this trip, however. We make friends easily with other moustachioed and bearded men. Kurdish men, Cretan men, Cypriot men in small villages and Iraqi men in Nicosia, they are all curious about these two Canadian men with facial hair. Are we friends? Are we something more sinister? Business associates? We must be business associates—business associates masquerading as American spies? (We could be American spies.) Nobody believes he is my dad. They think that would be too good to be true, a dad and son out in the world. When I agree that it is very good, and also insist it is true, they still do not believe. Where are your women? They are dead. The men get sad. They understand our trip. I ask: *do you have something similar in your culture*—going away in order to talk about it—*maybe in ancient times?* They don't answer, not exactly.

The unspoken terms of our language are different from those of these hairy men—we like to skip rocks across the Bosphorus, or if there is no water we kick them down the road, or throw them at trees or traffic signs, or off cliffs (a large part of our travel experience is about throwing rocks). Our subtext is more subtle even than the evolved spikes and dips in the inflections of these men. The women are more direct, they ask for every little detail about how we took care of her until the end, they say *oyee oyee oyee*—

+ what now?
– i'm not sure.
+ you need a plan.
– why?
+ you need to do something with your life.
– why?
+ WHY? listen, who's the fucking father here.
– i'll clean her stuff out of the house.
+ that's a good step—then what?
– i haven't decided.
+ will you find another woman?
–
+ i'd be ok with that. unless you bring home some skank.
– i wouldn't—
+ not this soon.
– so.
+

Ari is telling me about the referendum. He is a rare Greek Cypriot "yes" on Kofi Anan's reunification plan. I ask him how he could be a yes when the plan is fucking Greek Cypriots up the ass. He tells me that he has decided to stop saying no to the universe. He will only say yes now. *Is it working for you?* "It is working better than you would think." Nicosia is littered with characters like Ari—schemers and oddballs swathed in subtext, caught between worlds. We belong here right now. By day, working on the documentary, I interview terrorists, soldiers, refugees, unrecognized presidents of unrecognized territories. At night, my dad and I meet up in our room at Tony's B&B (which also rents by the hour). He tells me about his own interviews with local characters. I arrive dusty and thirsty. "I hope that your business goes well today," Assad, who runs Tony's, always says to me on the way up the stairs. I ask Assad about his new Russian girlfriend, we practise Iraqi salutes, and then Assad, who was once shot in the head and spent years on the run after Saddam killed his brother, says, "Your friend is a very good man."

I'm suddenly struck by a conversation, which I relate to Assad. It's one of those hypothetical what-the-wedding-will-look-like conversations that increase in frequency right before you break up when your mom is dying. The girl asks who my best man will be. I think for a long time and say that it will be my dad. I look at my watch. I tell Assad: "In a month, she is marrying a different man."

+
– can i ask you something?
+ anything.
– what happened with x?
+ we wanted different things.
– and y?
+ what we expected out of life—it was just different.
– and the new one?
+ she's kind of fucked up actually, she wants some of the same things.
– which is nothing?
+ also everything.
– how will it last?
+ maybe lasting isn't the point.

– what is the point for you?
+ i don't know if there has to be a point.
– i have to stop falling for them.
+ my girlfriends?
– ha.
+ no you don't.
–


She was curious about my life, and I was private. I had become something different to both of them. Like all sons, I had a secret second life beyond that of being their child. I wrote for a living, I wandered, I knew some ways of the world that they did not. Where did that come from? When she was in the hospice, the tumour pressed into a place that took away her speech, I taunted her. I said: "You think you will find the truth about me, but you will not. Right now I am getting all the wickedness out of my system. When you come back to spy on me with your new omniscient seraphic view, you will only see me reading a bible and drinking tea and arranging tulips." I had been feeding her some mango, and she spat it out her mouth in a gust of laughter. "Your spirit will not be able to follow me into the Congo." *Oh yes it will*, her eyes glowed. And I pretended to go damn. But in truth, I liked the idea. I wouldn't have to hide anymore.


+
– matt dunigan is the last straw.
+ you're cancelling your tickets? you and she had those tickets for
   years.
– the new owners have ruined this franchise, there are bleak years
   ahead.
+ i think love is the most pure as hope of future dwindles.
– how can you say that?
+ i never loved life more than those moments before that last
   breath.
–

We are talking some good shit with a civil engineering student, who would actually prefer to be a hospitality student. His English is good, he knows a lot of good things to do in Istanbul. *You'd be good at hospitality*, we say. But a swarthy man is whispering to my dad, and soon we are dragged into the Blue Mosque. The man keeps insisting that he is a good friend of ours. *Why are you insisting?* "I am telling you about the mosque. I want to have apple tea with you and your friend."

+ who is this dude?
– i don't know.
+ are we done talking to the student?
–

But we are in the Blue Mosque. I whisper to the man: *you're going to some crazy lengths to sell us a carpet*. "You are offending me," he replies. *We do not find carpets interesting*. "This is no way to talk to a friend!" *The civil engineering student is our friend*. The man glares. For five minutes, he glares. Maybe he is giving me a brain tumour with this glare. We are quiet for ten more minutes, absorbing the magnificence, calming down, getting into the silence. But the man is staring at his watch in an obvious manner. He blurts: "How do you know your friend doesn't want to buy a carpet?" *Carpet dude! You are ruining our Blue Mosque experience—we only want to spend the morning sitting beside each other in silence*. "Do not talk for him!" Now I hiss at the wretched man: *He doesn't want to buy a carpet!* And now I feel his breath; "STOP ANSWERING, he has a mind, he wants a carpet!"

The accusation is packed with such vitriol, with such absolute certainty that I question what my dad does want. Then I wonder if this man is not actually a wise man who can see things that we have become too close to see in the last two months. Maybe there is a mistake in the way we have recalibrated the authority between dad and son. I question, in that moment, everything that my dad might want and need in his new life. Maybe he needs a carpet.

+
– it will be my last car.
+ shut up.
– what do i have to live for?
+ what does anybody have to live for?
– YOU have work. YOU have the new girl. i don't know if i have
    enough withs to distract myself for a long life.

We are in Istanbul walking around in the middle of the night, lost
on an eerie back street, thinking that, well, it's not that big a place.
The world's not that big, really. It's a shame she didn't get to—
    Oh—
    We are in the wretched man's shop. Looking at carpets. Do we
agree that his carpets are the nicest in town? "To tell you the truth,"
my dad says to the man, "they are a little bit boring for me." Apple
tea rushes up my nose as I try to contain my glee. My dad does not
want a carpet after all. In these last weeks, we have collected pebbles
from her father's land, shells from ancient sites; we've plucked old
tiles out of crusty streets, plain dirt from beneath olive trees. We are
discussing a memorial. The sleeves of the shirts we are wearing today,
all this stuff will become material for the memorial. Wherever we
go from now on we will bring such material back. We will stack it in
her garden like an Inukshuk.

+
– how will i tell people about this trip?
+ what do you mean?
– there's so much, i don't know how to begin.
+ you will need a good listener.

It is our last day in Istanbul. Time is wasting! We need to be all over
the city right now, all over Byzantium and Constantinople, all
over existence, planting her everywhere. I throw rocks at a wall im-
patiently. I storm up to the room to say Istanbul is waiting. But he
is looking out the window, at Asia on the other side of the Bosphorus. My heart rushes into my throat. Ronald Reagan's son is on
CNN, on Larry King. This is the first time we've watched TV in

more than two months. He tells me that Ronald Reagan's son has been describing the way his dad slipped away, the final breaths, the calm. It was exactly like—

And then he shows me something he has been carrying in his wallet for a few months, and tells me a long story. And for the rest of the morning we chat about what we have wanted to chat about. Dad helping son through son's uncertainty.

+ i want you to have an action plan, a path to being ok.
– why do I need a plan?
+ i guess you don't.
–
+ the one-day-at-a-time thing.
– yes.
+ i think that becomes a rut after a while.
– our plans aren't that different.
+ no, not really.

The new girl is from Hamburg. Her past is dotty, and already my dad has fallen for her. Not only did she actually once run away with a circus, she can do a headstand on a galloping horse. She has trained with Michelin Star chefs. She is writing her thesis on endogenous theory in economics. She almost has the same name as the Flames' new goalie. And I think she might have been run out of some towns somewhere along the way too. She blushes when I karate chop her neck—

It is early in the morning, and I am going to Berlin to see her. The next day he will start his journey back to Calgary. He has stayed up all night to make sure I don't sleep through the alarm and miss my flight. There is a flourish of packing, there is a reluctant moment, there is the inevitability, we hug, and I am walking.

+ will you be ok?
– why do i have to be ok?
+ i guess you don't have to be ok.
– maybe i won't be ok.
+ i just want you to be ok.

*Ray Robertson*

■

# HOW WICHITA,

# KANSAS, MADE

# ME A MAN

When I was twenty-three, I wanted to own a gun.

Didn't have any reason to get one, mind you—not too many opportunities to flash your piece during Introduction to Metaphysics, no matter how heated the discussion, nor even on Saturday night when the arguing took place at a corner table at the Duke of Connaught over who was buying the next round—but I wanted one anyway. Maybe it had something to do with growing up in Southwestern Ontario, just an hour from Detroit, a city whose unofficial civic sobriquet had, by the time I was a teenager in the early 1980s, metamorphosed from the "Motor City" into the only slightly less hospitable "Murder City." Then again, you never knew when some depraved rationalist was going to get all Cartesian on you.

It also probably had something to do with the sort of non-syllabi-required reading I was knee-deep into at the time. In the fall of my last year as an undergraduate, between writing oh-so-clever essays demonstrating the falsity of Kant's ethical argument for God's existence and expertly refuting Hume's supposed negation of causality, as well as trying not all that successfully to get laid (the Duke of Connaught was a wonderful place to piss away, literally, one's student loan, not such a great spot to meet anyone under the age of fifty not yet suffering from cirrhosis of the liver), I discovered

contemporary American literature. The language was what did it—
the revelation that rock 'n' roll could exist inside an ordinary prose
sentence, that rhythm and snarl and swagger and melody could
be syntactically shaped in the composition of a short story or even
a novel—but one of the incidental by-products of this aesthetic
epiphany was an immersion in all things guns. The fictional worlds
of Barry Hannah and Thomas McGuane and Jim Harrison and
James Crumly and assorted alive-and-writing others were crammed
full of the things. I came for the poetry and stuck around for the
Colt .45s.

■

Besides, guns were sexy. Are sexy. Violence is sexy. You don't need
to have read Yeats to understand that on some level—perhaps not
humankind's most evolved level, but a very real, very ingrained
level, anyway—violence is attractive, that it possesses an undeniable "terrible beauty." Violence—whether acted out or vicariously
experienced or even simply imagined, as in a typical revenge fantasy—satisfies the deep, if rarely realized, human desire to *know*, to
*act*, to simply *be*; to, as with the incensed dissidents in "Easter 1916,"
live, if only briefly, as one of those with "hearts with one purpose
alone." Witness, whether in person in the arena or in a crowded bar
with the game on the TV, the collective excitement and fervour
when a simple hockey fight breaks out. Of course, much like the
mental illness of the famous and the dead, violence tends to be
more romantic when it happens to someone else. Or else in small,
manageable portions.

When I met my now-wife, she introduced me to the joy of experiencing physical love with someone you care about and respect;
I introduced her to all the fun that comes with chugging Old Crow
Bourbon and Molson Canadian boilermakers: namely, blackouts,
screaming matches in the street and the occasional bar fight, the
latter because some guy looked at you or your girlfriend, you know,
*wrong*. In the end, a few scars (outside and in) aside, no harm done,

and with some good stories to pass around later when we're both too old to do much else.

More: Mara had always been unequivocally against the dust-ups—"What if you really hurt someone?" was her most familiar reproach. "I work too hard for my money to waste it on a lawyer for you"—but, nonetheless, couldn't hide her obvious attraction to some of the post-punch-up residual effects. The black eye I woke up with one morning a few months after we'd started dating, for instance, an honour I'd earned the night before because another gentleman and I at the old Paddock Tavern couldn't agree on whose turn it was at the jukebox. Getting dressed, and after letting me know how idiotic I'd acted and how worried she'd been, "Put your contact lenses in," she said.

"I thought we were just going for breakfast."

"We are. But I want everyone to see your face. I always wanted a boyfriend with a black eye."

■

All of which meant that I didn't possess any of the usual tepid Canadian trepidation about living in the United States when I was looking around for an institution of higher learning foolish enough to pay my way through graduate school. For an ex-philosophy student by this time turned neophyte novelist, America was, granted, Coca-Cola culture, Billy Graham and Disney World, but it was also drive-through liquor stores, all-night diners, and Hank Williams's long lost highways. Somehow, the image of Margaret Laurence finding her novelistic voice on the wind-swept plains of Manitoba didn't possess quite the same appeal.

When the call finally came from Wichita State University accepting me into their Master of Fine Arts in Creative Writing program, my wife and I loaded up our Chevy Cavalier with as much of several years of Toronto habitation as its sagging shock-absorbers would allow and hit the highway, never once looking over our shoulders wondering what we were leaving behind, only what was ahead. By the time we were pulled over for speeding through a construction site in Indiana—wolfing down ninety-nine-cent Whoppers with Dylan's *Highway 61 Revisited* blaring from the tape deck—it felt like we were Americans all but in birth.

Who knows? I thought. I still might get that gun yet.

■

One of the things you always heard about the United States was how cheap it was, especially if you were used to paying Toronto prices. Gas in Wichita was a dollar a gallon, a six-pack of beer four George Washingtons (three, if you were willing to drink Pabst Blue Ribbon), and Buck's Barbecue offered all-you-could-eat ribs every Wednesday night for $5.99 with cole slaw, choice of potatoes and a bottomless glass of iced tea included. We rented a house for $395 a month and couldn't believe our good luck. Not only did we have an entire place to ourselves with hardwood floors, a sun room and a non-working fireplace, but we were also located not a five minute walk away from the university.

When Mara put the final scribble of her name to the lease, the real estate agent—a heavily lipsticked, diminutive blond with hair nearly as tall as her four-year-old daughter playing on the sun-streaked floor with her doll—said, "But I thought you said you two were married."

Mara and I looked at each other. Not that it was any of anyone's business, but, "We are," one of us said.

"Then why is your name different from hers?" the woman asked, looking at me.

"Well, I kept my last name," Mara said.

"Why?"

"I kept it for work purposes."

"She's a painter," I added.

The perma-smile of before returned to the agent's face. "Oh, you kept it for financial reasons," she said, scrawling an addendum to the bottom of the contract, explaining why it was all right that Ms. Mara Korkola wasn't Mrs. Ray Robertson.

Later, as we stood in our empty living room, waving goodbye out the large bay window at the agent and her child as they pulled out of the driveway in their SUV, "What the hell was that?" Mara said.

I slipped my hand around her waist, pulled her close. I felt like I'd failed to protect her somehow. But from what—and how, exactly—I wasn't really sure.

"I don't know," I said.

■

I go to bed late and sleep in later and wasn't about to change my snoozing habits just because it was our first official Wichita morning. Mara was getting a good start on unpacking some of our stuff when I awoke to the sound of her yelling my name. I'd heard her scream my name plenty of times before, but always when I was awake and usually only when I'd done or said something particularly stupid. This was a different kind of yelling. I tore free from the sheets and raced from the bedroom to the kitchen.

Where—the kitchen window suddenly now a television screen only slightly obscured by the newly installed jars of paprika, nutmeg and chili peppers sitting on the sill—we watched several policemen hugging shotguns to their chests tramp through our brand new backyard. Because we couldn't change the channel, I called out through the opened window, "What's going on?"

"Lock your doors and stay away from the windows," one of the cops shouted.

We didn't need to be told twice. Twenty minutes later, a couple of the policemen returning through the yard to a white van parked in front of our house were kind enough to inform us that they'd been after a drug dealer who'd gotten away on foot during an attempted bust a block or so away.

"Did you . . . I mean, did you get him?" Mara said.

The cop on the driver's side started up the van. "Call 911 if you see a suspicious-looking black male hanging around the neighbourhood."

We watched them drive away. Standing on our lawn, the forest of signs sticking out of every front yard on the block boldly proclaiming that this house was protected twenty-four hours a day by this or that security company suddenly made sense. Ours was the only yard on the street without one.

"Maybe we should get some estimates for a security system," Mara said.

"I'll start calling today."

■

When I was in grade school the student council president was black. The only celebrity of note to emerge from my hometown of Chatham, Ontario, is Fergie Jenkins, the baseball hall-of-famer, a soft-spoken African-American man that my father, a boyhood friend, introduced me to when I was eight. My grandfather used to cut Fergie's hair when he was a kid. Fergie's blind mother used to make sure that my dad and all the rest of Fergie's friends—all white—had had enough for breakfast before they went to school. The whole black-white dynamic, in other words, just wasn't something I really thought about—or, if I did, only in the most abstract, liberal-simplistic terms: people are people, people, and, hey, why can't we all just get along?

The reason, we discovered, that we got such a wonderful deal on our house was because most Wichitans, if they could afford it, refused to live where we did. The locals, with little trace of irony, called it "white-flight," the abandonment over the previous few years of the older neighbourhoods around the university and most of the downtown core for the far safer suburbs, gated communities and hive-like apartment complexes on the fringe of town with names like—again, without irony—Windsor Estates and Spillman Manor and Le Versailles. Those on the political right decried a nation-wide decline in morality beginning around the time of Roe vs. Wade, when the Supreme Court gave women control of their reproductive systems. (Don't worry, I didn't get it either.) Those on the left spoke of the collapse of the local rust-belt economy and the massive cuts in social services under Reagan's two-term reign of terror as president.

But no one could deny that Wichita was now, among other things, the central drug distribution point for the gangs dealing crack, coke and heroin to all of the larger Midwestern cities like Kansas City and St. Louis, and that the Bloods and the Crips, just like any other two companies battling it out on the capitalist playing field for the same lucrative market, weren't above cut-throat business tactics. Actually, drive-by-shooting tactics. Wichita had a population of approximately three hundred thousand—roughly the same size as London, Ontario—but in the twelve months previous to our arrival reported fifty-six murders, two less than Toronto over the same period of time, a city of more than three million. Seventy-five percent of the deaths were black males under the age of twenty. Most of the rest were citizens caught in the crossfire.

So we locked our car doors when we drove. We slowed down whenever we approached a red light, rarely making a complete stop for fear of a car-jacking. If we were forced to wait for a light to change, we kept our eyes off the car next to us in case it was full of black teenagers wearing bright red bandannas who might feel insulted that somehow we were "disrespecting" them. We called the police every time we heard the rat-tat of gunshots (quite literally, about every third day). We got our very own, very expensive home security system, in the process eating up a large chunk of the travelling scholarship I'd received from my University of Toronto alma mater, Victoria College, money that had been earmarked for assorted Yankee Doodle self-realizing shenanigans. And I started asking around about how one went about getting a hold of a gun.

■

Academically speaking, things weren't going so well either. I was writing a lot—grad school is one long working holiday if you've just come fresh from surviving a nine-to-five job, as I had—but the only teacher who seemed to understand what I was trying to do in my apprentice novel (or at least as much as I did) hadn't published a book in fifteen years and was an absolute, hopeless drunk. If you got him early enough in the evening, though, before the Dewars got him, he was witty and funny and lively company. He drank at the same bar every night, Larry's, and always in the company of Aaron, a large, bearded man in a camouflage hunting jacket and scuffed steel-toed work boots. I forget how they became friends—both had served in Vietnam, although not in the same unit or at the same time—but by 11 p.m. any night of the week you happened to drop by, there they were, sitting side by side at the bar at Larry's. However uninspiring Steve, my teacher, might have been as a practising, productive writer, he was a good man, I trusted him and, when I'd told him what I'd been thinking about, he told me that I could trust Aaron.

"Steve tells me you're looking for some protection for your family."

Steve was in the washroom; his empty barstool sat between Aaron and me.

"We actually just got a home security system installed a couple weeks ago," I said.

"That's not what I'm talking about. I'm talking about protection, real protection. All an alarm does is tell you that a rapist is in your house. An alarm doesn't stop him from raping." Aaron lifted his bottle of Budweiser, drank.

"Right. Well, I guess I was thinking about getting a gun."

"Now you're talking sense. How much money do you want to spend? What kind of protection do you have in mind?"

"I'm not actually sure if I want to go through with it," I said. "I haven't even talked to my wife about it yet."

Aaron took a long pull from his beer, carefully set the bottle down on the bar. He turned on his stool to face me.

"You don't need to talk to your wife about it," he said, "you're doing this *for* your wife. The person you need to talk to is me. Now: how much money do you want to spend? What kind of protection do you have in mind?"

■

Of course I wanted to protect myself. Protect Mara. Protect us.

A gun, though. Not a gun cleverly produced at chapter's end in order to expedite the plot or amplify the central protagonist's roguish character, but an actual, $129.95 gun ideally kept as close to your bed as possible in case of an intruder in the night, a gun to have and hold and cherish and potentially kill someone with.

On the one hand, the logic seemed simple: they had guns, we didn't, therefore we needed one. But logic rarely decided anything important. I knew, I did a degree in it. That was one of the reasons why I wanted to write novels.

Mara was as mixed up about it as I was.

"I guess I'd feel safer. Unless I had to actually use it."

"I know," I said.

"Not that that makes any sense."

"No."

"But it's true."

"I know."

Pause.

"So?"

"I don't know," I said.

"I don't know either."

■

One thing I did know was that I needed to learn how to drink and drive like everybody else in Wichita. Not because I wanted to, but because I had to.

There being virtually no cabs or system of public transit in town, combined with the fact that even the short jaunt from our house to a night class at the university was perilous—one evening, frustrated at being automobile-imprisoned, I risked walking to class only to have to almost immediately head back home because a jacked-up Cadillac with bullet holes in its side was slowly trolling forty feet behind me—meant that if we wanted to go to Kirby's for a beer we had to drive. And we had to go to Kirby's. And not just because pitchers of draft were five dollars each and longnecks of Miller High Life a buck seventy-five.

Part of a small, four-store strip mall erected during the late-'60s and left to rot but which steadfastly refused to cooperate, Kirby's was tiny—held maybe forty people if half of these were standing—had a gloriously catholic juke-box (early Stones, Webb Pierce, Bach), and was where every possible definition of a freak by Wichita, Kansas, standards hung out.

Grubby graduate students, the handful of gays and lesbians who were brave enough to be "out" in a community where G. Gordon Liddy's morning hate-radio show was the top-rated program, eighteen-year-old girls with purple hair carrying around Kathy Acker novels, aging hippies with friendly, time-carved faces: to them—and us—Kirby's was liquid salvation. It was also the only place where I regularly talked to a black person.

Dennis had a Mod-Squad afro, thick black plastic glasses and a quiet, confidential manner when he wasn't yelling out "KIRRRBBBY'S!," usually just after midnight when the place was really packed, the cigarette smoke was thick, everyone was well lubricated and things really got hopping. Other than that, Dennis wasn't any different from anyone else at the bar. His politics progressive, his sense of humour dry and smart, his conversation intelligent but never pedantic, Dennis was just one more Kirby's misfit happily afloat for a few oblivious hours a night in a sea of Wichita bilge water.

One night after closing time we corralled a few people from the bar into going home with us for the first time since we'd landed in town: Dennis, Shocker Wayne, a genial sixty-something pothead who could name every Wichita State University Shocker baseball starting line-up for the last fifteen years, and John, a Ph.D candidate in mathematics with girlfriend problems. No big deal—a couple more beers, a few more cigarettes, some familiar sounds on the stereo—nothing we hadn't done tens of times before back in Toronto. Dennis was the last to leave. We kept listening to Dylan's recently released *Biograph* box set and saying "Just one more song" until the beer was finally all gone and the last song played.

■

The next day, cleaning up the mess from the night before, Mara said, "Last night was fun," as she dumped out the ashtray into the garbage pail under the sink. Neither of us smoked, but we always made sure to have an ashtray in the house for friends who did.

"Yeah, it was," I said, picking up the empty beer cans.

"It feels good to have other people like us in the house."

I smiled and gave her a kiss on the cheek on my way out the back door, a plastic grocery bag full of cans hanging from my hand. Beer cans weren't returnable in Kansas, and our sage city council didn't believe in recycling, probably thought it was part of some nefarious liberal agenda meant to undermine the morality of the country's impressionable youth, but the local Humane Society took them, traded them in for cash at a scrap metal dealer. When I came back inside, Mara was placing the last washed glass in the drying rack.

"Did you put the cans for the animals in the bag I already started?" she said.

"Yep."

"It probably won't end up adding up to much, but every little bit helps, I guess."

"Absolutely."

She wrung out the blue-and-white washcloth, hung it out to dry over the faucet.

"I don't want a gun in the house, Ray."

"I don't either."

I went to her, held her; she held me, too.

"Good," she said. "I'm glad that's settled. So. Where do you want to go for breakfast?"

# *Ron Graham*

■

## GOODBYE TO

## ALL THAT

It was a particularly wet and bone-chilling afternoon in April, the rain pellets almost sleet, the four o'clock sky as dark as doom, when I walked into my father's brokerage firm in downtown Montreal to photocopy the final corrections of my graduate thesis and bid him goodbye. I was twenty-two years old. I had $3,500 in my savings account and six years of university behind me. Now I was off to visit friends in Sussex, roam around England for a couple of months and generally indulge my freedom, my youth and myself. If that was irresponsibility, so be it: I was taking a leave of absence from the woes of the world, on the lam from my duty to save humanity.

My father was sitting behind the desk in his subtly lit private office, which looked more like an elegant study than a place of business, talking on the phone. Not so much talking as listening. From the gravity of his few interventions and the intensity with which he drew on his unfiltered Player's, I gathered it was an important call. He gestured to me to take a seat. Time slowed down, almost to the point of stopping, while I waited, five minutes, ten minutes, fifteen minutes, for him to hang up. The wind flung the rain against the large corner windows, further muffling the din of voices, telephones, laughter and tickertape machines coming from the other side of the closed door. I studied the patterns of the drops running down the glass. I observed the microscopic human beings toiling away in brightly lit cells in the surrounding towers of the business district, I listened to the cars splashing through the waves and puddles on the boulevard below, all the while conscious of my father's eyes fixed on me.

As was often the case when he paid me any attention, I felt I was being judged and found guilty (of what I was never sure), or at least found wanting. A letdown, a write-off, not up to scratch or snuff. Not, I hasten to add, because he was a cold or angry-looking man. On the contrary, he had a pleasant Irish mug, kind eyes, a sweet smile, and clear, fleshy skin marred only by the web of deep furrows across his large forehead, which weren't frown lines but the result of a boyhood bicycle accident that had almost killed him; and though his paunch was neatly wrapped in the vest of an expensive tailored suit and his grey hair was fastidiously groomed and slicked down with Vitalis, there was something baggy and unthreatening about his general appearance. He spoke in a quiet and considered tone, radiated a calm and imposing solidity, and was at heart a patient, practical, philosophical man who knew when to cut his losses on an unprofitable investment without dwelling in recrimination and rancour. And yet, I couldn't help but project all my insecurities and inadequacies into his indecipherable stare, just as an actor might look into a mirror and survey only the flaws in his face, or a priest kneel before an icon and believe it to know his every sin.

My father was like a plump peach, his soft exterior hiding, at the core, an extremely tough nut that could break your teeth if you ever tried to crack it. As a child I had been afraid of him, without much justification. "Just wait till your father gets home!" was one of my mother's standard threats, as a result of which the poor guy had only to walk through the front door for me to shake in anticipation of a spanking. And though he was for the most part an even-tempered and tolerant parent, his occasional volcanic blasts were all the more terrifying for being unpredictable, as though a mask had been torn from his familiar face to reveal a diabolic stranger burning red-hot with suppressed resentment and retribution.

But what had really cowed me as a small boy, more than his physical size, more than his analytical mind, more than his formidable obstinacy, was his silence. His impenetrable, unbreakable silence. I used to assume that his strength, intelligence and stubbornness were connected with—maybe even followed from—his wordlessness.

With time I lost the sense of alarm he had evoked in me. As a teenager, heedless of the consequences, I recklessly provoked his fury with my confrontational politics and in-your-face rudeness. Yet I never got over the discomfort I felt at not knowing who he really was or what he was really thinking. Indeed, the more he studied my woebegone face and hangdog expression on that rainy afternoon in his office, the more I imagined him resenting the money wasted—his money, lest I forget—in preparing, writing and now duplicating my thesis on the concept of federalism in Canadian socialist theory. Just as well, I thought, as I gripped the manuscript in my lap, that he hadn't shown a minute's interest in what I had been working on for the past two years. Or perhaps at this moment he was inwardly irritated by my striding into his territory, looking like a vagabond with my jeans, sneakers, knapsack and thick dishevelled hair, past the colleagues and receptionists who held him in such high regard as a captain of industry and master of finance. Or, unkindest cut of all, maybe his mind was on some balance-sheet number or banking clause and he wasn't thinking about me at all.

One possibility I didn't consider—and it occurs to me only now—was that my strong, successful father envied me, his weak and unconfident son. For I was going off to Europe at the very age that he had gone to war, and though my father seldom spoke about his experiences as a tank officer in the Italian campaign, his regimental years may well have been the longest and most intense period of happiness in his life. Fighting overseas had been his duty, of course, but it had also been his Grand Tour, his rite of passage, his great escape. In discipline, he found freedom. In danger, he found confidence. In exile, he found friends. While peace brought him the many comforts of home, the initial excitements of business, and the domestic satisfactions of starting a family with the childhood sweetheart who had awaited his return, a part of his soul must have felt he was walking the plank as he descended from the ship with his kit bag over his shoulder and his medals on his chest.

Years later I heard, though not from him, that his dream had been to study architecture. But his own father, who had initiated him into the differences between stocks and bonds at the age of ten, was eager for him to assume the mantle ordained by birth as the heir apparent of a financial dynasty in the making. His bride, desperate for him to rescue her from the clutches of a domineering mother by setting her up in a house with babies and servants of her own, apparently put her foot down at the notion of his spending time loose among the young coeds at McGill. And so, ever reasonable and perhaps too responsible, like so many others of his generation, he resigned himself to what was expected.

Is it gallantry or cowardice that causes men who are capable of standing up to the guns of a bloodthirsty enemy to buckle before the tears and scowls of a woman? In my father's case, the war over and his destiny foreordained, I think he simply wanted to be left in peace. He was certainly not the type to complain about his lot, of which in purely material terms he had no cause for complaint. If he ever thought about taking off in another direction, he never did anything about it—whether out of love or laziness is anybody's guess. Instead, he withdrew into absences and silence.

After buying a small company that manufactured wire screens for pulp and paper machinery, he disappeared for weeks at a stretch on the mill-town circuit, as though he were one of its travelling salesmen rather than the proprietor. Even when he became a wealthy stockbroker and corporate director, he rarely arrived home before eight on weeknights. Rather than join his wife and children, who were invariably gathered around the television set in the master bedroom, he preferred to retreat to the small yellow den off the living room to read a book or the evening newspaper, play game after game of solitaire, ruminate upon a deal, sip his Dewar's, smoke a pack of cigarettes, and eat the desiccated dinner that had been left on a hot plate in the dining room a couple of hours earlier, an offering placed on the household altar to appease the all-powerful, invisible guardian of the family's prosperity.

"If I came in at six o'clock, I'd never be allowed out again, so I stay out until I'm ready to come in," he once explained after I had confronted him about how cruel it seemed never to let my mother know where he was in the hours between his leaving the office and returning home. "And if she knew where I was, she'd keep phoning me every fifteen minutes. Besides, it's none of your goddamn business."

For many years it was his custom to hang out at the St. James Club after work, talking business, discussing current events or exchanging stories with whomever else was around that inner sanctum of the Montreal Establishment. Though he had few intimate friends, he was personable enough, liked ideas, enjoyed a good laugh and was part of a circle of peers who held him in high regard as a thoughtful, open-minded and thoroughly honest gentleman—a bit unambitious and standoffish, perhaps, in not wanting to be out and about with the local who's who, but better that than a snob or social climber. Despite having been an enthusiastic camper and sportsman in his younger years, he gave up hunting and fishing, lost his keenness for golf and poker, never developed any interest in tennis or horses, and rarely bothered to use the tickets that were available to him for hockey and football games. Nor did he care to join prestigious boards, lead philanthropic campaigns, attend society balls or have his picture taken with politicians, almost all of whom he held in complete contempt.

He prized his independence above all else and didn't spend a lot of time worrying about what people might think of him. Indeed, he prided himself on being self-sufficient emotionally as well as financially, and he sought to protect himself against any eventuality, be it rampant inflation or personal tragedy, that might make him vulnerable or beholden to others. For he harboured a mercenary and somewhat cynical vision of a dog-eat-dog world in which idealism, altruism, romanticism and spirituality are for hypocrites and suckers. Call it selfish, call it wise, call it a consequence of war, but he presumed that most human beings are in pursuit of their own profit and security and that nothing or no one else really matters as long as they and their families are prosperous and safe.

Growing up, however, it wasn't quite clear to me whether my father's love and labour were primarily for his wife and six children or for his own father, his five brothers and his seven sisters. When he was only thirty, my grandfather had charged him with setting up and looking after a private holding company that was intended to bolster everyone's level of comfort for a generation or beyond, and for the next thirty years that remained his main preoccupation and heaviest burden. Whenever he took a risk in a capital investment or made a mistake in the stock market, he wasn't jeopardizing just his own well-being but also that of his dozen siblings. Though some of them came to share the decision-making responsibilities with him, most of them remained dependent upon his work, his intelligence and his success.

Moreover, he was bound to them by something much stronger than any shareholders' agreement or annual dividend: an Irish joy in being together. Even if my father had been born a loner, who claimed not to have uttered a word until he was four because he had chosen not to bother, he had been born into a Hibernian tribe of loud, loquacious talkers. His father, whom he truly adored and with whom he spoke at length most days even when they lived a continent apart, was a garrulous extrovert with opinions and stories about everything under the sun, and he presided over a large brood of forceful, articulate boys and girls who laughed uproariously, yelled to make their know-it-all arguments prevail and shared the confidences they trusted to no one else. My father, in the role he came to inherit as pater familias and chairman of the board, may have seemed the still centre at their gatherings, older, quieter, more refined—indeed, a maître d' once made the mistake of thinking him the father of his brothers—but I used to observe how unusually happy and relaxed he was in their midst, with an amusement in his eye even when he was exasperated by some of their antics. He was among family, or what I assumed that expression to mean, in a way that he rarely seemed at home.

I envied my many uncles and aunts the easygoing, no-holds-barred rapport they had with my father and I sometimes wondered if they weren't family enough for him, in the sense that they provided all the sentimental and psychological nourishment he required, leaving little or no need to talk, laugh or even fight with his own children. (I remember being inordinately impressed by a 1960s bumper sticker that read, "Even a punch in the nose is human contact," which may have accounted for my being such a royal pain in the ass for most of that decade.) Perhaps, as youngsters, we didn't engage his mind the way his adult brothers and sisters could, or was it that we didn't engage his heart?

Whatever the reason, by the end of the day and at the end of the week, he rarely had much more of himself to give. He had given at the office. Not only did he make it evident that he preferred his own company to ours, he was remarkably indifferent to what was going on in his own home, except to bark at us from time to time to keep the noise down. He paid almost no attention to the food that was placed before him, the paintings that hung on the walls or the furniture that filled the room. Anaesthetized by alcohol, pacified by tobacco, he generally went along with my mother's vacation plans, her French poodles and her all-night radio, and his only idea for a Christmas gift or graduation present was a cheque. Nor do I remember him giving any thought to my schooling, my grades, my university selections or my career.

Later I would occasionally hear through the grapevine that he had been impressed by something I had written during more than a decade as a journalist and author, but he never let on to me personally, either by way of praise or criticism, that he had even read any of my books or magazine articles. To the extent that my motives for success had been rooted in a desire for some attention from my father, I needn't have bothered.

While I know the cause of the scars across his forehead, I can only speculate (not least because he never did) as to the cause of this reticence, which seemed no less a wound. Maybe it had to do with the dominant culture, which inculcated in men like him the starched reserve of upper-class Victorian England. Maybe it had to do with the stiff-upper-lip fortitude demanded of a generation that had had to deal with depression, war and recovery. Maybe it had to do with the premature death, from cancer, of my father's pious mother; the unseemly haste with which his father wed another, much younger woman; or the despondent loneliness and mid-life funk into which he sank for a few years following my grandfather's death. Maybe it had to do with the disappointments in his own marriage and the tedium of parenting. Maybe it had to do with the power that comes with keeping secrets, withholding confidences, playing your cards close to your chest, whereby others imagine a knowledge, wisdom or winning hand that may or may not exist. Or maybe it had to do with some sort of (unspoken) contract by which he agreed not to ask anything of me if I agreed to ask nothing of him.

However uncharitable his stoicism may have seemed to others, it served its purpose for him. It enabled him to withstand the horrors of battle, the loss of good friends in a hunting accident and a plane crash, and the stresses of business. Later it would give him the courage to deal with the laryngectomy that took away his voice, of all things, as though God had wanted to teach him a cruel lesson for undervaluing the divine gift of speech. It would give him the stamina to clean and nurse a tube the width of a bullet hole in his neck from which spewed gobs of bloody phlegm and chunks of crusted mucus. It would give him the fortitude to endure the humiliations of a handicap that many people found disgusting or creepy. It would give him the dignity to carry on as usual even though he was reduced (and there's no more descriptive a word) to learning to speak like a robot through a buzzing hand-held microphone he had to press against the vocal vibrations in his throat. And finally the equanimity to receive the news, without a bleat of self-pity or regret, that the cancer had spread throughout his body and he was to die within a year. If there was nothing he could do about it, seemed to be his reasoning in this and every other matter great or small, what was to be gained from talk?

And yet, as my father's life wound down, I came to see his silence more as a weakness than a strength, a model better to avoid than to emulate with my own children, whom I elevated above the advancement of my own career and taught the importance of opening up. His was a well-fortified bastion, to be sure, but behind its wall huddled a brave little soldier, besieged by unexpressed passions and unfulfilled dreams, profoundly hurt, often lonely, fully cognizant of what he was expected to do to die like a man, but ultimately baffled by what it had meant to live like one.

When he was literally on his deathbed, no longer able to walk or sit up, with my mother already suffering paroxysms of grief, round-the-clock nurses waiting on his needs, and the unique odour of cancer filling the darkened room like the smell of decaying flowers, I begged him to try to declare his love. But even when he made the effort—a physical effort, in his case, as well as a psychological one—to voice his feelings and his thoughts before he was condemned to eternal silence, he found himself incapable of speaking the language of his heart and so remained to the end as indecipherable as the Sphinx.

"Perhaps," he confessed, softly, after a long pause, with the voice of a machine, "perhaps I just haven't got anything to say."

All that was decades yet to come, but I intuited in his office on that rainy April afternoon before my departure for London that all was not well within my father. It was there in the grey hair that made him look much older than fifty-one, the pastiness of his skin, the paunch, the Scotches, the chain-smoking, the absences, the unuttered malaise that was driving me away from him and his life. I was seeking happiness, and I had seen up close from an early age—perhaps the single greatest advantage that an advantaged upbringing can bestow—that power, wealth, reputation and duty don't guarantee it. Why struggle then to the top of the greasy pole, unless doing so be a kind of competitive sport or self-expression, if only to slip from an even greater height into the ennui of every other pensioner who has nothing better to do while serving out his time than watch CNN, *Wheel of Fortune* and weekend football?

Yes, yes, I knew my father's retort, if everyone thought that way, there would be no society, no economy, no civilization, and by whose labour and sacrifice did I think I owed my education and my liberty? It was an accusation with which an entire generation of Western youth stood charged in those days. Millions of spoiled adolescents were taking off to the mystics of India or the mud of Woodstock, taking up marijuana or macrobiotics, taking on the military-industrial complex or the plight of grape workers, anything and anywhere to escape the sterility and boredom and unquestioned duty that were the dark side of post-war peace and suburban prosperity. As their representative seated in the docket of history before my father's stare, I understood the weakness of our defence against all the evidence of hypocrisy and ingratitude—hence, in part, my hot-bloodedness, my pig-headedness, my nervousness and my urge to get away. The alternative, whether draped in the guise of social responsibility, filial obligation or intellectual maturity, was to become a servant to my father's reality or, worse, to his imagination.

At some point during my university years he must have given up on the unspoken assumption that I, the eldest son of the eldest son, would someday follow in his footsteps directly into the boardroom of the family company. Any grand aspirations he might have had for me were reduced to wishing I would drop my socialist cant and get a decent haircut. Now I sometimes wonder if he hadn't wanted to give me the freedom that he himself had never known. Why else hadn't he instructed me in the difference between stocks and bonds when I was ten? Why else had he spared me the daily phone calls and the burdens of family obligation? At the time, of course, instead of thanking him for his extraordinary generosity or benign neglect or whatever impulse it was that prompted him to set me free without penalty, I interpreted his tacit manumission as further evidence that he didn't really care.

At last I got up and shook his hand. He wished me a good trip and turned back toward the papers on his desk. As it turned out, I wasn't to see him again for two and a half years. My visit to England became an unexpected journey through Europe, across the Sahara, into Africa, through India, to Asia and the South Pacific, to the world itself. And, though I tried to keep in touch through letters every fortnight or so, the only communication I had with my father in all that time was a letter I received from him in Nairobi. It came from his office, on thick vellum with his name elegantly embossed on the envelope, and I trembled opening it. Had something terrible happened? Was he going to berate me for being away so long? Was he going to say he missed me?

Clipped to my driver's licence was a note, signed by his secretary, which read, in full, "Your father thought you might need this."

# *William Randall*

■

## THE HAPPIEST
## HOUR

I

You died at the happiest hour:
Ten past ten, the position most visually appealing;
So the hands pointed when you left,
The watch you gave me told me so.
Candino Saphir Chaparal, small on my wrist
The faintest tick, the slowest second,
Eternally rock. The elements revered you;
*Es bravo, Don Ronaldo, es bravo . . .*
The kindest man in the pampas is laid to rest.

II

In books I shall always find you: hard covered versions
In blue, brown, and age-darkened fabric, spilling their secrets
From faded pages. Your humility is echoed in the actions of
    Kumalo,
Dignity in the quiet pride of our Prince, adventure in Lawrence's
    heart,
And wisdom in the stutter of Claudius; you handed them all
    to me.
In words I shall see you, understated but enthused,
Guiding my thoughts along the worn and traveled road that
You have concluded. And as I delve into worlds yet unknown

Undoubtedly you will appear in shadows and in sunlight,
From the heights of fantasy or the forceful nature of truth,
Springing from a sentence that may remind me, curiously,
Of your perpetually white hair, the gentle laugh,
Your wrinkled hand, the BBC, or a worn armchair by
    windowpanes.
I shall walk the length of your bookshelves in years to come:
Colossal epics of anger and betrayal, depictions of war,
The conquering of civilizations, the dominance of barbarians,
Residing, side by side, with the saga of English families
And the carriage-driven days of a lady in autumn.
Among them I will never find the love you have given,
Handed to me not in bound objects of foreign creation
But in the painful gesture of concealed disappointment
Or the tender smile hiding behind your eyes,
Warmth wrapped in security, my eternally there;
Now gone.


III

Let the eucalyptus stand tall and troughs cease their crying,
Dust the books on his shelves and beg Wagner to continue
    playing,
Call the pigeons out of mourning and the cattle to their feeding
    ways;
Let all things natural resume on this saddest of days.

Let the park unravel in disorderly queue and join the procession,
As the radiant sunflower heads follow their newly found sun;
Hear the dust settle lightly for a moment of stillness,
When my grandfather joins the earth, forever his.

Let the tosca lie rigid in statutory salute, watching tears drown
In great domes of salt: a crystal realm he can call his own;
Order the parakeets to line his fences in colourful display,
Let all things natural resume on this saddest of days.

Look up, watching the heavens cry tears of clear domain,
Shedding life where it now seems impossible to regain,
Call the clouds from beyond horizons so that they may witness
When my grandfather joins the earth, forever his.

∎

# WAYS OF SEEING

Sometimes, I remember it as if it were all a dream, in that fragile, unfocused way where the edges lose their definition. And maybe there are parts of it that were. I remember my father on the stairs, holding my brother in his arms, and me to blame—but I don't remember where it fits. Whether it all happened the way I think it did, or whether it's just scattered memories that I gathered in, sticking them all together in ways that suited me.

That happens sometimes, and men don't always like to admit it: you stick something in the wrong place, use it as justification for scars and recriminations when really it comes from another day, another week, another month. You don't mean to, it just happens. The only reality you have is your own, so you come to count on it.

I remember a summer cottage we once had in Owl's Head, Nova Scotia. I remember a neighbour named Gallant, Vin Gallant, who always smiled and who always smoked Player's Lights. I remember the bearded sturdy sailor inside the life-ring on the front of the package. I remember the way Gallant would twist the silver foil from the packet into a tight ball and then flick it at you from the hollow of the palm of his hand.

"Gotcha," he would say, the same way he would say it when he did that trick with the strike-anywhere matches, flicking them so they tumbled toward you, end over end, one end flared and suddenly burning.

My parents remember locking the door, and expecting to come back the following week to find the whole place had been burned to the ground, for no other reason than the simple logic that's sometimes found at the bottom of a case of Oland's Ex. They imagined a jut-jawed man from small-town Nova Scotia with a lit Player's Light between his first and second knuckle, smiling while leaning toward you like he meant to punch you in the mouth, then climbing into his car and fishtailing away down the gravel road. Dust in a rooster tail behind, climbing into the air.

I remember the sun shining down there hard and bright day after day, remember collecting mussels off the rocks in the cold Atlantic, reaching down into the water as far as we could reach and for as long as we could stand the chill, the small boat rolling in the swells, the water so frigid that it made the bones in your arms ache. My mother remembers a dead mouse, always, in the kitchen sink near the drain, where it had fallen in and had found itself unable to escape the vertical stainless-steel sides, until we came back to find its furred and forlorn carcass nose-down.

I remember a lot of things, and I'm sometimes unable to sort out the difference between what is actually empirically true, and what is just my version, the version that gives me the most comfort. It's the way you might remember an incredible drift of laden raspberry bushes—just the raspberry bushes and the sweet, rich tang of the berries' juice—without ever choosing to remember that they sprouted up among a pasture of wrecked and abandoned cars, and that you picked the berries by jumping from one car roof to another, feeling the thin steel cave and dent beneath your weight, hearing the rusted metal kink loud in a boy's ears.

I think I remember the tack—and afterwards, although sometimes it seems very much like a dream, my brother in my father's arms, and the way it all happened: one brassy bright thumbtack that I remember leaving, point-upward, at the very top of the basement stairs. It was the start of one more late-night trip to the hospital, the kind of trip every parent makes and dreads.

I remember putting the tack there, and planning that my brother would sleepwalk to the top of the stairs and step exactly there, that the tack would sink into the ball of his foot, and he would awaken suddenly, the way sleepwalkers are never supposed to wake. And it would be perfect, the perfect revenge for whatever latest sibling slight I might have suffered. That's how I remember planning it. And that's the way I remember it happening.

The cool, smooth feeling of cotton sheets, white and cold against summer skin. That first shock of cold that gives way so quickly to body heat, the stiff surface of the fabric. Sinking against the pillow's deep give of feathers. Waiting for sleep, surrounded by the scent of sheets fresh off the clothesline—the smell of sun and salt and juniper—burrowed in, while all the sounds topple over themselves; the familiar thump and bang of the house being readied for night. A cupboard door in the kitchen, water running in the tub, the bleating distant single note of an outdoor car horn. The tick of cooling roof beams and boards. Mother's muffled chuckle, from their room. Until eventually there is only the even breathing of sleepers.

I remember the night with the tack as being one of those nights, a summer night, although I have no idea whether that was the case. It could just as easily have been winter, it could have been any season, and, even more unsettling, I sometimes wrestle with a fear that it may never have happened at all, because it was never spoken of in my family again.

But I wanted it to happen, wanted it to happen with every scrap of my nine-year-old being, and I see it as clearly as I can see anything in memory: that tobacco-tasting teenaged boy's first kiss—completely offhand for her, completely riveting for me—or the slippery-cold eager first touch of the strange fingers of a new love.

But just because you remember it, doesn't always mean it's exactly true.

Like the way I remember my mother jumping out of a closet in my room, growling like a bear, as I came in from the bathroom. I was ten, wrapped in a towel, fresh from the bath, thinking already about pyjamas and bed. I remember that she was smiling that wide, eager smile she has, the smile that's supposed to pull you in. She swears it didn't happen, that she would not have done anything like that. That she would obviously remember it clearly if she had.

Yet I remember it just the same, surrounded all in a flare of yellow-white light, as if the entire room had burst bright with shock.

I can even hear the sharp high shriek of my own voice, hear it filling the room, hear it rattling around, jagged.

And I can convince myself logically, rationally that she's right, that it didn't happen, yet I will never, ever find a way to forgive her for doing it.

■

My neighbour drives too fast. He drives too fast for a residential street, too fast for a street where kids play ball hockey during the day. He drives without turning his head, a permanent profile rushing by me like a head on a postage stamp. When he gets to his driveway, he cuts the wheels sharply and goes in real fast. Some day on thin slick driveway ice, maybe that sudden jamming-on of the brakes won't be enough, and he'll pile into that steel front door, the brass number 61 falling off the door frame and ringing on the ground.

He reminds me of Vin Gallant, my neighbour Verd does, something about his jaw and the way he knows there's no need to ever look around. It's as if he can control everything he sees, as if he can dictate shape and speed and colour by what he chooses to focus on.

It's a kind of unshakeable confidence, as if he's able to simply impose his will on the world. The confidence of a man who can deliberately choose to exclude anything he doesn't like in the world.

At night in the summer, I can hear them through my open bathroom window: Verd and the woman he lives with, coughing and yelling and fighting, the dogs exploding into paroxysms of manic, furious barking whenever they think they hear footsteps on the gravel driveway between our houses. I imagine the small, brightly lit kitchen they sit in—I can see only one corner of their kitchen table from my bathroom, along with the big fan they've got fixed in the window, huffing air inside. She coughs and coughs, desperate wet gasping coughs, the kind that make you feel like you should be doubled over as well. And sometimes you wonder if she's ever going to come up for air—she never speaks when she's outside, and she looks away from your eyes if you try to talk to her. And Verd—slender, small, angry Verd—walks the dogs, three big frightening dogs, his control over them absolute. King, the smallest, is a mixed-breed, brown and black and white with short hair, whippet-thin. King can turn on a cat and Verd can call him off in mid-charge with one sharp word. It's hard not to admire.

At the same time, you can't help but have the feeling it might work the other way, too, that Verd could just as simply tell King to come at you and he would. Just the way he'd break away from attacking a cat, he'd be on you, too afraid of Verd to stop for anything.

Verd didn't speak to me for the first two months I lived here, up on the second floor of an old St. John's house that had been turned into two apartments. I live in what had been the upstairs bedrooms when the house was all in one piece. Old windows, hard to open in the heat, some painted completely shut. Up there, I look out over the neighbourhood on every side except the front, higher up than all my neighbours. In the back of the house, a tight shelter of the tops of maple trees, and in the summer wind, the leaves swish together, a slithery slick whisper that is as familiar as the smell of smoke.

And who am I? Just a sometimes too-intense forty-two-year-old, caught in the hard, bright glare of a divorce in progress, trying hard to define exactly what place I inhabit.

I'm still rocked by dreams, still shaken by the repeated stabs of that sharp little knife of regret, a knife you hardly feel going in, but feel real well when it twists between your ribs. I can still feel the telephone bite my neck like a poisonous snake, and I can feel the world getting away from me, twisting away out of my hands and speeding up with a dangerous, unsettling wobble. I got an unlisted telephone number to avoid the calls, and then immediately surrendered and gave her the number when she asked. Every step you wonder whether it's a step ahead, or merely one foot in front of the other. There are pathetically few dishes in your apartment, and they all seem to be the already-chipped ones, the ones that might otherwise have been thrown away. It is amazing that someone could remember every wedding present that came from your side of the family nineteen years ago, and send them all to you in a box.

But I'm either getting ahead of myself here, or running away with myself entirely. Because I was trying to explain about Verd— and, I guess, about me.

I'd say hello, and Verd would walk by without turning, holding me arm's-length and out of existence every time. He could do that. Hold me out of existence by simply refusing to acknowledge that I was even there. I sometimes admire that too.

I've been there six months now, and I can hardly go into my boys' room when they aren't with me, when they're with their mother. Can't go in the room without bunching their rumpled sheets against my face, trying to catch some hint of them, the lead-pencil scruffy smell of their necks. I leave things where they lie, the blankets bunched, their pyjamas half inside out and stuffed under their pillows. They have big pine bunk beds, and they hardly ever sleep the whole night on their own, one or the other of them stumbling into my room in the middle of the night, their pyjama legs jammed up around their knees from thrashing around when they sleep.

You can feel danger, sometimes, feel it as thick and heavy around you as summer humidity. So that you wade through it when you walk, push against it with every step, feel the weight of it when you swing your arms. Oh, and I didn't mention this: Verd feels like danger.

Danger is never far away when you have children. When they are really small and completely perfect, just babies, dread diseases seem to swirl around them like gnats. Every cold, every flu seems to have its own mysterious high fevers, and when they sag boneless and unmoving in your arms, flattened by their own temperatures, it's hard not to believe the worst in every moment. And when it does happen—to other children—you have a strange and unacceptable feeling of relief, as if, statistically, there are a certain number of children who will somehow be permanently stricken, and that every other child who slips under makes it somehow less likely that your own will.

And that's just part of it. Then there is the talking to yourself—if you have children, you know you do it, too. Making bargains—you do it as if something out there, God or whatever you like, is some kind of bookie, someone you can stack the odds with, if you only could take enough time to get to know him real well. Just do this for me, you ask the shadows. Just save me from this, and I will believe.

I will believe, I will behave, I will be beholden.

What are my children like? Like little boys. Just like little boys, because that's exactly what they are. One brown in summer, the other one pale; one is ten years old, the other seven. I could tell you their weights or how tall they are, how one devours math and the other makes scores of friends in the offhand way the clumsy spill water. I could say that the oldest has a ball-hockey slapshot that will eventually drop you to your knees; I could tell you how different their hair feels between my fingers.

But the whole equation is far more complicated than that: the seven-year-old, spinning quickly down the sidewalk on his impossibly small bicycle, his brown head huge and bulky in the helmet, getting precisely to the driveway before locking up the brakes and leaving a precocious and thin rubber strip of a skid behind him on the pavement. Your heart stops every time, watching the back wheel start to slide as the bike pulls to one side, and you can feel your own body reacting instinctively, your muscles trying to ease off on the brakes before the bike crashes. And he does it himself, just in time, that small, perfect effort, and you feel yourself melt right through fear to love. You watch that, and see him growing up, just a tiny piece of growing up, the way their adult faces can occasionally show through their soft, unformed child's skin for one heart-stopping, shifting moment.

They stay with me most weekends, and the first weekend in July is when the heat really weighs down. Making dinner, cutting up the broccoli, starting to cook the meat, and I'm all by myself. That's one thing you miss, the casual ability of two parents to tag-team, the ability for one person to be busy while the other keeps half an eye out the window, keeping a careful ear on the tone of the noise outside.

You tell yourself, when you're alone, that it will be all right if you can just hear them laughing through the open summer window. The way you look at lottery tickets—imagining that you will necessarily win if the digits of your birthday magically appear. Hanging your hat on imperfect signs, like counting crows—"one for sorrow, two for joy." Creating your own omens, your own small guarantees. That if you hear the screen door slam, they will have to be safe. That they will just have to be safe.

And then, magically, they are. This time.

And you know you have committed yourself to a deal that you cannot ever keep—a deal you cannot possibly even begin to keep. That you have made promises that you are already breaking—that you will never fall victim to lust, that you will be fair and honest with everyone else, that you won't get unreasonably angry when the now-safe boys leave their room in a mess or spill milk from their cereal down into the cracks in the floor. That you won't lose your temper or make selfish choices.

And there's that emptying feeling of relief, that drain-pulled, emptying feeling when they are both back inside. That no one's hurt, that you haven't left them alone for too long, for that fateful moment that you always read about in newspapers—*But I only left them for a moment*—while the police are stopping cars or fire-department divers are searching the river that runs, ungated, fast and silty under the parking lot. But anyone—man or woman—who has children spends some time imagining the worst. Looking into that dark little room, and then slamming the door shut as quickly as possible. We have that in common, at least.

My parents were right, you know. In the end, they knew Vin Gallant better than I did. They knew eventually he would get exactly what he wanted—they could read the possibilities behind those steady, cold, light-blue eyes. Eventually, they sold the cottage at a loss, sold it to Vin because he wanted it.

My mother said Vin was sitting on his front steps when she got there, looking up the low hill across the narrow dip between his place and ours, that dip I remember as being filled with a wide swale of raspberry canes. She saw Vin's face was completely expressionless.

When my parents went to get the boat out of the shed, my mother said Vin was taking an old foundation down with a sledge-hammer, his shirt off, and he didn't stop once the whole time they were there. And she told me later they drove away and talked about how they both felt that they were lucky, that they had escaped something far worse.

■

The sound: the sharp shrieking chuck of the tires skipping on the pavement, the crump of the car hitting something. That's all it took; I didn't need to go outside, didn't need to see the bicycle that his big brother had ridden safely for so long, wrapped around the front of that red car.

I can see it in my mind, the parabola of Verd's red car roaring in across the sidewalk, his head square to the front and unwavering. The inevitability of its intersection with the too-small, speeding bike, a bike with its little pilot concentrating on one last long tire-rubber skid before dinner, before sliced strawberries for dessert.

You're supposed to rush outside, and I almost did. I halfway did. But I went back up the stairs with my hands over my face.

I didn't have to see. I knew my deal was suddenly null and void, and that was no surprise whatsoever.

I'd spent months in my head, planning for exactly that; sometimes for Verd, sometimes for a careless pickup truck shrugging through a street hockey game, sometimes for the results of a child's too-singular power of concentration focused on a vagrant ball.

I knew it already, had seen it a hundred times in that raw spot of imagination: the white of ribs sticking out through his shirt, the small, frothy bubbles. That keening shriek that fills the air around you. Someone screaming, you think detachedly. Someone screaming. And even the person screaming doesn't know who it is.

So I went back up the stairs and I stayed there.

Because if I stayed there, a shivering, shaking crying ball leaning against the refrigerator, it could still be my imagination. Because the sirens might mean something else. Can't they please mean something else?

Please. Just one more screen door slam. Just one.

I'll make any promise you want. I'll do anything.

Never look, I tell myself. Never ever look, so you don't ever have to see. So it all has that strange and airy soft-edged, impossible feel. That comfortable distance that, once you have kids, you will never, ever really have again.

Oh, please.

Let it be a dream.

Then the screen door slamming, and two sets of feet coming up, coming up fast, boys excited, boys with news to share. Shaking with relief, I am unable to speak, unable to even make a noise. Listening to them chatter excitedly, the way their words build higher, the crescendo of what they have both seen.

And then wonder: what deal have I made? And who have I made it with?

# Michael Redhill

■

MOTHERHOOD:

Three *pensées* and an interview

with the author's mother

## 1. Matriarchs

Every family has one. She's dead and you never met her. She gazes
sternly out of an old photograph taken in a town that no longer
exists. She's the one that bribed the Cossack or stole the chicken or
convinced the landlord to let the family stay. But that's not entirely
why she's remembered. She's remembered for her baking, for her
girth, for a laugh the person who's telling you the story never actually heard. She's remembered as a living archetype.

The fathers are never remembered this way, they lack staying
power. All that stomping around and finger-shaking turned out to
signify nothing, just as you had always suspected. In my family, the
husband-to-the-legend was Naftuli, a small man with a moustache
and a black hat, eyes romantically kohled by the fading of the photos
he's in. He's always described as "kind," which is a euphemism for
"we don't really know what he was like." Standing beside him, a
force of nature almost twice his size, is Channah Dina. She was my
maternal grandfather's mother, my great-great-grandmother. Like
the head of a crime family, she was the one whose approval everyone sought. She came last to Canada from Poland, waiting until her
entire family had made the passage over safely, before she came herself, the mothership.

She died when my own mother was eight, but Channah Dina cast a shadow over my mother's generation as well as my own. She's better remembered than some of those who came after her. In some ways, she's more alive than her one remaining child. There's a picture of her in almost all the great-grandchildren's houses and she comes into conversations easily. Meanwhile, her son—my great-uncle—is alone in an old folks' home in North York, and I have yet to visit him. I'm ashamed of, but not surprised at, myself.

What is it about mothers that causes them to ripen into legend? Fathers inspire gestural stories, but a woman like Channah Dina has an actual presence in the remembrances of her kin. They remember her touch, the sound of her voice, and when they recall her failing health they can see her sallow skin, sense her power ebbing, and they still feel for her. Maybe it's that men get the lion's share of attention in their lives, while the constant, quieter insistence that is the life force of a woman like Channah Dina is something that deepens after death. No one is named for Naftuli, but my sister and a first cousin are named for his wife. I can still eat her cooking because I make a number of dishes that come down directly from her.

For my sons, the legendary matriarchs died in my lifetime: Bubby Freda and Nanny. There was also "Big Nanny" (Nanny's mother) and "Little Nanny" (Big Nanny's mother). My sons' grandmother is Nanny's daughter, who, just to keep things clear, is known as Nanny. Practised in the arts of making these wonderful women even larger in death than they were in life, we tell our sons the famous stories, and so they will carry images of these women as I have carried Channah Dina in my mind.

I watch their mother carry some of her great-grandmother in her body. The young hands I touch now in our bed will be recalled as greyish and thin by our sons' grandchildren. Amazing to imagine Channah Dina as a young woman, and so odd to think that we imagine ourselves as young for so long, when the ones who will be with us at the end will only recall us as elderly. And the grandchildren's children will be told about someone probably called Nanny, who laughed easily and made a mean *pudding chaumeur*. "Oh, Nanny loved beer," they will say, and it will seem cute because they won't have any way of remembering the woman I know, who dances barefoot in the summer, hair wild, a bottle of Keith's in her hand.

The great-grandfathers are remembered for broad backs, bad stock picks, stories they told. But I'm certain my sons will be able to smell these women we speak of. The matriarchs come down as a scent in time; the men are only voices, fading. I hope I won't fade away, but probably I will, the wild-haired old guy in the corner with a book, asking the grandchildren to keep it down. Lord, I'll probably smell funny, too. The matriarchs will all be there though, standing on their clouds with their lightning-shaped cooking utensils.

## 2. Lust Bears a Son

I have sometimes had the thought that nature is using me. That the feeling of being in love is a chemical vector designed to get me to impregnate someone. If this sounds darkly cynical, it's only because what I'm saying is true. I may love my wife—and I do, truly and with all my being—but the fact is, my "being" is the figurehead on the ship of my genes. My genes want what I want, only they know by its real name: the future.

And if this is a profoundly operative force in me, I can only imagine how it functions in the body of the sex that actually has to do the work of reproduction. Once my ship reaches port, it is the woman who does all the heavy lifting. To recognize that you and your loved one—both with all the appurtenances of personality, values, fears, ambitions—are really only partners in what amounts to a dance of legacy-building is to admit to one of the darkest facts of our own existences: we're not what we think we are. We're machines designed to make more machines.

Most of the time, we do a fine job of masking that fact. We do it with lacy underwear, brunches, walks along the Scarborough Bluffs, sea-kayaking, oral sex, shoe-shopping, hyacinths, flights to Quebec City, and all the other good things we do that amount to eye-averting. But reproducing strips it all away.

The raw fact of childbirth is the real moment of truth. There's a reason why the *Alien* movies are so frightening. The concept that a parasite has taken hold of your innards and will shortly, regardless of your wishes, burst out of you is the right set of images for pregnancy and childbirth. The relentless Hallmarking of the "birthing experience" has made it much more difficult to feel the horror and awe that is rightly associated with reproduction. Perhaps it is to lessen the trepidation of those who have not yet reproduced that such unscary imagery is bruited. But when the one you love is writhing in mortal agony with a needle in her spine, inside a cold, space-age room, and the result of her pain is something that resembles nothing more than a huge grub covered in cottage cheese, then you have to know someone's been telling whoppers about childbirth. When my first son was born, there was a brief pause in my partner's birth throes when his head was fully out of her body. He was face up, just a head, with eyes and a nose and a mouth, all its features squirming, stuck there between her legs. He opened his eyes and pinned me with a look—only the first time I would see such a look on that face—and if I hadn't already been awake, I would have woken up screaming.

Fatherhood was a notion I took to uneasily, focused more on the inevitable ways I would screw it up than on what it might turn me into. I wanted to do everything right; I was deliberate and cerebral. On his second day of life, I held Benjamin up to a stereo speaker and played Mozart into his ear. He seemed not to care, but I was certain I was grooving neural channels. This was what I believed I was supposed to be doing for him.

My partner had no trouble adapting. I witnessed striking skills— a natural outgrowth of babysitting? I knew it must be more than that when I saw Ben, belly-down, in his mother's hand in the tiny washtub. Asleep in her palm, suds slowly coursing down his back, his mother utterly at home in this dangerous task. Drowning! Dropping! Soap-in-eyes! Accidental breakage! Mushy fontanelles! None of this fazed her and afterwards she threaded the tiny, rubbery limbs into a sleeper. While I tried to dream up ways of getting him to sleep for longer than an hour at a time, she washed underthings as if they *weren't* stained with shit, proudly wore the white epaulettes of spit-up on her shoulders. She'd spent the first trimester vomiting, but nothing made her sick now, while the wafting, slightly acrid scent of digested formula almost made me swoon.

Watching the one you love become a mother is a startling thing. You realize with a shock that God had other plans for those body parts you've so adored. All of them. You suddenly understand why what happens to a male preying mantis happens: he might as well make himself useful. A mantra heard and felt by any man in a household with a new baby. So you hop to it—you take control of those things that make you feel your sex actually has a reason to be out there in the world. Brake shoes get changed, driveway pebbles get raked. A new barbeque bought and fired up. Manic activity, while inside the house, mother and child *bond*, as if what went on before birth *wasn't* bonding.

There is a tiny voice in all men that speaks up when a baby appears: *is that it for me?* What a rotten, selfish instinct that is. But while mother is leaking actual *food* from her body and both grandmothers are passing the secrets of motherhood through the ether, there you are, standing in a door (and not with your own father, who sure as hell doesn't want to remember what this all felt like), and you do have to think: I kind of mattered before all this, didn't I? But the thing—and a great thing it is if you can handle it—is that you don't matter and you never did. And therefore, you're sort of free. To invent this thing you've suddenly become. Not all gaping existential maws have emptiness in them.

A fearful wonder, all of it.

## 3. Boys and Mothers

My mother was the first person to level with me about death. I wanted to know and she told me. But what she told me was not what I wanted to hear: I wanted to know that there was a nice big bright room with all your friends in it and plenty of good food. But she told me that, as Jews, we believed that there was no afterlife, no grand reopening of graves and mass migration to Paradise. No, this was the real thing, this was life, and there was nothing after it. Death was final, death was black and silent and it was forever.

Imagine my relief when I ended up with a Catholic.

Not that my boys, at six and four, aren't any less mystified/terrified by death. The recent return of Terry Fox to the news has my four-year-old convinced that every time he bumps his leg he's "caught" cancer.

In my sons I see that dawning awareness that something *particular* is going on around them. Something they are a part of, and that their part is highly contingent. They worry about what they're doing here, although they don't think of it that way. Rather, they wake up sweating in the night and crying, unable to recall what frightened them so. They turn to us for answers.

■

I watch my sons with their mother. She is their first *other*, their first encounter with that-which-is-not-them. She is on their side with everything, another odd trick the species plays on you: that won't happen with another woman for a good long time. But for now, she's the Garden of Eden.

Still in their early years, I think my sons suspect I'm just another, albeit older, boy that lives in the house with them and belongs to her as well. Not far off. Any son who had a caring mother struggles with the warring urges to be wildly desired as well as excellently fed. A really honest man would say his dream lover would fuck him like a wildcat while playing with his hair. One must not think too hard on it; it's disturbing.

My sons have no sisters, so the presence of this über woman in the house is all they'll know of girls or women for the most important phase of their life. They're lucky: she's a good one. She's a born encourager, not afraid of white glue or sprinkles, doesn't get all anxious when, while baking, the floor gets covered in powdered sugar. Adds just the right amount of guilt to the narration while she cleans it up: *you guys get to have fun and I get to mop it up, huh?* They agree it's a fine arrangement. They have no idea what's coming. Not with her, mind you. Just the world, when they're in it with women who aren't their mothers. Look out boys. It gets to be fun, but you have to clean up a lot more.

My recollections of myself as a son are the kinds of memories I hope my own sons will have of their mother. My mother was creative, funny, patient—maybe a little too honest about the existential realities, but a good mother. My brother and I respected her, but probably not enough (I have an odd memory of breaking into laughter whenever my mother got *really* angry, as if I couldn't believe she was capable of being *really* angry, as if the performance of anger simply wasn't credible). My sons' mother won't have that problem. Given that she is from no-nonsense French and Scots stock, they know to come to attention whenever their mother roars. It's interesting to see. My own authority is wobbly—after all, all I can do is cancel television—but if their mother calls down thunder, it could mean they won't eat. But worse than that, I think, would be simply having to live with the knowledge that they have disappointed her. I fear I'm the parent whose anger will be laughed off. *Go write a poem, Dad. Christ.*

To be *of woman born*. It's everyone's karma, and we need not speak here of how complex women's relationships with their mothers are. Men have a much simpler task: love and be loved. When a man speaks of hating his mother, it strikes me as an unexpected tragedy. I resist the notion that "bad" women could somehow also be bad mothers. A son who hates his mother immediately seems to me a profoundly flawed human being. It's like being angry with the stars—what on earth have they ever done to you but moulded your poor dust into life? Ease up. Even if she's a coked-up crack whore who beat you daily with a willow switch and let your poor little ass get so red and chapped it almost fell off, she's still been through a lot, and she's *still* your mother. She built you *in her body*, man.

I asked my sons to tell me what they thought about their mother. I said, "Describe Mama to someone who's never met her." My six-year-old talked about how beautiful his mother is, how she comes to him in the night without fail when he's had a bad dream. He said she makes the things he likes to eat and picks out clothes he looks good in. I remember feeling all this (except for the clothes thing; for some reason my mother thought it was okay to dress me in corduroy T-shirts)—how capable my mother was, how she seemed always to know what I wanted. But for some reason, it was Benjamin's little brother who boiled it down best. I asked him the same question and he said, "I think that Mama's nice and I think that Mama works good. And that's all."

## An Interview with the Author's Mother, 39 (since 1981)

Linda Redhill: You shouldn't call your child a "grub."

Michael Redhill: It's just a comic exaggeration.

LR: *You're* a comic exaggeration. And you make me sound like a mean rabbi or something. I never told you there was nothing after death.

MR: I even remember where we had this conversation. It was at the kitchen table at Old Colony and you were in a housecoat, and you said there was nothing after death. Isn't that what you believe?

LR: I don't know what I believe.

MR: Well that day, at least, we were all rotting in the ground forever.

LR: And *schoen*.

MR: Anyway. Was the stuff about Channah Dina right?

LR: I don't think she spelled her name that way, but yes. One thing I remember about her—and I *do* remember her, very well—is that she was very strongly tied to Judiasm. She was also a woman of action, and I think she was fairly well known in the Toronto Jewish community of that time for raising money for Israel—she was a staunch Zionist, that is until she *went* to Israel. She went in 1949, she went by herself by boat. And when she returned she was disappointed because she thought Israel was too secular. She was ill when she came back and died shortly after that.

MR: Can you remember what kind of a mother she was to your father and aunts and uncles?

LR: She was a wonderful mother—she really was the matriarch of the family. Irving and your *zaida* used to go have lunch with her every day, they'd come home from work on Spadina and she made them lunch. You really should go visit Irving by the way. He loves you.

MR: I know, Mum.

LR: Then why don't you go?

MR: I'm worried he'll be angry at me.

LR: For what?

MR: I don't know. Let's go back to Channah Dina.

LR: She was a good mother, that's all. I think all of her children admired her and loved her and looked up to her. She was really the glue who held everyone all together. It was a very close family. The only vibes I ever got from my mother about her mother-in-law was that she loved her. From my child's point of view, she was perfect, and I've never heard anyone ever say a bad word about her.

MR: What kind of influence did having this iconic role model in the family do for you or your own mother?

LR: I was too young when she died for her to have an effect on my ways of mothering. My own mother had more of an effect. We often think about what our own mothers did wrong and try to do the opposite. My mother used to do cartwheels to try to get us to eat. If she made something we didn't want to eat, she'd make something else, and we really used this as a way of controlling her. I never wanted to do that. If you guys didn't like what was on the table, you could go make yourself something else, but I wasn't going to cook three different dinners. I think I was a much more selfish mother than my own mother was. She was very giving, but it was too much . . . for everybody. Perhaps it didn't seem that way at the time, but it never taught us how to do things for ourselves. Maybe because she lost her family at such a young age, she felt she had to do everything for us. There have been times in my life when something has come up and I've gone to talk to Channah Dina in the graveyard, to ask her to watch over us. She's a talisman for me.

MR: Do you remember what it felt like to become a mother?

LR: Remember, I was married when I was nineteen and I had you when I was twenty-four.

MR: You were a child bride.

LR: Not quite, Michael. We grew up faster in those days. Becoming a mother was something I really wanted. I had a miscarriage before you, which was a very difficult thing to go through, especially with a first pregnancy because then you think you're never going to have a child. We were thrilled and I was very happy to be a mother. And I think that until we moved back to Toronto when you were fourteen months old, it was really quite idyllic, because most of the time it was just you and me; Dad was working most of the time. And you were such a good baby the most clueless of women would have been able to look after you, and I wasn't clueless. Remember, I was a pediatric nurse.

MR: Excuse me, weren't you *completely* paranoid that I was going to get sick and die just about every minute of the day?

LR: Well, of course I was. Every time you looked the wrong direction, I thought you were dying. I would put you in the playpen after breakfast and all of a sudden you'd be sleeping, so I was convinced you had either sleeping sickness or a brain tumour and I'd call the doctor and he'd say Linda, you're the only mother I've ever known who complains her kid sleeps too much.

MR: So it wasn't exactly heaven then, being a mother.

LR: No, it was. Although—did I ever tell you this?—when you were just a few weeks old, I thought you weren't breathing properly, and I was convinced you were going to die. It was on a Sunday, and we called the pediatrician at home and he said to bring you over to the house, which was the other side of Baltimore. So I said to Daddy, you take him, because I don't want to be there when he dies but Daddy said I had to go and we drove the forty-five minutes to the doctor's house. And you have to remember this doctor isn't one of Dad's peers, he's an established doctor, and we take you in and you're crying and yelling and carrying on and he looks at you and he says you're fine, and of course being the pediatric nurse and the obstetrics resident, we have gone out in the night with this very young infant with no diaper and no bottle, and no wonder you were screaming.

MR: Didn't you have a breast with you?

LR: I only breast-fed you for four days.

MR: Why did you give up after four days?

LR: My milk didn't come in and I was alone in Baltimore and every-one said stop. That's why you're the way you are: I didn't breast-feed you and I threw the toys at you.

MR: Do you want me to talk about the toy-throwing episode?

LR: If you mention it, I'll kill you.

[When we were kids, my mother had a wonderful chest of toys at the cottage that she filled every summer and that we'd get to choose from if it rained and we had to stay indoors. During this one summer, the weather was impeccable, and we began to pray for rain just so we could get our hands on these toys. We started driving her crazy—if so much as a cloud covered the sun, we'd run into the cottage hollering that it was going to rain, and finally she got so mad at us that she opened the chest and threw all the toys at us. But I just want to go on the record and say that we deserved it.]

MR: I think that's it. If I think of anything else, can I call you?

LR: Are you going to say anything about the toys?

MR: No.

LR: Well, don't call me today. I'm going to have a nap. And Daddy is taking me to see the horsies tonight, so call me tomorrow.

# Chris Nuttall-Smith

■

# THE GAME
# OF THE NAME

We're trying to have a baby. Carol and I got married last year, then we bought a house, a little semi-detached on a quiet street with a good school. Our house has a couple of extra rooms upstairs. We both love kids. So of course that's what we're doing. I've begun to prop Carol up in a headstand after sex lately. Anything to give sperm and egg a little extra help.

We've picked a first name if it's a boy. Jasper. We agree on that, at least. I want to give him my last name, too. It's more important to me than just about any other thing. It's important to Carol that we don't.

This has nothing to do with vanity. (I can't stand the way my last name sounds, to be honest; I've never been able to pronounce it.) I don't think that passing down my name is my God-given right as a man. My grandfather died in the war when my dad was a boy—at least that was my grandmother's story. Frederick Nuttall-Smith left their home near London for the front when my dad was seven years old. Soon after, my grandmother told my dad that his father was gone forever. She met and married another man and changed their name before the war was even over. My dad, a strawberry-haired, Oxbridge-accented boy born Bendt Holger Nuttall-Smith, became Benoit Boucher overnight. He lost his name like he lost his father.

I grew up as a Boucher, too. I had the name until I was six, until I got the name that I have now. My father always knew somehow that Boucher didn't fit.

■

Me: "Why don't you want our kid to be a Nuttall-Smith?"
Carol: "Because I want him to have my last name. We're all girls.
     We're the last in my father's line."
Me: "What about your uncle Eric? He's got sons. They have your
     last name."
Carol: "Well. Yes. But they're still not my father's line."
Me: "What about my name?"
Carol: "Well. That's not the point."

But it is my point. I'll compromise on just about any other thing.
I always do. My father has no brothers. I am his only son. He already
lost his name once. He almost lost it for good. There is no way I'm
going to let it die.

Long before my father came along, my grandmother was married to Alex Nuttall-Smith. Alex was Frederick's brother. I guess
Alex didn't make her happy. She started throwing pebbles at Frederick's bedroom window. Her name was Alice Weber. She had red
curls and fair skin.

Alice and Frederick ran off to Tanganyika together, where he
worked for the colonial office. In 1933 she gave birth to my father.
You didn't do that then, not with your brother's wife. The colonial
office sent Frederick and Alice and their illegitimate son back to
England. Frederick lost his job. Alice's family sent money, but her
family lived in Denmark. The war put an end to the money. She
told Frederick to sign up for the war.

■

In our house I am the wearer of pants. Without pants I could not
also be the hammerer of nails and filler and painter of walls and
unclogger of hair-clogged drains and digger of garden beds and in-
staller of extra locks on the back door because Carol doesn't feel safe
alone at home without them.

Carol is a modern woman. She is smart and funny and independent and wise. Like a lot of modern women, Carol does not do domestic. She does not clean. She rarely cooks. I am Carol's kitchen bitch. I bring her cappuccino in bed every morning. I keep the cupboards stocked with groceries. I make breakfast on the weekends and dinner nearly every night. I do the laundry and clean the bathroom and dust and mop the floors. I do take-out, as well, I'm learning: twice this month she's volunteered my chocolate raspberry cake when we've been invited out to dinner parties. Forty years after *The Feminine Mystique*, I am Betty Friedan's Happy Housewife Heroine, except that I wax my shoulders sometimes and I've also got a day job. And you know something? Most of the time I don't mind any of it.

What I don't do is what my father's generation did. I do not expect her to obey me because I am the man of the house. I do not "call the shots." I do not yell at her or tell her how to vote or what to read or what church she should pray in. (To the contrary, she insisted long before we were married that any child of ours would have to be baptized. I am an avid atheist. After arguing for a day I relented. I even agreed to bake a cake for the post-baptism celebration—this, assuming, of course, that the crucifixes don't start spurting blood when the child is dipped in the baptismal font.)

I will never expect her to sacrifice her career for the sake of mine. I don't tell her who to be friends with or how to spend her money. And when we got married I didn't insist that she take my name. I didn't consider asking, even. She is not my chattel. I am not the patriarchy. I'm not even close.

I'm willing, up to a point, to pay for the sins of our fathers' generation, even though neither Carol's father nor mine was by any stretch of imagination the "boss" of his house. I admit, too, that a lot of the time I love cooking for her. (And, in Carol's defence, she's never demanded that I do this stuff; it's that if I didn't do it, it would never get done. I am her kitchen bitch by default.) I get a disturbing sense of satisfaction when I clean; I would renovate and dig flower beds for a living if I could swing it.

But at what point do the sins of the fathers become absolved? Must we discard every tradition that somehow favours men over women? Have we not more than evened things out by now? How much more time has to pass before I get a little more give to go with all that take?

In England, at least, this habit of taking men's names started to catch on in the 1300s. Fathers began passing their names down the line. "It came first among the most consequential families, those that were proud of their achievements and whose descendants wished to parade their paternity," Eldson C. Smith wrote in his influential book, *The Story of Our Names.* "The hereditary quality, slowly over five or six centuries, filtered down through the most humble classes."

But sometimes the mothers passed their names down, too. In 1772, Henry Birch Smith of Clareen married Eleanor Nuttall. Eleanor was an heiress. Heiresses did not take their husbands' names, they kept their fathers'. Eleanor passed her father's name to their son, calling him George Nuttall Smith. George, in turn, passed the name to his own son, also named George. And for reasons of vanity, or because he wanted "to parade his maternity," perhaps—no one seems so sure anymore—George II promoted his middle name, making it part of his last. George Nuttall Smith changed his name to George N. Nuttall-Smith. My family name was born, and from a mother's name, no less.

■

*Sunday, August 20th, 1944, Fircraft, Broadbridge Heath.*
   *My darling husband,*
   *Your lovely letter of the 15th arrived yesterday—just the kind of letter I needed.*

It is my grandmother's handwriting, tidy on lined letter paper in medium blue ink. She is writing to her second husband, my father's stepfather, the man who replaced Frederick Nuttall-Smith when he was, as she maintained, killed in the war.

*Your answer to the problems over Benoit is just what I expected &*
*darling I am so looking forward to the time when you can help me*
*with him . . . darling, I must admit that if it wasn't for this child, life*
*would be simple and wonderful. He makes me feel very unhappy at*
*times.*

My father was eleven then. He felt very unhappy at times, too.
He felt very unhappy for a very long time. He could never make his
mother feel happy, and his stepfather never seemed to like him. I
flip through the papers in search of an envelope. Alice's handwriting again. It is addressed to Francois.

*Major F. Boucher*
*14 Cdn. Aux. Serv.*
*Canadian Forces.*
*Netherlands.*

Of course Frederick Nuttall-Smith is gone by then. 1944. My
father's father is long forgotten.

■

It made sense for those few hundred years, even if it wasn't always
right. The sons inherited from the fathers. The daughters married
other fathers' sons. Then inheritance customs changed. Until late
in the last century, however, naming almost always stayed the same.
Wives took their husbands' names. There wan't any question about
the children. Then over time it started to change.

Writing on Salon.com a few years ago, a woman named Carol
Lloyd complained that "most women make their first public act as
mothers an etymological suicide, obliterating the most visible identifying link between their children and themselves.

"Just because women are blessed and cursed with the vital um-
bilical connection, it doesn't mean that we have to relent on every
symbolic front," she wrote. Patrilineal naming, she continued,

serves no reasonable purpose except that it "assuages both marital conventions and male egos."

Which yes, in fact, it does. But Ms. Lloyd makes it sound as if women have no rights at all; as if North America's men still own their wives and their children. She writes as if nothing in these hundreds of years has changed.

What "symbolic front," other than children's names, is left? For most middle-class North American women, the old patriarchal order of domestic servitude and forfeited dreams died a long time ago. The "Comfortable Concentration Camp," as Betty Friedan once called it, isn't mandatory anymore. It's an easily avoided option.

And is the "most visible identifying link" between a woman and her child really the child's last name? For most of the mothers I've ever met it's three long trimesters of elasticized pants and maternity sweaters. It is a rush of baby showers and "Congratulations!" cards and swollen breasts and a nursing baby. It is a being born of the female body, and forever tied to that maternal body, as to no other body, for that very reason. It is birth stories and hospital pictures and a year of maternity leave while dad trudges off to work every day. (How many young fathers these days would not love to stay home with their children for a year? I would sign up in a second. Most of my friends would, too. But that won't earn us the rights that bearing the baby does. I dare any prospective father to utter the words "We're having a baby" in a room full of modern women. If he doesn't already know how utterly unnecessary he is, the glares will surely tell him.)

Amy A. Kass, a senior lecturer at the University of Chicago, and her husband, Leon Kass, current chairman of President Bush's Council on Bioethics, put it like this in their celebrated 1995 essay in *First Things: A Journal of Religion, Culture and Public Life*: "Although we know from modern biology the equal contributions both parents make to the genetic identity of a child, it is still true to say that the mother is the 'more natural' parent, that is, the parent by birth . . . there is no way to deny out of whose body the new life sprung, whose substance it fed on, who labored to produce it, who wondrously bore it forth. The father's role in all this is minuscule and invisible; in contrast to the mother, there is no naturally manifest way to demonstrate his responsibility."

And yet: for most of us, the surname we are given at birth will never change. At the very least we will never forget it. It is concrete, as solid a detail as you can give a child, a sayable thing. And it is the best answer to an unchanging, undeniable reality. Everybody knows who the mother is. The father? That isn't so easy sometimes. In other words, that last name is the only firm part of a child a father can have.

■

*After a very long voyage I eventually ended up with the Royal Army Service Corps in North Africa, facing Rommel and his part of the German Army. Here I was for a long, long time, writing frequently but never getting a word from her.*

This is Frederick's writing. It is scrawled in black ink, shaky. He writes like a palsy patient. Each line takes a lifetime to decipher.

*Eventually I asked the army welfare organization to make inquiries. After a considerable lapse a lady welfare officer told me, with tears in her eyes, that they had heard from England that my unmarried wife had married a Canadian officer and had gone with him to Canada.*

■

The Spanish put the father's surname first, followed by the mother's. A baby born to Maria Ruiz Verdugo and Ernesto Chamorro Barrios, for example, becomes Baby Chamorro Ruiz.

It preserves the woman's name for a generation at least, but after that the maternal name is lost. (And the maternal name, for what it's worth, still comes from the woman's father, not from her mom.)

Mennonite women take their mothers' maiden name as their middle name until they are married; at marriage they drop it in exchange for their father's name.

Here in North America we've begun to do it differently. In a much-cited article in 1993, a writer for the *New York Times* caught the leading edge of a wave of parents who weren't passing down their own surnames but were choosing, instead, to create entirely new handles for their children. One couple, Dean Skylar and Chris Ledbetter, named their children Skybetter. Another couple, Elyse Goldstein and Baruch Brown, thought it important to preserve their own family identities in some way, but they didn't want to follow the patriarchal pattern of passing down their fathers' names. They found a mid-point somewhere on the colour palette between Gold—the root of Goldstein—and Brown, making their kids' last name Sienna. (One does begin to wonder how many generations it will take for the Siennas to become the Veal Greys or the Burnt Almonds.)

Many other couples choose to hyphenate. This system is probably the most equitable of them all: both parents' (fathers') names are preserved, and in North America at least we haven't yet developed a standard for which name goes first and which goes second, the maternal or the paternal. There's equal opportunity for either name to achieve primacy of place (though negotiations for such trivialities can easily become as complicated as anti-ballistic missile treaties); the father gets his definitive linguistic umbilicus to the child, the mother gets one too.

Such a system, of course, eventually forces a child to choose one parent over the other. In a world of children with double-barrelled surnames, naming successive generations becomes a matter of either selective ancestral pruning or of untold cruelty (will these human hyphenates' great-grandchildren have seven hyphens in their last names? Baby Tennant-Willersley-Salvadurai-Marshall-Brown-Schaeffer-Geddes-Carsley might be a bit of a mouthful when making reservations at TGI Friday's; believe me, Nuttall-Smith alone is already a colossal pain in the ass. For this same reason, Nuttall-Smith-Toller is not an option).

The double-barrelled solution will be a passable one for the next 20-odd years. After that we'll all look back on hyphenated last names in the same way we'll remember the introduction of the Hummer H2, or those first highly entertaining but ominous episodes of *Survivor*: we'll shake our heads and wonder, "What in Christ were we thinking?"

Amy and Leon Kass, the husband-and-wife ethicists, put the case of newly created last names—invented and hyphenated alike—in a somewhat sterner light. "What [these parents] have creatively managed to 'pass on' is a name with no past; and the so-called 'family' name is in no case the name of the entire family, but of the children only. The children are thus, already from birth, nominally (in the literal sense of the word) emancipated from all links to their parents, nominally identified as being unrelated to either parent, let alone to a married couple whose common name would symbolize the couple's union in a new estate and its potential to be a unified family with offspring."

Maybe the Kasses take their argument a bit far. They give every indication of being old and cranky, and they insist, they somewhat smugly write, on being called Mr. and Mrs. Kass. (They do not divulge whether her stationery is engraved "Mrs. Leon Kass.") But something an acquaintance of mine said the other week captured the entirety of the Kasses' point, while bringing the tone down a notch.

"Do you have any idea what a pain it's going to be to go on a simple family holiday to Disneyland when your kids don't even have the same last name as their parents?" he said. "Good luck trying to get across the border."

■

A name can reach through time and place for years once memory has failed us. The immigration card is pale, yellow, stamped with the date and the port and the name of the ship. March 24, 1945. Halifax, N.S. RMV *Rangitata*. To all the world my father has become Benoit Boucher by then, but the name change hasn't been made official. So the port official fills in the immigration card, typing what he sees on my father's documents. Bendt Nuttall-Smith. It is a strange name. The official types an "x" where the hyphen should be. Bendt NuttallxSmith. What kind of kid has a hyphen in his name? But after a minute he gets it right. Bendt Nuttall-Smith. That name keeps coming up somehow.

In 1980 a family friend, a priest, tells my parents he is about to travel to England. A memory, somewhere, is ignited. Could the priest have a look in the London phone book? Frederick Nuttall-Smith is dead. My father has no good reason to doubt it. But Alice has never explained things. My father wants to know what happened.

■

I've started to soften my position in the last few weeks. It came from talking with friends, in part, and also from reading a little more of the rhetorical company I've been keeping. I never want to be confused with the "family values" crowd.

Amy and Leon Kass, the most eloquent of the old system's supporters, argue not only for keeping the father's surname; they also believe that a wife should always change her name as well. What's worse, they dress it up in Focus-on-the-Family speak.

"The wife does not so much surrender her name as she accepts the gift of his, given and received as a pledge of (among other things) loyal and responsible fatherhood for her children," the couple writes. "A woman who refuses this gift is, whether she knows it or not, tacitly refusing the promised devotion or, worse, expressing her suspicions about her groom's trustworthiness as a husband and prospective father."

All of a sudden, reading them almost makes me want to get my tubes tied.

An acquaintance of mine, a well-known author, told me the other evening that both of her boys have her last name rather than their fathers'. Her first son's father abandoned them, she said. So she changed the boy's name to her own.

The choice of a surname for her second son never was in doubt. Her partner's father had "drunk himself to death," she said. They didn't see a need to celebrate his name.

I concede the old way doesn't always make sense. If my father or my grandfather were drunks or racists or louts I might be happy to dump their name. If Carol's family had an extraordinary history that was just about to die I'd think more readily about a compromise. But it doesn't, and it's not. My family does. And it is. Maybe that sounds convenient; the convenience does not trouble me, in any event.

But this thing I will fight for. I only wish I knew how far.

■

We take the tube from London Heathrow. It is my father's first time in England since his childhood during the war. From London we ride a train north, staring out through rainy windows as the city gives way to Essex.

An old man waits on the platform when we arrive. He is short and stooped, but white haired with a beard and a long, slender nose and eyebrows that peak upward like rooftops. He looks exactly like my father. Frederick Nuttall-Smith died in the war when my dad was a boy, and then he wasn't dead anymore. The old man doesn't even have to introduce himself. My father knows his name.

# David Hollingshead

■

## SOMETHING
## ABOUT FATHERS
## AND SONS

I am with you when I am nine years old, following you through these empty halls. I don't know what your job is, but I know we always take a grey staircase to get there—never the elevator. I run my hands along the uneven cement walls, wondering why they were made so rough and hard. There is no one else around when you and I are here.

You let me play on your typewriter while you work at your desk. I sit beside you and mash the keys, imagining I am working hard too. I like the noise of the typewriter. I like the way all the insides work. Every fulcrum and every hinge. I mash the keys so each letter pivots forward. I can see everything happen all at once.

Dad, I can watch the river from your office window. The trees are green in the summer and white in the winter, and in between during the in-betweens. When we are on the other side of the river, in the car, I ask you which building you work in, which building has your office and the typewriter and the rough walls. You point and say, "The one that looks like a layer cake."

Dad, I don't know what a layer cake looks like.

You and I have a problem with words. You mean well, but I don't know what you mean.

We sometimes go to pick up your mail from your office. In the mailroom, you find the small box with your name on it. Inside are papers. What do they say? I promise I will try to understand.

I can never remember why I come along to your office, Dad. Maybe I have to. Maybe Mom makes me go with you because, to her, love is the time spent close to others. Maybe you ask me and I can't say no because saying no to you is like denying a quiet part of myself. A part I desperately need, and a part I desperately shake off.

Dad, I think you thought that I got bored always following you. Sometimes you asked me if I wanted to wait in the car while you ran up by yourself, because you thought I didn't want to be there with you. Like the way I always refused to give you a hug goodnight, and eventually you stopped trying. So I would wait for you in the car, but my heart would pound. I would think about growing up and losing everyone. I would think about my house being as quiet as the halls where you work, the walls just as rough.

There are times, like in the stillness after a nightmare, when I have called out for my mother, and your voice has answered. I just ignored you, and called for her again. I hope this does not keep you awake or make you sad.

Most nights I think about what will happen when you die.

First, your mail will collect—it will spill out of the box. I know this.

I would come and get it for you, Dad, but I wouldn't know what to do with it. I don't know what your work is, but I would run my hands along the rough walls without you, if you were not around to take me. I would be scared, but I would do it, if it's important to you.

Once I asked if you ever talked to yourself when you were alone. You said you did, and I thought that maybe that's where all the words go. There, and into all the lonely books in your office.

Dad, my brain is filling up the silence between us. There's such a sad cadence playing in that space. Can you leave the light on in the hall before you go to bed tonight?

Dad.

You are everything that is unspoken in my childhood.

I am with you when I am twelve years old, watching you read your stories to people in a small bookstore in British Columbia. Half the chairs are unoccupied. I shuffle my feet and watch your hands on the podium. I've heard this story many times. It's about your grandfather.

Mine is a story about fathers and sons.

I want the story to end, but I can't stand the pause before the clapping. I want the story to end, but listening to the measure of your voice makes me want to cry. I want the story to end, because I am bored, I tell myself. But I am not bored, shifting on this uncomfortable seat, watching you sip from a glass of water. I'm scared.

I have so many questions for you that I don't know how to ask, and you are up there reading a story about your grandfather. I am too young for these things, Dad.

And it's not fair. You are vulnerable in ways I didn't know fathers ever were.

It's not fair, like when you congratulated me between the rows of endless tombstones at Dieppe for finding my great-uncle's grave.

Like telling me about your own father, who died at the racetrack and sold cars, and who everyone says you take so much after.

Like telling me where you want your ashes scattered.

It's not fair the way the pages pour you open in front of us.

Promise me you won't die in your suit jacket, Dad, at a reading, or when you're on stage. Not when your voice is so clear like this. Not when you are telling all these important things to all these people, with your son in the crowd. Your only child, who is sitting there thinking about fame and death. He's thinking about tomorrow too, and what it was like before he was born.

Beside me is my mother, your wife. Sometimes she cries at your readings. Sometimes she yawns, but she is always there. Tonight she will tuck me into bed and read me a book you recommended. I have never read your books, Dad, because you have never recommended them to me. But if you want, I will come and listen to you read them all across the country.

And I've learned to laugh when the audience laughs. I laugh loudly so you'll hear me.

And that one line in your story, Dad. That one line that is always followed by a hush over the crowd. The line when your grandfather meets an Indian boy travelling, and the Indian boy compares a picture of his god to the picture of Jesus your grandfather carries in his wallet. I've learned to love that line, Dad, what the Indian boy tells your grandfather, though I don't understand what it means.

*"Your God is finished,"* says the boy.

I smiled when you read it, Dad, I did. We all smiled.

But my smile was the heavy kind.

The kind that hides the toil of growing up.

■

I am with you when I am eighteen years old, watching you scribble your black ink over an essay I have written for class. Commas, spelling, verb tense: you know I am past these now. Your x's and scribbles efface my work, make it almost unreadable. You say that the style is fine but that, structurally, it's flawed.

Dad, you are an ellipsis in my sentence.

I read an interview with you in a newspaper the other day. The first line said that something Freudian is happening in our family. Something about fathers and sons. I promise I have never done anything to hurt you, Dad. I am writing because of reasons bigger than us. The reasons stretch back into the dark, mute histories that steer us all. There are no causes and effects.

Dad, I have finished mashing the keys.

Now, when I read out loud, and I see you in the audience, I tell myself to breathe. I want you to be there to hear every word. I want you to walk through the empty hallways with me. I want to call out in a bad dream, hear you call back, and let you know that nothing of you is lacking—I would not prefer it were someone else. I want you to see me with all my in-betweens, and know that my story is about fathers and sons, too.

Dad, one night when you and Mom were out I got drunk with a girl. We came home together, and before we had sex on the futon, we lay on your office floor and read your books. We pulled them from your shelves and spread them across the room.

I read them all, but just the endings.

I think that, structurally, Dad, we are all flawed.

■

I am with you, now, in every word on the page. My lilt is your lilt, and my hands are yours. I promise nothing I have become is for you, if you promise nothing you have become is for me. Instead, we have written each other onto our own lives. I am *by* you, Dad, and you are *by* me, and we are not the same. Our stories are due, but it has taken so long to find the words.

Like a newborn adjusts to the daylight.

Like breathing the buried air of long voiceless years.

# Andrew Pyper

■

## ME, THE UNMARRIEDS AND UXOR

Some months ago, as I stood at the altar of the same church I was christened in thirty-six years earlier and watched as my bride-to-be was led down the aisle on her father's arm, it occurred to me that, for the first time in my life, I was taking a voluntary step into Foreverdom. Unlike Neverland, Foreverdom is for grown-ups only. Only men who are at least dimly aware of the rules of mortality end up sweating in tuxes, their left nipple throbbing from the wayward pinpricks of a corsage, standing before friends and family, fighting tears as their co-pilot for the years ahead glides toward them. While most other coming-of-age events in a man's life come upon him whether he likes it or not, marriage is something you choose. This is what threatened to take the legs out from under me on the golden afternoon of October 2nd, 2004: I didn't have to be here, and yet I was.

What doubled the strangeness of this recognition is the fact that the men I see the most of these days—those I went to school with, bump into at professional boondoggles, join for occasional weekend benders at cottages, casinos or, once, unaccountably, Buffalo—are unmarried. Some have found themselves in this state having come through marriages (or *de facto* marriages) with kids, diminished assets and resolutions on how to play it all differently the next time around. Others have never married and it looks as if they never will. We were all born in the sixties. We all still have most of our hair. None of us have wives.

Except for me.

This exclusive status is something that I'm at once proud of and puzzled by. Why was I the one to go down? I sometimes wonder if my matrimonial inclinations are a sign of weakness. I'm an *artist*, after all. One of the last vocations (along with professional athlete, movie star and crime lord) where boundless self-absorption, skirt chasing and the unconditional pursuit of pleasure is both expected and forgiven. Other men who avoid marriage into the first greyings of early middle age are invariably tagged with having a "fear of commitment" (at least by their ex-girlfriends). But artists? Our random shaggings show not fear but liberation, an anti-bourgeois boldness of imagination. I had a licence to be *bad*. But on the day I signed the registry that records the names of history's Forever cadets, I voluntarily handed my licence in.

I knew this was the right time for me—and the right person— some months before I proposed. That is, I had gone from idly wondering if I would get married some day, to idly wondering to whom, to—and this seemed to happen overnight—the stylistic concerns of how best to pop the question. The Big Thinking supposedly involved in the determination of Is She the One? passed me by, or was carried out in my dreams, which may be the best forum for such referenda. For me, there was no protracted analysis of my intended's merits and faults, nor of my own. I asked my girlfriend to marry me in the same way I bought the house we live in today—abruptly, after visiting fifty previous open houses.

My bended-knee moment took place on the eighth day of a nine-day paddle trip on the Yukon River, just the two of us for fifty miles in any direction. It was a hell of a long way to go for that extra kick of romance, I admit. But if you have any doubts whether the woman you're with now has the right stuff to be Mrs. [Her Surname]–[Your Surname], take her in a canoe, alone, through grizzly country, preferably with neither of you having much experience with such an activity. Why? Let's just say you *learn* things. About her, about yourself. About the limits of your patience, the limits of hers. How you handle fear, discomfort, a map. What both of you truly smell like.

Most men prefer hard evidence over mushy impulse to figure out matters of the heart. To this end, consider a canoe trip a fact-finding mission. For instance, my paddle mate, Heidi, smells surprisingly good even at her ripest. We've decided that I'll handle the maps from now on (though I make mistakes reading them from time to time, Heidi is among the severely direction-challenged). As for patience, we now know I'm not so good with the chit-chat before noon, and her skin gets somewhat thinner prior to her afternoon snack. How tough can a life be together when you come into it equipped with this kind of data?

Even now that the wedding day has come and gone, canoes have continued to assist me in gaining insight into my wife's capacities and my own limitations. Last summer, on what was supposed to be a much tamer trip into the backwoods of Algonquin Park, I saw a side of my wife that I hadn't really noticed before, but am glad she possesses—a surprise, post-marriage bonus.

We had camped on an island and decided to take a day trip to another lake, have lunch and be back at our island by dusk. It was a three-mile portage in, three miles out, over steeply hilled, rock-stubbled terrain: not too tough for hardcore canoe carriers, but definitely something to think about for a thirty-something novelist coming to this fresh-air thing rather late in the game. On the way in, we noticed pieces of gear left alongside the trail every few hundred yards. A fishing net. A pair of child's sneakers. A jumbo cooler. A fold-up Toronto Maple Leafs chair. Together, it told the story of campers somewhere ahead. Ones who'd packed their canoe as if it were a minivan.

Once we made it to the interior lake, we paddled around its shore for a time, looking for a good place to eat our sandwiches. We were completely alone. At least we thought we were, until we heard the "Hulloo!" of another voice, loon-like, from somewhere on the opposite side.

We floated closer and found a father in his fifties with his twelve-year-old daughter and her friend, the three of them squeezed together on a tiny square of beach. They'd arrived the night before after ditching half their equipment on the portage (including most of their food), the father tearing a muscle in his leg pushing their canoe off in the dark, and all of them getting soaked in the morning's thunderstorm. They were in good spirits, all things considered, but I detected that slightly shrill, false jokiness in the father's voice that signals barely concealed desperation. He'd brought these girls out here to retrace the same fishing trip he and a buddy had undertaken as "kids" over twenty years ago, but he'd learned that his body and brain had softened since then, and now he was screwed.

Given where we were and what we had with us, Heidi and I could do nothing more than offer them our food and water and wish them well. Yet that night, back at our island, we couldn't help wondering how the three of them were going to make it out of there on their own. They couldn't, we concluded. Not without leaving half a Wal-Mart aisle's worth of garbage behind.

In the morning, we paddled back in to help. After hauling our own canoe the three miles in to the interior lake, we found the father and the two girls, already beaten. The man's leg was shot. He'd have trouble limping out with nothing more than the Tilley hat on his head, never mind a canoe on his shoulders. I stepped up and boldly offered to carry it the whole way out myself. After some very Canadian negotiations ("No, we're fine! Really!" "Hey, it's no problem. I *want* to do it!") I set off with their much heavier boat on my back, the others following as best they could behind me.

The morning became hot, even in the humid shade of the forest. I kept up a running, wheezing pace, as though being timed for a qualifying heat for an as-yet-unnamed competition. By the time I made it to the portage's starting point and dropped their canoe, I was dizzy. The bottle of water I'd brought along was empty. Walking straight was harder than it is on New Year's Eve, but I had to head back to get our canoe.

One by one I passed the two girls, Heidi, and, last, the father, making their way out. The man in particular was grateful in a way that tested his abilities of articulation. I pretended it was no big deal. But by the time I collapsed at the far end of the trail, I was in truly bad shape. My guts churned volcanically hot, though my skin was cool to the touch. I had trouble focusing. All sound, all air, all motion seemed to be sucked out of the woods.

Some time later Heidi made it back and, when she saw me curled up on the ground, immediately set to work starting a fire. She pushed squares of chocolate into my mouth. She covered me with her rain jacket to ward off the chills. In short, she did exactly what the survival guide would have your backwoods companion do for you when suffering from exhaustion, low blood sugar and mild shock.

A couple of hours later, I had our canoe back on my shoulders, taking my time and Heidi letting me do it, in the name of preserving whatever remained of my never-especially-convincing-to-begin-with tough guy pride.

Over the miles out, I made my first mental jottings toward what I now think of as the Marriage Formula:

$$(x-y)b = a$$

This, where $x$ is what, at best, you're capable of on your own, $y$ is your own multiple shortcomings and visitations of bad luck, and $b$ is the factor to which a loving partner can help pick you up off the ground when in the negatives, or assist in and celebrate your triumphs when in the positives.

The $a$, of course, is the resulting you. A man, at least potentially, improved.

■

Back home in the city, I would tell this story and add at the end that it was one of the reasons behind my "uxoriousness." It was my word of the month, and I threw it into conversations whenever I had the excuse. Some would ask what it meant, and I would explain that an uxorious husband defined an enlightened man who loves and respects his wife. The trouble is, as I later discovered, it doesn't mean that at all. That I was provided this erroneous definition by a newly remarried woman trying to tell her second husband that there was a word for what she expected of him should have put me on alert. In fact, according to my Webster's, to be uxorious is to be "foolishly fond of or submissive to your wife." Or, in modern phrasing, whipped.

There are worse failings than foolish fondness or submissiveness, I suppose, but it's still a descriptive I'm glad to fall short of. The truth is, the word "wife" has yet to pass easily from my lips so far in my married life, at least in any non-ironically, quotation-marked usage. There is something about it that, like a dark spell, makes me worry I will instantly age thirty years if I utter it without the protection of self-consciousness. Maybe this is what my unmarried friends are most wary of: finally and irreversibly becoming their fathers.

Just the other day, driving on the murderous QEW, we (my wife and I) passed a car bearing a sticker in the rear window which read "I ♥ my wife." Heidi and I both laughed at its lame simplicity, the public advertising of such a banal claim. We figured the driver's wife bought the thing and made her husband stick it on the car after a week or so of his repeatedly "forgetting" to. "Poor bastard," I said, and we laughed again.

But now, recalling the glimpse of tartan cap as we zoomed by, I believe the fellow slapped his declaration of love onto the back of his Buick out of an entirely voluntary (albeit borderline uxorious) impulse. So the guy still loves his wife after forty years on the inside, and he couldn't give a hoot who knows about it. If that isn't bumper sticker boast-worthy, what is? Perhaps my and my young wife's laughter had more of the nervous titter in it than we'd like to admit: from the point of view of those on the married side of the wall, those two in that Buick are living examples of the best-case scenario. The fact that the man looked a little like my dad only drives the point rather uncomfortably home.

■

To the aging and still unmarried men among us, I say: Think of what comes with the deal! A wife can assist her husband in often unexpected ways. Remind him of his own parents' birthdays. Kick him under the table when halfway to revealing a secret shared in strictest confidence that he'd mistaken for common gossip. Point at a lump on his neck he hadn't noticed and ask, "What's that?"

The doctor squeezed it and called it a swollen node. When he asked if I'd had any cat scratches, flu or signs of fever in the past weeks, I said no, thinking this was a good answer to give. He only pinched his chin in a severe way I didn't like. Then he admitted he was stumped, and told me I'd have to get the thing biopsied.

I wandered out of his office, weightless and mournful as a ghost. Went home and paced. Though I work on my own every day, I felt alone in my house for the first time. I struggled against thinking of my dilemma in clichéd terms, but so many have faced just this situation over the centuries, there are few if any original ways of conceiving it. Death had popped its unwelcome face around the door and stuck its tongue out at me. I thought things like *Well, this is it* and *Why me and not that guy on the corner who drinks a gallon of sherry every day?* and *I don't want to go just yet* and *Fuck, fuck, fuck* and couldn't stop.

When Heidi came home from work I told her that my lump might well be something very, very bad, and we both cried. It wasn't self-pity alone that had me in its grip, but the profound injustice felt by those, still young, taking their first glimpse into the Void: *Hey, I was just getting started!*

It took ten days before the test results came back. I'm not claiming that my anxiety and gloominess over that week and a half were any worse than the suffering of others in the Suffering World. In fact, I was aware at the time that I should try to snap out of it, given the state-of-the-art anguish being borne by the millions of refugeed and tsunamied and starved and blown-up in the morning paper. But it's hard to think in relative terms when faced with the possibility that you might soon be leaving this life without having gotten around to having a child, without doing your best work, without being able to fully enjoy some serious mileage with your new wife. The days were raw, and I passed through them wondering at how easy it is, when things are good, to stupidly live without being aware of it.

I also wondered how this time would have passed had Heidi not been there with me. What if I had been awaiting the results of a test like that while single? I'm lucky to have plenty of excellent friends, but friends generally don't share your bed, bring you tea, hold your head as you cry in their laps. I literally thanked God for my wife. And not just silently in my head, either. But on my knees, aloud. I thanked Him for the gift of her strength, because I was weak, and needed it.

A nurse called. She sounded nice. She told me my results were in, and that the lump was reactive, or normal.

"That's good, right?" I asked, idiotically. But she was a nurse who dealt with people at junctures in their lives when they were permitted to act like idiots.

"Yes, it's very good," she said, and to me, it sounded as though she were commenting on the general merits, despite all contrary evidence, of life itself.

■

All of this is not meant as a recommendation for marriage on the grounds that it's nice to have someone around in case you think you're going to die. (While this seems like a sufficient reason on its own to me, it's not the argument I'm making here.) What I've taken from my recent speed date with Death is essentially nothing more than what should be universally obvious: we will all have our day, and it will come sooner than most of us would like. In the meantime, if you are in a position of choosing (and that would be every one of us), what's to be made of this marriage thing? Is it an enhancement of our numbered hours, or a squandering of them? Does a wife make life better, or merely make it seem longer?

Ultimately, whether one should be married or not cannot be decided by debate. It's not an issue to be voted on by the Parliament of Contemporary Men in the way we might one day resolve questions such as Two- or Three-Button Suit Jackets? or Is It Okay to Have a Roommate Past Your Thirty-Fifth Birthday? There is no ethical aspect to walking down the aisle versus lifelong bachelorhood, no social compulsion one way or the other worth mentioning. There is only the matter of determining what might make one happy, which, as anyone who has ever been unhappy knows, is a far trickier business than it sounds.

As for me, I can report that, as of the date of this writing, my wife makes me—and this is a word I didn't necessarily expect to rank first—happy. But then the doubter's follow-up (and I can hear it coming from wherever you sit, dear Reader, married or single, man or woman, snorting into the pages you hold open before you): *For how long?* I have made oaths before God, family, friends and a Presbyterian minister that I will remain a good and faithful husband until the Shadow of Death and beyond. Really, though, all I can be sure of is to do my best. Marriage isn't easy, after all.

(Nowadays everyone tells modern-day newlyweds this, I've found. *Everyone.* Divorced friends, blithe swingers, bartenders, cab drivers, Dr. Phil, your mom. "Marriage is hard work," *every single one of them say*. And I'm certain it is. But wasn't there a time when this grim truth was withheld from the giddy kids getting hitched at least until after their return from a sweaty weekend on a heart-shaped bed in Niagara Falls?)

But no matter how hard one clings to hopeful visions of the future, current domestic peace and conveniently unlimited libidinous work-outs, the point must inevitably be conceded: marriage *is* hard work. It is also capable of delivering sharp pains in the ass, as well as other symptoms, including (but not limited to) fatigue, poor sleep, weight gain, swollen liver and vertigo. So if you're not already in the middle of a marriage, if you have the option not to go there at all, why bother? Who needs more *work* in their lives? Especially when all that labour and self-sacrifice and *Who's Afraid of Virginia Woolf?* mind-gaming so often leads to lawyers and U-Hauls anyway? I'll be the first to admit that the empirical support for the Stay Single case is overwhelming. The detractors of marriage can (often gleefully) cite both the anecdotal and StatsCan evidence of the increasing number of broken homes and miserable marrieds in our land. The odds just aren't that great for staying together long after an early twenty-first century walk through the confetti.

But it's one thing to face the discouraging statistics, the endless tales of thwarted ambition and sad, Updikean adulteries, and another to find yourself in love with a woman, who, even in the sober light of day (and the sober light of the day after that), you see as someone who could deliver you Forever. That's the only test, as far as I can tell.

As for what to do if you feel you've passed that test but still don't know whether you actually want to ask her to seal the deal, that's up to you, my brother. The only wisdom the ages provide on the question is that marriage is a risk.

But then, so are most of the best things—the flying leap decisions, the changes that change everything—and when you come out on the other side, your new life announces itself as miraculously as any birth: you didn't have to be here, and yet, thankfully you are.

# CONTRIBUTORS

*Bert Archer*

I write and have written, edit and have edited, for all sorts of people and publications over the past decade or so. The one book I've written so far, called *The End of Gay (and the death of heterosexuality)*, was published in Canada and, more recently, in the UK and the US.

*Douglas Bell*

I am a Toronto writer and occasional actor. The paperback version of my first book, *Run Over: A Boy, His Mother and an Accident*, is due for release in September 2005. I can also be seen in seasons two and three of the CBC television comedy the *Newsroom*.

*Ted Bishop*

I live in Edmonton, teach English at the University of Alberta, and have published on James Joyce, Virginia Woolf, and motorcycling, all of which conspired to produce *Riding with Rilke: Reflections on Motorcycles and Books*.

*Ian Brown*

I was born in Montreal and now live in Toronto with my wife and two children. I currently work as a roving feature reporter for *The Globe and Mail*, as the host of "Talking Books" on CBC Radio, and as the presenter of TVOntario's documentary series, *The Human Edge* and *The View from Here*. This is my third book. The first two were *Freewheeling* and *Man Overboard*.

*David Eddie*

I was born in Boston, and came to Canada with my family in 1971. I've written a novel, *Chump Change*, called "brilliant and funny" by *The Wall Street Journal*; and a non-fiction book, *Housebroken*, translated into five languages and optioned for a sitcom by Fox/CBS. I also write a column in *Toro* magazine called "Damage Control: Advice for Guys in Sticky Situations." I'm currently working on a screenplay called "Overexposure," about a man who tries to overcome an extramarital crush by "overexposing" himself to the source of temptation. I live in Toronto with my three boys, ages 8, 5 and 3; and my wife, Pam, a TV news reporter.

## Max Fawcett

I'm one of the newest writers in this anthology, a mere twenty-five years young and fresh out of seven pointless years in two of Canada's finer post-secondary institutions. I'm a contributing editor at Dooneyscafe.com and my first book, due to be released in the spring of 2006, will introduce Canadians to my generation.

## Don Gillmor

I am a senior editor at *Walrus Magazine*. For twenty years I have been a magazine journalist. Occasionally I write books for children (*Yuck, A Love Story, Sophie and the Sea Monster*) and for adults (*Canada: A People's History, The Desire of Every Living Thing*). When possible, I work in my office at home.

## Ron Graham

I am a freelance journalist who has written several books about the politics, religion and history of Canada, as well as numerous magazine and newspaper articles. Married with three teenage children, I divide my time between downtown Toronto and a cabin in the woods of Quebec. My website is www.rongrahamcanada.com

## Bruce Grierson

I am, among magazine writers, what's sometimes called a "generalist"— which just means I have trouble focusing. I've written about spelling bees and squash, the Russian space program and experimental dental surgery, for various publications, over many years. I live in Vancouver with my wife, Jennifer, and daughter, Madeline.

## David Hayes

I am a freelance writer and author whose work has appeared in publications such as *Toronto Life, Saturday Night, Report on Business, The New York Times Magazine, enRoute* and *The Walrus*. I've published three nonfiction books and am at work on a fourth. I also teach magazine feature writing at Ryerson University.

### Geoff Heinricks

I'm living the life of Odysseus's pop Laertes, quietly hoeing my vines. My wife and I fled the city ten years ago, and quietly struggle to raise four children in Prince Edward County. A satirist, a cartoonist, and now winegrower, my last book was *A Fool and Forty Acres*, published by McClelland and Stewart.

### David Hollingshead

I am a twenty-one-year-old undergraduate at a western Canadian university who finds writing well extremely difficult. I am uncertain if my goals are the same as yours. If you want to talk moral disposition, fine: I lean toward semi-lawful deference, but if given access to the karaoke microphone, I will not behave myself.

### Greg Hollingshead

I have published three story collections—*Famous Players* (1982), *White Buick* (1992) and *The Roaring Girl* (1995) (which won the Governor General's Award)—and three novels: *Spin Dry* (1992), *The Healer* (1998) and *Bedlam* (2004). I live in Edmonton with my wife and son. Some of the year I spend at Banff, where I direct the writing programs at the Banff Centre.

### Brian D. Johnson

I'm employed at *Maclean's* as film critic and senior writer. I've written some books, including *Volcano Days* (a novel), and *Brave Films, Wild Nights: 25 Years of Festival Fever*. I've contributed to a bunch of magazines that no longer exist, and some that still do, from *Rolling Stone* to *Saturday Night*. And I play percussion in a Toronto band called Baltic Avenue.

### J. M. Kearns

I left Toronto many years ago, a hitchhiker headed for L.A., with a knapsack, a guitar and a PhD in philosophy. I now live in Nashville, Tennessee, record indie artists in my digital studio and write songs, novels and non-fiction. My next book will be called *Why Mr. Right Can't Find You*.

*Chris Koentges*

My work appears sporadically in leading Canadian magazines and sometimes on the CBC program IDEAS and also in miscellaneous vestpocket letterpress editions. I am currently entertaining bids for my 3/200ths stake in the Aegean villa mentioned earlier in this book. Send reasonable offers via the publisher.

*Martin Levin*

I am books editor of *The Globe and Mail* and moonlight a little writing about music, movies and baseball, three cornerstones of a man's life. I've long ago (alas!) given up my dream of pitching for the Pittsburgh Pirates, but hope to live to see a play I co-wrote (with Peter Kenter) about über-awful film director Ed Wood produced.

*Jake MacDonald*

When I was an unpublished writer, living in the woods and taking a writing course in Winnipeg, I walked into class late one night all frazzled from the highway with woodsmoke in my sweater, and my classmate Sandra Birdsell said, "Oh good, our token wilderness writer is here." I've lived in the city for ages and have written eight books since but I think she got me.

*David Macfarlane*

I'm a writer—the author of *The Danger Tree, Summer Gone* and a play, *Fishwrap*. I've written newspaper columns, magazine articles and film scripts. My most recent project is a book of non-fiction about the marble quarries of Carrara. I live in Toronto with my wife and two children.

*Chris Nuttall-Smith*

I recently returned from Sumqayit, Azerbaijan, where I was completing research for a novel to be published in 2007. Born and raised in Banfora, Burkina Faso, I now live in Toronto with my wife, Carol, and a three-legged dog named Banjo.

### Ian Pearson

I am a writer, editor and radio producer. I live in Toronto. I am also proprietor of Zedtone Records, a company dedicated to the music of Eleni Mandell, who is the second-greatest woman singer-songwriter living in Los Angeles.

### Philip Preville

I am the youngest in my family, the fifth of five boys. I know what you're thinking: "Oh, your poor mother." Bullshit. We handled all the household tasks that would otherwise have been relegated to our sisters (vacuuming, washing dishes, disinfecting toilets) in addition to lawn care and trash disposal. The biggest problem with raising a house of boys, said Mom, was that "girls are such a mystery to them," in other words, we were a family of suckers. In my career as a writer and, now, a senior editor at *Saturday Night*, I have steadfastly avoided writing about gender relations until this book.

### Andrew Pyper

I am the author of three novels, *Lost Girls*, *The Trade Mission* and, most recently, *The Wildfire Season*, as well as *Kiss Me*, a collection of short stories. I live in Toronto.

### William Randall

I have been living in Toronto for the past six years while completing undergraduate and graduate studies in geology at the University of Toronto. Work will take me to the Ungava Peninsula, after which I plan to return to Argentina to visit family and friends before discovering Africa.

### Michael Redhill

I live in Toronto with my partner and our two young sons, where, when I'm not driving someone somewhere, I also publish *Brick* and write novels and plays.

*Ray Robertson*

I'm a Toronto-based novelist (*Home Movies, Heroes, Moody Food,* and *Gently Down the Stream*), literary critic (*Mental Hygiene: Essays on Writers and Writing*) and a contributing reviewer to *The Globe and Mail.* I've got a wife, a dog and a heart full of soul.

*Russell Smith*

My most recent novel, *Muriella Pent,* was shortlisted for the Rogers/Writers' Trust Fiction Prize and the Toronto Book Award. I also write the weekly "Virtual Culture" column in *The Globe and Mail.*

*Russell Wangersky*

I am a writer, columnist and newspaper editor with *The Telegram* in St. John's, Newfoundland and Labrador. As a columnist, my work has appeared in newspapers across the country. I have published both fiction and creative non-fiction, fought fires for two different volunteer fire departments and played competitive rugby for more years than was reasonably sensible.